55^{00}

Epicurean
Awakening™
- The Cookbook -

Dear Bill -
Exciting times ahead!
♡ Rebekah Kee Maya

Rebekah Kee Maya
Epicureanawakening.com

Copyright © 2023 by Rebekah Kee Maya. Epicurean Awakening, LLC. All rights reserved.

No portion of this book may be reproduced in whole or in part, stored in a retrieval system, or transmitted in any form or by any means- electronic, mechanical or other, without written permission from the publisher, except by a reviewer, who may quote brief passages in a review or author, except as permitted by U.S. copyright law. First Printing, March 2023

ISBN: 979-8-9877283-0-7
Published by Epicurean Awakening LLC

Printing: ADI
King Printing Company, Inc.
181 Industrial Avenue East
Lowell, MA 01852
Phone: 978-458-2345
Mobile: 937-789-0810
Fax: 978-458-3026
www.kingprinting.com
www.adibooks.com

Wholesale orders at EpicureanAwakening.com

Library of Congress Control Number: 2023902815

Front Cover Design by SMK Marketing at www.sabrinamknapp.com and Louisa Firethorne at www.firethornedesigns.com
Back Cover Design by Rebekah Kee Maya, Epicurean Awakening LLC.
Cover Photography by Claire Johnson Photography, Brewster, WA.
Interior Photography by Rebekah Kee Maya, Epicurean Awakening LLC.

Disclaimer: This book is for educational purposes only and is not intended to treat or diagnose any health condition. Please seek professional help regarding any health conditions. The author is not responsible for any adverse food or health reactions from any of the information and recipes contained herein. No expressed or implied guarantee of the effects of the use of the recommendations can be given or liability taken.

Dedication

This book is dedicated to the loving memory of my Grandma.
Her encouragement of my being with her when she was working her
Kitchen Magic continues to bring me joy as I explore living Fearless in the Kitchen.

Acknowledgments

Epicurean Awakening™ has been an awakening for me. A labor of love. The courage, commitment and dedication has been a 30 - year journey for me. Well, actually, longer than that. It is true, we learn best with contrast and that is just how this book was born. Through much contrast. Contrast in my health, in my relationships and in my love of cooking and baking.

And adapting over and over and over to fit my ever-changing dietary restrictions. And now, to finally get it right. To finally align with the bigger picture. To finally have the ability to share it with the world. You make this worthwhile. Thank you.

Here is where the love came from in the way of family, friends and sometimes, critics...

I'd like to first thank Katherine Ingrish, with Divine Desserts. A wonderful bakery just outside of Chicago, in Geneva, Illinois. Thank you for believing in me. For helping me discover just how much I love decorating cakes and making pastries. Your faith in me was the seed that grew me into the confidence I have today. You and your business brought me tremendous joy. And I'll always remember the leap of faith you had in hiring me. Thank you from the bottom of my heart.

I'd also like to thank B & O Espresso, Charlotte's Heart Bakery, in Seattle, Washington, and the many bakeries where I was able to perfect my craft. And Earth Save Seattle. And the community colleges and continuing education programs in both Seattle and Whidbey Island that supported my contemporary cooking classes as a Vegan Baker/Pastry Chef and Whole Foods Culinary Artist.

To my Angels, both embodied and ethereal, a big thank you for keeping me inspired and following my bliss with creative cooking. You know who you are.

Thank you, John Hannam, from Seattle Earth Save, for encouraging me, believing in my creativity and enjoying my vegan recipes.

To my dear friend, Dr. Bill Mitchell, co-founder of Bastyr University, who supported me in many, many ways as my yoga teacher and doctor. I'm grateful for the dots you continue to connect for me, and how you believed in me and my gifts. I'll never forget your kindness, your impeccable intuition and your passion in your work.

A big thank you to Cassandra Knight-Lac, EAMP for educating me endlessly with 5-element Acupuncture. And Dr. Nashalla Nyinda for educating me equally with Tibetan

Medicine, and, specifically, what my body needed. You gave me exactly what was needed and helped me to never give up. Helping me over the years to build my health back from my pregnancies and the times I had been sick. Your wisdom has been one of the foundations to my recipes.

I'd also like to send a big thank you to Jessika Neuert, Nutrition and Wellness Coach, for being there all these years, 18 to be exact, with your incredible support as I was going through some of the hardest parts of my life.

Thank you, Shawna Pavliga, and Annapoorne Colangelo, my dear friends, for always believing in me, laughing with me and loving me...enjoying our friendships and all of my cooking. For celebrating with me all the crazy recipe ideas I develop and create.

Thank you, Dr. Thom Rogers, (ND) and Dr. Alicia Capsey Rogers, (ND), for referring patients to me that allowed me to support their health through dietary changes. Researching, finding and experimenting with creative recipes to help others is what inspired me to create Epicurean Awakening™.

To Dr. Sodhi, an Ayurvedic Doctor, in Bellevue, WA., who educated me on my journey, along with Paltul Rinpoche, Tibetan Doctor from New York. The tag team of you two continued this evolution of both healing for me and my body type and how to learn to cook for many other kinds of diets. Without your knowledge and expertise, I wouldn't be where I am today.

A massive thank you to Dr. Said, DC, ND, for being the GPS helping me find my way to my truth. My true health. Inspiring me to finish my cookbook and supporting me in ways I never thought possible. Your wisdom, expertise and intuition have saved my life and opened new doors for me that I never thought were possible. I can't thank you enough for the kindness and ongoing support you have been for me and my children. The recipes developed in this book are for all your patients. May this book serve, heal and save many lives.

To my editor, colleague, and best friend, Tim Holman. I am forever grateful for the countless hours you've supported me, inspired me and loved me through some of the most difficult and challenging times in my life. You have shown me the space to find my strength and courage to finish this book. Thank you for believing in me and encouraging me to show up in ways I never thought possible.

And a huge thank you to Claire Johnson Photography. I love how you have captured the visual artistry of my food, teasing our hunger, desire and curiosity.

Sabrina Knapp, with SMK Marketing, thank you for all your encouragement and business support. Especially for the suggestions with the book cover design.

To my children... thank you for endlessly testing recipes, eating the results and helping clean up the kitchen… on a daily basis! Your feedback has been super helpful, as now, I trust many of these recipes are kid friendly!!

Lastly, I'd like to thank my sister for listening to me, celebrating me and acknowledging my creative cooking talents. No words can thank you enough for being my number-one cheerleader and your loving support.

To all the "Brave Taste Testers" who have eaten my unorthodox recipes, thank you for your valuable feedback. I appreciate all of you. This has been a monumental community undertaking!

Sincerely,

Rebekah

Table of Contents

Foreword: Dr. James Said, ND, DC…..………....…..8

Foreword: Kari Halligan, RN, RNC, BSN………....17

About the Author………………………………....…..19

Introduction: Jessika Neuert, Nutritionist………25

Your Awakening Begins……………………..……...29

What is Aquaschata™?...35

Let's Get Started…………………………….………39

Health and Vitality…………………………………..42

Menu Planning………………………..……………...44

Comfort Foods………………………….…………….45

Food Alignment; Food Frequencies……………...47

Choosing You………………………………………..51

Personal Accountability……………………..……...56

"Finally Free," a Poem by Rebekah Kee Maya…60

Risk Taking … Fearless in the Kitchen……..…...63

Food Magic………………………………..…...……..67

Table of Contents,
Continued ...

Alternatives
- Baking Powder..69
- Caramel..69
- Cashews...69
- Coffee..69
- Dairy..70
- Egg...70
- Extracts and Flavoring....................................72
- Flours..73
- Food Coloring...78
- Gelatin...78
- Potatoes..78
- Sweeteners...79
- Inulin...79
- Stevia/Sugar Chart 82
- Oils..83
- Wine..83

Equipment..84

Quick Reference Guide............................85

Resources...88

Juices & Smoothies
- Additives...92
- Juice Machines...93
- Blueberry Smoothie.......................................96
- Oat Nogg..96
- Maple Pecan Swirl...96
- Flaxseed Shakes...97
- Juicing for Well Being...................................98
- Symptoms of Healing..................................101

Table of Contents
continued ...
Butter, Cheese, Sour Cream, Aioli, Cream Cheeses & More

Riced Cauliflower……………………………………106
Angel Butter……………………………………………107
    Basic……………………………………………107
    Herb……………………………………………107
    Sundried Tomato…………………………108
Vegan Sour Cream…………………………………108
Macadamia Cauliflower Ricotta Cheese………109
Basic Cream Cheese………………………………110
    Cashew………………………………………110
    Flavored Cream Cheese ………………110
    Pumfu…………………………………………111
    Chive…………………………………………111
    Basil……………………………………………111
    Cilantro………………………………………112
    Hazelnut……………………………………112
    Faux Lox……………………………………112
Mayonnaise……………………………………………113
Aioli………………………………………………………114
    Cilantro Garlic……………………………114
    Basil……………………………………………114
    Roasted Red Pepper/Smoked Paprika……115
    Basil/Artichoke……………………………115

Herbs for Cooking & Baking………………………117

Sauces & Salsas………………………………………118

Happytizers……………………………………………127

Salads, Salad Dressings, Pesto & Soups…………142

Crackers…………………………………………………170
Bread, Bagels & Pretzels……………………………183

Table of Contents
Continued ...

Tortillas and Wraps...229

Entrees, Breakfast Style..236

Entrees, Dinner Style...247

Pasta...270

Desserts..282

Baking Tips...284

Pies, Meringues, Cakes, Cupcakes & Cake Pops......324

Basics & Bonuses..360

Frostings and Whipped Toppings.......................376

Cold Drinks and Treats.......................................394

Index..411

Foreword
by Dr. James Said, ND, DC

Rebekah Kee Maya has written a cookbook.
This cookbook.
Epicurean Awakening™.
This is an entirely plant-based (vegan), sugar-free, with no added fats or refined oils, using some nuts and seeds, gluten-free cookbook.

Rebekah grinds her own flours as a way to promote eating unrefined carbs. With no refined sugars included, as she uses stevia, xylitol, monk fruit, dates and other low-glycemic alternatives. The diet being promoted in this cookbook is exquisitely simple. Using simple foods to create a complex and rewarding flavor. And it's healthy.

I'm going to address the issue of refined fats and oils and our body's ability to metabolize them.

Fats and oils require very specific kinds of digestion and metabolism in order to be used efficiently by our bodies. And many people, genetically, cannot metabolize fats and oils efficiently. Now, there is a caveat... As a doctor, I find that some patients require fats and oils. They can metabolize them well, and they need them to thrive. Maybe 1 or 2 percent of my patients are like this. Most people need essential fatty acids to thrive. But they don't need excess fats and oils. So, it's not the mainstream requirement of our bodies to process fats and oils. And what our body tends to do with excess fats and oils is drive up LDL cholesterol numbers. And here's why.

The cholesterol mix comes as HDL, IDL, LDL and VLDL. Each one is an identifier in the relationship of density in proteins. You have high density (HDL), intermediate density (IDL), low density (LDL), very low density (VLDL). And they have different functions in terms of transporting fats. For example, the LDL cholesterol is a Lipid (fat) cell and protein cell complex that carries fats from the liver, after they are metabolized and used by the cell. HDL carts the cell back to the liver where it recirculates with the other excess fats. It's just a cool system. Now, many people genetically can't hold on to too many fats in the LDL molecule and those excess fats end up getting dropped along transport through the arteries, where it's highly oxidized. Since arteries are for carrying oxygen as well, we end up with oxidized LDL. The cause for hardening of the arteries.

Do you know why you cannot get hardening of the veins? Because there's no oxygen in the veins. Therefore, no setup for oxidization in the venous return.

And it's mainly HDL that comes back through the veins. So it's the LDL that is oxidized on the way out through the arteries. If they have to dump fats excessively, when they carry too much, it can create what's called a fatty streak within the artery. This, along with oxidizers and other lipids damages the tunica intima of the arteries, the innermost layer of the arterial wall. Over time, that then allows the arterial wall to erode. So, now the body has to protect itself. To not allow the artery to blow out. As its first line of defense, it creates a plaque. First, a soft plaque that basically becomes hardened. And, I'm sure you are aware of what plaque does to the arteries. Even though there are different ways of treating arterial plaques, it's not the scope of this description. Prevention is. Through eating choices.

Now we look at the quality effects. When using fats and oils, for people that cannot metabolize fats and oils effectively, it is necessary to keep their consumption at a minimum. They genetically can't manage them. And I've seen the numbers between 40 and 60% of the population who, genetically, are not able to metabolize fats and oils. In my practice, it's closer to the upper range. Keep in mind, I see the part of the population that's concerned about their health and vascular integrity. And they tend not to do well with fats and oils. Easily 60% of my patient load is not. Now, the other 40% can tolerate some but not much. Fats and oils in moderation at best. It's the rare person that I actually recommend fats and oils to. Maybe one or 2% of my patient load, where they have to have fats and oils. And then they fly. That's right. I've had some really interesting cases, where they couldn't respond until they started eating fats and oils. And then they did well. But that's very rare. Most people are the other way around.

Now, this brings me to make a comment about sugars for a moment, I'm going to come back to fats and oils. I have yet to see anybody do well with refined sugars and refined carbs. It is a classic triggered inflammation, generally, body wide. And pathology always starts with inflammation; all pathology, including cancer, and heart disease. It always starts with inflammation. When I first work with a patient, I take out all of the inflammatory triggers in their diet and lifestyle. Then they can begin to actually recover. I inquire about if the person's eating foods to which they're forming reactivity, like inflammation. Sugars, refined carbs, or stimulants like coffee, tobacco, chocolate, black tea, or bad quality fats or hydrogenated oils, dried fats, or animal fats ... this becomes my focus. Starting in the gut. They have to get these out of their diet; the excitatory neurotoxins, like heavy metals, drugs, artificial sweeteners, flavors, colors and dyes, derivatives and free glutamates, etc. And heavily preserved and artificially preserved foods and food additives and colorings. These are all neurotoxic. They literally bind to receptor sites, on proteins of foods, blocking enzymes from breaking down those protein structures to access amino acids. Now you end up with undigested proteins that are tagged as foreign proteins, generating alternate autoimmune reactivity. What is called molecular mimicry. In other words, these molecules mimic molecules in the body but see them as foreign and attack the body. This is known as autoimmunity. There's plenty of published research now. It's well known. Let's get back to fats.

I have read several articles recently on the issues of linoleic/linolenic acid. But there are two schools of thought. One is based on real biochemistry. The other, not so much. It's based on "food science." A so-called "science" derived or funded by the food industry to promote their profit. Precisely! Profit-driven science. Not about what works for you, rather, what works for the food manufacturer.

Let's check out a biochemistry chart and see what I'm talking about.

I'm looking for the prostaglandin E to cascade here. This is a chart showing the cascade of omega six and omega threes. So omega threes are alpha-linolenic acid and Omega six derives from linoleic acid.

Linoleic acid derives down to arachidonic acid. Arachidonic acid is the fatty acid you find in animal fats, meat, fish, fowl, eggs and dairy. Our bodies contain Arachidonic acid. That's animal fat. This animal fat drives what is called the COX and LOX pathways. These are all pro-inflammatory pathways. We know it causes inflammation, vasoconstriction and platelet aggregation. That's the net effect of COX and LOX pathways. This creates a number of spin-off chemistries that are all pro-inflammatory. That's the simple version of it. And the Omega threes generate eicosapentaenoic acid (EPA), countering COX and LOX pathways by creating anti-inflammatory pathways. And vasodilation and anti-aggregation. It's just the opposite. Simply stated, the Omega sixes from the linoleic acid through arachidonic acid, and your animal fatty acids all generate pro-inflammation in our bodies. The Omega three's, from alpha-linolenic acid, generates eicosapentaenoic acid (EPA), which generates other chemistry that is all anti-inflammatory, causing platelets to not aggregate (clump) and stimulates vasodilation. Net result; improved circulation.
This is basic biological science.

This is biochemistry. I'm reciting biochemistry 101. We all learned this in science. As opposed to wishful thinking from food scientists. My agenda, here, is to bring your awareness about food back to the basics of science. To not let you get swept away by the inaccuracies of the profiteers. After all, they make it so shiny, pretty and easy to swallow.

In order to stay abreast of their deceit, I read their propaganda and I apply my background and knowledge of biochemistry to what "food science" offers.

In fact, I used to teach this in medical school in biochemistry. And then I started seeing papers coming out in favor of omega sixes. I thought, "What is this work? They're trying to negate biochemistry. They can't negate biochemistry. It's been known for a very long time. The pathways are well known and well established, well researched and well documented. And, well taught over many, many, many, many, many decades." And now we see information starting to come out and trying to negate or cast doubt on biochemistry. Sadly, I'm seeing this across the board. This is not the forum to go into the politics of it. Big money is behind it. I am staying with the science, here. Pretty basic.

Speaking of basic ... let's look at Dr. Caldwell Esselstyn, who wrote a book called "Prevent and Reverse Heart Disease." Out of the Cleveland Clinic, he took the worst cardiac cases available at the time. They were called terminal cardiac patients. The clinic had sent them all home to die. They had all the medical interventions that medical science could provide. They had the drugs and bypass surgeries, they had the stents, they had replacement surgeries, and, in the end, it all proved to be unsuccessful. 20 people were sent home to get their affairs in order and sit in a rocking chair and die. The medical field had failed them. I'm not exaggerating, 20 people.

Dr. Esselstyn took them all and put them on a 100% plant-based diet. Oil-free. Zero fats and oils. Not some oil, zero. They all started his program with exorbitant LDLs. They continued this diet until the LDL's came down to under 80. Normal is regarded as below 99. But we know from the Framingham Study, which began in 1948. 74 years of following people through their lives, monitoring fats and cholesterol, reporting that anybody with total cholesterol of 150 or less, with an LDL of 80 or less, has never suffered a terminal heart condition. Making an LDL marker of 80 or less the target.

That's a big deal.
That's our target.

Medical science can't touch that. Because in their paradigm, normal just means 95% of the population fits in a specific range. And 95% of the population does not fit in that range. 95% of the population is very, very sick. That's why Heart Disease is the number one killer in this country. Ironically, it's also the number one moneymaker in hospitals. They can't afford to conservatively manage heart disease. Hospitals would go bankrupt. They'd have to change their entire model to a healing, wellness-based model. They'd thrive if they were to make that change. But that's not their model. They don't think in those terms. Although I saw Kaiser has started to promote a plant-based diet for their physicians and nurses. Just recently I saw that. I find that interesting. The point is, that, Dr. Esselstyn's research proved the reversal of heart disease, using an exclusive plant-based, oil-free diet. It didn't just slow it down. It stopped and reversed heart disease. That was demonstrated clearly in imaging studies of the cardiovascular system to the heart and to the vascular system of the heart.

Then he did a second study of 200 patients. Same protocols, same outcomes. Every single patient that did the protocol and stuck it out, reversed their heart disease. There is a documentary called "Forks Over Knives" that details the work of Dr. Esselstyn. And Dr. Colin Campbell.

Dr. Campbell is a doctor that had similar results with similar protocols, only his research was with cancer. Dr. Campbell, professor emeritus, at Cornel University, studied and researched nutrition and biochemistry his entire professional life.

Dr. Campbell showed the reversal of cancer using the same strategies. A plant-based diet. The irony is, he set out to prove that people on a meat-eating diet had a lesser chance to get cancer. His research found the opposite to be true. It blew his whole hypothesis. He had to change the direction of his research since the outcome was contrary to his original thinking.

He published a book called The China Study, because his research was done in China. It is the largest study ever done on nutrition and cancer. He had the full support of the Chinese government because the director of Preventative Medicine, at the government level, had been diagnosed with cancer. And he knew of Dr. Campbell's research and wanted to be healed. All of this research was for the country of China, though the results have been shared worldwide. Dr. Campbell proved the reversal of cancer using a plant-based diet. And he showed the mechanisms behind the trigger of cancer.

With these kinds of results, it's no wonder why Dr. Campbell and Dr. Esselstyn were featured in a movie called "Forks Over Knives." I used to lecture after every show with three other doctors. We would travel all over Southern Oregon, encouraging people who had just watched the documentary. This created such excitement for information that we brought Dr. Esselstyn to lecture in Southern Oregon, in 2011.

He lectured in the largest venue Southern Oregon had to offer. He also lectured at the hospital and changed cardiology there for the next decade. Until those doctors retired, and the new ones didn't understand or want to understand the value of his research. Sadly.

Anyway, I got to meet him and his wife. And he was telling a story of a gentleman whose numbers had gotten worse after his findings had been published. And he asked, "What's going on here, your LDLs are starting to climb back up?." The gentleman had changed directions from the eating protocol because he read something about the Mediterranean diet and the olive oil diet being good for him.
He added olive oil to his diet and was reversing the trend. Instead of maintaining his improvement. He was going back to the way he was when in the hospital. He was heading for heart disease. Dr. Esselstyn had him go back with zero oils, zero fats until he brought the LDL back down. Return to how he had already reversed and survived heart disease. There's proof at many levels. The greatest proof was in the actual imaging studies before and after the reversal of plaques and atheromas and the reversal of heart disease. This dietary change had pulled him and these people out of their prognosis.

I see similarities in my caseload and with my patients. Usually, in my practice. I see many patients with heart disease and coronary heart disease and shift them to that same kind of plant-based diet. Oil-free or minimal fat, depending on the level of advancement of the disease and what is required to reverse the pathology.

One other point in current research in medicine, in cardiology, in particular, they're showing that optimizing a plant-based diet, in fact, is reversing many forms of heart disease. And I just recently took a couple of courses from a world-class cardiologist who is also a naturopath. A naturopath and an MD cardiologist. Great combination. He is showing, from the medical literature, the downside of most of the drugs used for treating heart disease. And the upside of using a plant-based diet in conjunction with an appropriate, nutritional-based, botanical medicine. So botanical formulations are on the rise now, allowing us to do what classic medications can't do anywhere near as effectively.

The bottom line is that we need to start with a plant-based diet, minimizing fats and oils or reducing them to zero. Bottom line. And that's becoming more well-known in the cardiology world.

Now, one other point, there are many who have jumped on what I call a bandwagon. Or a fad. Called the Paleo system. High fat, high protein, minimal carbs. And we are starting to see it backfire. Some claim it is to stabilize blood sugar levels to have people eat every two to three hours. That will definitely backfire. It takes an average body four to five hours to digest what's in the stomach and small intestines. Eating as often as encouraged on the Paleo diet will mess up the digestion of the previous meal. Ending up with more and more undigested proteins and therefore, more chances for metabolites, molecular mimicry and autoimmunity. This is well-known and well-documented. This is how the body responds to excess protein, carbs and fat. This is a bandwagon that's doomed to failure. I'm seeing it widespread. Sadly, people are losing sight of basic science and physiology. And we know the politics behind it though I won't touch that aspect of it here. Be aware. Do your own research.

I truly appreciate what Rebekah is doing here. And I've been asking her, and others who are vegan chefs, to create cookbooks that are healthy, that are minimal to no fats. No refined sugars, no refined carbs and gluten-free. Rebekah has done that masterfully. And with delicious flavors.

Many, many of my patients are gluten intolerant. There's something called non-celiac gluten neuropathy or gluten sensitivity. You don't have to have celiac disease, an autoimmune condition, to not tolerate gluten. And gluten is a common inflammatory protein for many, many people. And they don't even know this until they have stopped eating gluten. And we know much of the mechanisms behind it ... wheat has been hybridized to be 50% Gluten instead of 5%. With that kind of increase, the average person can't break down that protein, effectively. We end up with undigested proteins that create problems in the gut lining, leading to a leaky gut, or hyper-permeable gut. Now you have avenues for large molecules, like undigested proteins, going across the gut barrier into the bloodstream. Circulating through the entire body, including across the blood-brain barrier, activating the immune system of the body and the brain as well. This system is called the microglial adaptive immune system.

This system is activated globally. When something triggers an active microglial adaptive immune system, the brain, the entire brain, swells and goes into inflammation all at once. So when people eat foods, like wheat, that trigger a reaction, they don't feel good in the tummy and they want to fall asleep. Or they get a foggy brain. A common problem. And if people don't notice much of a change, they say, look, I didn't eat wheat for three weeks, nothing made any difference. However, I find that people who are sensitive, have other foods that are also reactive and will eventually realize a problem. They just don't know it, yet.

Ideally, we test to see what their needs are with a larger diet picture. At the very least, I get my patients off of gluten, almost universally. Then we test, to see how they tolerate Gluten or gliadin protein.

So, gluten-free is important. Fat-free or fat-minimal is important. And plant based is important.

Removing Omega six and linoleic acid is key to removing the triggers that drive inflammation, aggregation and vasoconstrictions. As opposed to bringing in the Omega threes and converting Linolenic acid to the Eicosapentaenoic acid. In turn, aiding the prostaglandin group that generates reduced inflammation, reducing platelet aggregation and vasodilation. That's what we look for.

This is why we get people off of the fats from animals, especially from Linoleic acid triggers. And then, we get them off of all fats that are derived from plant oils like corn oil, canola, vegetable etc. Introduce them to high-quality fats, which are nuts, seeds, avocados and olives. Get them away from processed oils.

I appreciate that Rebekah has done this in her cookbook. She's done it. No added oil. She understands the value of high-quality fats. And how most people can tolerate them well. Although I do get patients who are allergic to certain seeds, avocado oil, or olives. On those occasions, we have to test for that. There's no way to know that without evaluating it clinically and testing for it.

Rebekah's gone the healthier route. Without sugars, without added oils, without gluten and plant-based diet. Exclusively. She's covered all the points on the triggers of animal fats, Omega 6, Gluten and sugar.

The need for this approach is huge. Many, many people suffer from gluten intolerance. Many more suffer from intolerance to fats and oils and the effect it has on the cardiovascular system. Or genetically, the inability to metabolize them. Eating this way is going to have adverse effects with the creation of inflammation, autoimmune disorders and a poor quality of life.

The need is large. Larger than most people realize. It's time. If people move in this direction and follow these kinds of recipes and start purchasing and planting foods that work this way ... their health will improve. They'll feel better. They'll have more energy, typically better sleep, less inflammation, fewer aches and pains, and they will think more clearly. They become more available for healthy relationships. And they'll have more compassion. No longer driven by the cruelty that comes from eating flesh foods. And people tend to mentally bypass this part of the equation. But you can't. It's inherent when eating meat as food. Not to mention the hormones that are coursing through their entire bodies at the moment of their death. We can clinically see what happens with this.

I see people coming in with a typical Standard American Diet (SAD). High proteins, high fat and highly refined carbs, wheat, gluten, sugar. They come in sick and in pain. They can't think clearly, have foggy brains and they know something is dreadfully wrong. They don't know what to do about it. This cookbook has the answer.

With the input that Rebekah is providing in *Epicurean Awakening*™, supporting a dynamic way of eating and cutting those things out of the SAD diet, she is providing easy-to-follow recipes, that taste good, and are getting you way ahead of the game. People can actually start reducing inflammation and getting help.

I have great respect for what Rebekah is doing.

We need this kind of information out there.

Foreword

By Kari Halligan

Registered Nurse, RNC, BSN and Holistic Health Coach.

My joy is that you have found this cookbook. It means that you are ready to revolutionize your relationship with food, cooking and your own well-being.

My name is Kari Halligan and I am a Nurse and Personal Coach, working to assist others in achieving their greatest well-being, both inside and outside the hospital setting.

Often, I work with people healing from chronic digestive issues, healing from surgeries, bladder and pelvic floor issues, hormonal imbalances, prenatal and postpartum Moms, as well as people who just want to maintain their health and well-being.

One of the foundational conversations we have is always about diet. How can we create a diet that allows the body to heal and have the proper nutrients it needs? For most people, the first three days are the roughest. Once they get past that, they make it about another two to four weeks and then they start to drop away from their plan. It starts with a little something here and little something there. Then a full blown cheat day!

Why?

Because they feel deprived and unsatisfied by the bland food they are eating. Or eating the same recipe every day with maybe a slight twist ... kale instead of collard greens 😖.

I went to a birthday party for a child once. The child had food allergies and we were given cookies as the birthday treat. After one bite the grandfather leaned over and said, "Wheat free, gluten free, dairy free, sugar free, taste free." Yep ... that about sums it up.

What if we didn't have to go through those first 3 days of intense cravings that leaves us unfulfilled? Or drop off because we wanted something that felt more satisfying?

Now how do we do that?

How do we keep food from feeling boring and unsettling? Meet Rebekah Kee Maya. With her revolutionary cookbook, ***Epicurean Awakening*™**. Rebekah Kee Maya has a creative and inquisitive mind. Going through personal health challenges and with her background in the culinary arts, she began the quest. Like all good scientists, she started with a question ... How do we create healthy whole foods that are nourishing to our bodies and souls? And naturally bring the body to healing and balance? That is exactly what she did. Over several years, decades actually, Rebekah used her background in the culinary arts, healing food knowledge and food elimination skills to play with foods and recipes. She combined and created recipes for things you could never imagine! Donuts?! Bread?! Pasta?! Cake?! Gluten free! Oil free! Sugar free! And Flavor Full!!

Now, she is sharing this knowledge with you. To make it easy to have a wonderful, fulfilling, tasty relationship with your food, cooking experience and your body.

Bringing you back to center.

Bringing you back to balance.

Bringing you back to life.

Kari Halligan, Registered Nurse, RNC, BSN, Holistic Health Coach.

About the Author
Rebekah Kee Maya

"Never let your music die inside of you."
Wayne Dyer

My music was always found in the kitchen. I was born to cook. I was born to bake. Most importantly, I was born to create.

As early as I can remember, I would sit and watch my grandmother bake. She would let me help make the cinnamon rolls and Mandel bread. My favorite part was whipping the cream by hand, not to mention licking any bowls of chocolate cookies or cakes. I think my all-time favorite was her black-bottom mini cupcakes. Chocolate cake on the bottom with cream cheese and chocolate chip topping. I would sneak in the kitchen to steal them after they would go to sleep.

By 8 years old, I had an Easy Bake Oven™. I remember making brownies in them. In high school I was making chocolate mousse, grasshopper pies and my favorite, black bottom cupcakes.

By college, the food scene was revolting. And my state of health was consumed by stress more than anything. In fact, that's when I learned I had high cholesterol. It made no sense to me. I was so active with dance, ice skating and playing volleyball daily. All three of these activities were part of my day. How could I have high cholesterol?

In the fall of my second year in college, I moved out of the dorms and finally into a house with roommates. I was in a small town in New Hampshire outside of my college town. Fall was breathtaking. Exquisite colors and steam came off the ponds in the early morning as I drove to campus to start my classes as a wildlife student. I had a roommate that liked to cook and began showing me some techniques. My very first thing I remember making with her was a pasta salad. It wasn't any pasta salad. It was loaded with veggies and herbs. It was incredible! She showed me how to be bold in choosing flavors. How to let go of being intimidated and to have confidence in whatever I was making. That pasta salad was the beginning of my **Fearless in the Kitchen** adventures. And I've never looked back.

At 23 years old I moved to Chicago after a very frustrating time finding work as a floral designer in New Hampshire. The economy was in a depression of some kind and

I was begging to be a floral designer. So off to Chicago I went. There I trained as a floral designer and found work immediately upon completion.

At this time in my life, my health needed attention. Stress seemed to be the #1 factor for my health issues. By now, I had experienced many skin issues and made countless trips to my dermatologist. This actually began when I was 8 years old with rashes, rough skin and hives.

My health journey as a child was that of a typical Standard American Diet (SAD). And it was definitely SAD. My parents were clueless when it came to food and health. Not once did they connect what you eat and chronic ailments. As a child, I had IBS, severe acne, rashes, hives, etc. ... my mom would say I just had the Katz family digestion. Never once looking further into it. And the suffering was brutal. At 13, I had begun an unknown rash at the beginning of spring and it seemed to be connected to the sun. I was put on so many creams or pills, year after year, as well as allergy shots, year after year. My dad believed that doctors "fixed" everything with a pill. No one considered a dairy allergy or gluten or sugar intolerance. This all came later ... so from the age of 13 to 19, I was at the dermatologist regularly. It wasn't until I was 19, in New Hampshire, that this dermatologist concluded I was allergic to the UVB (sun burning rays) of the sun. Again no one made any connection to food yet. And no one made any connection to stress yet ... sort of. It was complicated. Very complicated ... and until I was older, I didn't know how complicated it was.

At 21, I had a car accident that led to a stress fracture in my lower back. There went my love for ice skating, dancing and volleyball. Inflammation and Advil were a way of life now. And my constant companion, stress, continued to be in my life. In my second year of college, I thought I had an ulcer and lived on Tagamet to get me through. Only leading me straight back into the dermatologist's office. With pityriasis rosea. A virus that looks like chicken pox. And I was miserable. Stress ... diet ... still no one connected the dots. Well, maybe not no one. There was a psychologist that tested me for a learning disability in the second semester of my freshman year. After finally getting "diagnosed," I went into a funk. And when he discovered my stress with my family, my childhood and my father, he began seeing my learning disability as the least of my concerns.

Finishing up school a year later than expected and moving to Chicago seemed to be the fresh start I needed. I didn't realize just how life-changing it really was. At 23, I had one of those life-changing moments standing in a health food store in Geneva,

Illinois. Soup to Nuts it was called. I remember how ready I was to lose the weight of my stress. Little did I know that the two books I walked out with were the first steps in embarking on the next chapter of my life. The path of greater health.

Fit for Life, by Marilyn Diamond and *Real Magic*, by Wayne Dyer. These two books shifted my perspective. One on diet and one on spirituality. The latter is a whole unique universe of its own. At 23, I became vegan overnight after reading Marilyn Diamond's book. My body, for the first time in its life, had relief.

The crescendo didn't come until working as a pastry chef and a floral designer in a suburb of Chicago. Two of my favorite things to do. Creating beautiful things. My joy. I was lit up all the time, even though I was working two full-time jobs. Baking 10,000 chocolate chip cookies once a month. It was at this pastry job, which I absolutely loved, that I could see the connection between sugar and my mood swings. It was here that I could connect the dots with how Dr. Jekyll and Mr. Hyde I became during my monthly cycles. It was here that I learned I had to stop eating white sugar. How can something I love so much be poisoning me? Definitely a conundrum. I eventually left the flower shop to work only at the pastry job. My love for baking, cake decorating and creating pastries was my dream job.

I believe this was the driving force to learn to make desserts healthier so I could enjoy them once again. My desire to learn alternative ways to bake was born.

Being vegan was another joy for me. My body was thriving in this way of eating. Never did I feel deprived. If I did, I would experiment and figure out how to make a delicious dish. Inspiration was and is still always there for me. My mind comes up with ideas and then I find ways to create it. Thirty years later, it is no different. My joy of creating food is right there. My journey of health continued with Acupuncture, network chiropractic care and learning what you put into your body really matters. However, skin issues continued. Why?? Oh, and so did my high cholesterol ...

At 26, I moved to Seattle and had several different pastry chef jobs, until finally landing at a vegan bakery. I was well-known in Seattle for my vegan desserts. I was also teaching cooking classes, cooking for private retreats and catering for many years. I had doctors hire me to help patients learn healthier ways of eating.

It was when I moved to Whidbey Island and began milling my own flours that I understood I had a wheat allergy. I was making fresh whole wheat bread regularly and could see how it impacted my skin with eczema. It became really evident that I had to stop eating wheat. But, it was confusing to me, as sometimes I could eat it and sometimes I couldn't. Again, my body and diet always seemed complicated to me. Not to mention stress ... again. Childbirth, stress, eating meat again due to blood deficiency and living in an emotionally toxic environment was now my new norm. Again, with the stress. Even after two years of working with an Ayurvedic doctor I felt like I had stalled out. Did I have a leak in my lungs where my life force was seeping out of me, from exhaustion? Through a series of events, I was led to the next chapter of my life. Meeting a Tibetan doctor, Paltul Rinpoche. He gave me Tibetan medicine and 3 days later, the sense of my life force seeping out of me stopped. Just like that. And so began my learning about Tibetan medicine. Eighty percent is diet. And the joy of cooking for my body type (Tibetan understanding) began. It all clicked. My body type is such that I have to eat one way spring and summer and another way in fall and winter. The season and the environment play a huge piece in how we feed our bodies. Our bodies parallel the environment. We are the elements of nature. Water is the fluid in our body. Earth is the physical body. Metal is the iron in our blood. Wood is our growth. In Chinese medicine, the wood element is our liver and gall bladder.

I became an energy medicine practitioner with flower and sea essences, learning from a woman on Vancouver Island. Again, my love of flowers, and healing the body were connected to a bigger picture. During this time, I was one of my own case studies with my skin and the sun. For once and for all, I was going to heal what my "sun allergy" really was. To my surprise, it was very meridian based. Meaning the rashes would run on a line connected to an organ. Chinese medicine has a very holistic approach to the body. And I could see that the sun was actually cleansing me. I just didn't know anything about toxic loads at this time ... stress was just a way of life. And the sun was powerful enough to cleanse the toxins out of me. And the liver represents the skin. Resulting in a 27-year journey of detoxes and kidney cleanses. Maintaining a body is work when stress is the go-to. If I managed my stress better and chose joy over stress, I don't believe I would have had to do so many cleanses. However, being born and raised in a very stressful environment kept me locked into this loop. My diet at this point in my life fluctuated immensely ... vegan, vegetarian, omnivore, opportunivore ... Is it right for me or is it hurting me? You can be doing all the right foods in the wrong environment and still have "dis-ease." The definition of diet is "a way of life." My way of life was high-stress survival mode.

My second child was born when I was at age 42. And eating meat was still required for me. Ten years later, it is no longer required but I have grown to like it. A lot.

However, stress dictates the direction of what's required. Time for another kidney cleanse. Time to reset my body. At this point, I hadn't connected the dots of being an empath and a highly sensitive being with eating meat. Again ... it's complicated.

Until I stop making it complicated.

Choosing health and vitality is not the same thing as choosing stress and living in a toxic environment. No matter how much health and vitality you are wishing for, if your environment is toxic, as in toxic people, the emotional stress will overtake any good you are doing with your diet.

I was drowning. My life was steeped in stress. And, at the same time, I was trying to heal my body. It was like taking a bucket and emptying a boat with a hole in the bottom and it keeps filling up with water. I was sinking.

Toxic load is just that. Toxic load. Learning what the toxic load is and taking the right action will turn poor health around. Fatty liver disease is rampant in the US. Is it diet? Is it stress? Is it in your DNA? Getting informed about your body type, your blood type, your DNA will paint a clearer picture of what health and vitality will look like for you. One person's medicine might be another person's poison. Therefore, my recommendation is to gather information first, from several perspectives, and then make informed choices.

It comes back to where is your joy? What brings you the greatest level of happiness and fulfillment? It's quite possible you are not filling yourself up. Are you drowning? Is your boat sinking? Is it time to pivot? Is it time for a new chapter in your life?

Awakening to your illustrious journey. It all begins with a choice. One new choice.

The 4 core choices for your desired outcome are...

*I choose to live a life I love.

*I choose to create health and vitality.

*I choose to live my true nature, on purpose.

*I choose to be the predominant creative force in my life.

Are you ready to choose for you? Are you ready to be big and bold in the kitchen? Are you ready to be **Fearless in the Kitchen**? Being fearless means being willing to take a risk with something new. It means being curious. When you are curious, everything is an experiment. When you experiment, you are not attached to the outcome. You have no point of view as you are willing to try something. You might like it. You might not. You will, however, expand. And inside that expansion brings new growth. And with that new growth brings flexibility, new beginnings, direction and even joy.

When a toddler is given something it loves, like a toy, it will hold on to it for dear life. When you take it away, the toddler throws a tantrum. The only way to prevent this tantrum is to give the toddler something else. Equally pleasing. In doing so, it will release the other toy effortlessly. Without any tantrums. It's a simple formula for creating ease.

When food is one's comfort, be it eating sugar, meat, potatoes, etc. ... it will be difficult to let go of the attachment to it. Unless something equally pleasing comes to you. Being satisfied is one of the biggest keys to living a fulfilling life. It is natural to desire things. However, that desire creates a silent message in our brains. If something is better outside of ourselves, then the silent message is "I'm not good enough," "I don't deserve it" or "I'm not worth it." These silent messages stop satisfaction. These silent messages sabotage growth. If you truly choose to live a life of good health, vitality and Well Being, then being satisfied is the key to feeling successful. Starting with food is a great step in that direction.

The recipes in this book are designed to satisfy you. To satisfy you visually, through smells and through flavor. Being completely satisfied is aligning you with creating a life you love. It is aligning you with the awakening you are here for. To be the fully satisfied lover of life you've always dreamed of.

Introduction
By Jessika Neuert, Nutritionist and Wellness Coach

Metabolism. Everyone has heard of it. Everyone has it. What can I do to maximize it? Start by stopping the consumption of food combinations that reduce your body's natural ability to assimilate nutrients. Sounds pretty simple, right? Yet, most of us break what I consider to be the number 1 rule of food consumption ... That is, eat no sugar. When you consume sugar, your body is not able to assimilate fat properly. Basically, metabolism is reduced by eating sugar. Would you drive a car with one foot on the gas and one foot on the brake? If you did, you would not get anywhere. Either the brakes would fail or the engine would fail. Is this what you want for your body? Of course not. That is why you are reading *Epicurean Awakening*™ and learning how to cook in a way that supports your Well Being.

Because of having seizures at 8 and 9 years old, I decided to find out what was causing them. I was scared. The doctor gave me anti-seizure medicine but could give me no reason for why I was having them. He called it Epilepsy. So I went to the library and read everything I could find about the cause of Epilepsy. Sugar kept coming up as having an association with seizures. And I was definitely over-eating sugar. Since I had no parental oversight, I ate sugar every chance I could.

Until I became determined to stop having seizures. Again, at 9 years old, I knew that something had to change, and I found that eating a ketogenic diet would be a big help. I began eating a bunch of fat. And protein. But the thing that really changed my life forever was that I stopped eating all processed sugars.

Today, as an adult, and having continued my research into eating for greater health, I find that eating all of the non-seasonal fruits and veggies, sugars, preservatives, GMO's, glyphosate and other chemicals, while having a considerable lack of "good" bacteria in our gut, it's a wonder anyone is alive anymore!

These days, we are ingesting more histamines than our bodies can realistically filter. Histamines come from unripe fruits. Fruits that are grown out of season, shipped to us green, and eaten as if it is a normal thing. It may taste good, but it has increased histamines. So, coupled with eating all the sugars, the liver cannot process, cannot filter the way it's supposed to.

I'll call it what it is, Toxicity. And Toxicity creates a toxic environment that in turn, creates inflammation. Yes, toxins create inflammation, resulting in histamine activation in an already histamine-rich environment, as your body attempts to eradicate the toxins. Combined with the big blobs from oils and indigestible fats that are cruising around in your system and adding to the inflammation, from the sugars. This is what I call a mess!

We don't digest proteins properly when we consume sugars. A major part of proper digestion starts in the tastebuds. The tastebuds need to be stimulated by naturally occurring bitter compounds in the foods. For example, let's say you were to eat radicchio or Romaine lettuce without sugar, like honey mustard dressing, and you get the bitter stimulation on your tastebuds, the body actually tells the liver and the gallbladder to start making the enzymes to break down what you are eating. It's basically turning on the enzymes needed for digesting the naturally occurring sugars.

But if you're constantly eating sugar, the body never gets that mechanism turned on. The body actually cannot function properly. it becomes stuck. It's asleep or dormant. Removing the sugar wakes up healthy digestion. And eating foods that are not over-processed, not sweetened and are savory, activates an entire system of digestive stimulants.

Now that the enzymes and acids are getting produced, the body can actually start metabolizing in a strong and healthy manner. **Without those bitter compounds, the body accumulates toxins.**

Read that again. It's literally just like pouring sugar into your gas tank. It's only creating long-term issues. You're not going to go anywhere. The toxins are just floating around. Now you have these oils, sugars and toxins floating around in your bloodstream. And you wonder why you have brain fog, you feel tired all the time, your body is achy ... The thing is, you know why you can't move. It's because of the choices you have made. So, removing the sugar is a key.

By alleviating the body from the histamines and sugars, you're actually allowing the body to do its job and clean you up. The biggest problem is we don't stay in Healthy mode. Are we addicted to pleasure mode, or comfort mode? Our liver isn't getting the nourishment it needs and is not capable of filtering out the toxins at the level they are coming in. All the excess and unprocessed histamines, sugars and chemicals cause the body to rebel against you. Then you end up with allergies, nasal congestion, chronic digestive issues, skin issues ... whatever is your most vulnerable point of immunity gets attacked. That's why it's called an auto-immune disorder.

It doesn't matter if you are eating a million supplements, or doing cleanses or following treatments ... it's really all about clearing the way to make the change in your eating habits. It's literally about clearing the way so that your body can do its job. That's the biggest thing that you can do. Simple. It is so incredibly simple. And, I believe this is the most important thing to remember ... that it's simple. It doesn't involve hundreds of dollars of supplements. It doesn't involve expensive medical treatments. It doesn't involve any procedures. It's literally just getting out the toxins and getting your body able to do its job. Out-of-season and unripened fruits have histamines, and if you are eating sugar, the liver cannot filter it out as it should.

Remember, it actually goes back to the flavor. It goes back to the senses. Why are we doing this? We're trying to please ourselves, we're trying to satiate ourselves, we are trying to comfort ourselves. One way or another, we are actually the ones doing "it" to ourselves.

Empower yourself. Put the control of your health back into your own hands. Reclaim your Well Being. Rebekah is giving you your life back through *Epicurean Awakening*™. Don't just read it. Embrace it as your commitment to clearing out the toxins that keep you from living life with energy, vitality and great flavors.

Having spent most of my life guiding and supporting people toward their best possible personal health, I find it exciting to see people taking hold of their health. Watching, as you literally are putting your life in your own hands. Each time you reach out for food and put it into your mouth, you are dictating your health and your life. Rebekah has put that control back into your hands by writing this really great manual, so that you can take your life back, seriously. You've literally been given the opportunity to get your life back and your joy back and your comfort, too, because you are getting satisfied through this food. And the food actually nourishes you, without harm.

Jessika

What Will YOU Choose … ?

Your Awakening Begins!

Let the Fun begin ...

How to take advantage of natural ingredients, achieving results that create pleasure ... without the foods you can no longer eat.

"The original meaning of the word 'bless' was to consecrate with blood or to strike. I think often our blessings come to us disguised as suffering, to cut away the deadwood in our lives and enable us to move in new directions. Pruning can be painful, but in the hands of a Master Gardner, great beauty is created."

Anonymous

What is disease? It's a question that is often followed with, why is there disease? The SAD (Standard American Diet) is consumed with processed sugars, high sodium, high fats and little nutritional value. Coupled with life stressors, such as uncertainty, fear and anger. It's easy to believe that something has to change. With ongoing stressors, at some point the body begins to break down without proper nourishment. What change is possible? That is what *Epicurean Awakening*™, The Cookbook, answers. Awakening to rich foods that are loaded with nutrition, full of pleasure and filled with satisfaction.

Change doesn't have to be hard, it just needs to be understood.

A dietary approach to the seasons and environment we live in, creates harmony or disharmony in the body (ease vs dis-ease). Diet, like the environment, is dynamic, not static, and constantly changing. Our bodies are in the same constant transition. And our bodies must meet our constantly changing biological needs.

What happens when we live in limitation?

Resistance, attachments, beliefs, habits, fear (**F**eeling **E**verything **A**s **R**eal) and many unwanted circumstances, set up our path. The simplest way of saying this, is to think of a baby being born, living in innocence, and as this baby individuates between 4 and 7 years old, the child learns how to play the "game" in order to get its needs met. We define ourselves not through who we believe we are but as those that have defined us growing up. We become the circumstances of our environment, our family, our teachers, classmates, etc.

Limitations are experiences that define us. And those "ceilings" that we carry within become deeply rooted.

Perhaps if people followed the path of gratitude as the go to, there wouldn't be as many chronic illnesses. After all, illness is defined as a "deficiency." Lack is considered a deficiency. Lack of love, lack of joy, lack of abundance, lack of family. They possess the same qualities in the body as they do in the mind. What if the body is a reflection of the mind? Holistic medicine is treating the whole person. The Body, Mind and Spirit. Each is interdependently connected. And when you nourish one aspect of yourself, another aspect receives it as well. Similar to entrainment. You are entraining your Body, Mind and Spirit to live in harmony. This is the beginning of a wellness plan.

Therapeutic Diets

Diet comes from the Greek word *diatia*, meaning a way of life. Embarking on a whole-foods plant-based diet is a lifestyle change. Becoming sugar-free, oil-free, gluten free, all fall into the category of a lifestyle change. If you are new to this, you are changing from what you are familiar with to something you are completely unfamiliar with. In other words, you are getting out of your comfort zone, away from your comfort foods and you are choosing to "live" with new ideas and concepts.

For some of you, this brings resistance, revealing where you have food attachments and beliefs that may create more struggle. This concept of "struggle" is a pattern. It may even be hardwired into you. It means that you are not going to make this easy on yourself. Unless you come from a place of curiosity, gratitude and allowance. Welcome to surrendering.

If you are in a health crisis, I refer to this as the "Do or Die Diet." You have to do it or you will die. It's that simple. However, the "fear" of deprivation and the "now what can I eat?" feels a bit overwhelming. The intention of this cookbook is to take the "fear" and the overwhelm out of your "mental association" of diet. It's designed to allow for the *Epicurean Awakening*™ to grow inside of you. To take flight and open your senses with a new way of seeing. A new way of being in your body and in the world. This book is meant to "transform" you with grace. Not to consume you with deprivation.

When you understand the natural order of the outer world, the inner world finds its harmony. A dietary approach to seeking balance doesn't exist. A dietary approach to seeking satisfaction, no matter what circumstances arise, is what we are after. Balance lives in polarity. You cannot have light without dark. Contraction and expansion are the same. If you choose to live in the contraction, you will find the darkness, the agitation, the fear, the lack and the excuses to not change. When you choose expansion, you allow, seek greater clarity and are open to embracing what's possible. Some of these recipes in the book need you to go beyond what you "believe" they will taste like. They will test your ideas, beliefs, attachments and conclusions. Your tendency will be to identify the recipes based on what your mind says and not what your taste buds say. Remember, this is the type of thinking that got you here in the first place.

What is Aquaschata™?

Aquaschata™ is the FIRST EVER cooking oil alternative, helping you live a healthy heart and liver focused lifestyle. It is a compound ingredient used in cooking AND baking, made primarily from butternut squash. Because of its Superfood ingredients, it has a fraction of the fat content that traditional cooking oils consist of. It is also sugar-free and unlike most processed products, it can stand on its own, without adding sugar to compensate for being Fat-Free!

Over 80 Million Americans battle Liver Disease and its side effects. Doctors have found that Non-Alcoholic Fatty Liver Disease (NAFLD) can be mostly controlled with dietary changes and lifestyle alternatives.

Even more alarming, there are more than 130 Million adults living with diabetes or are pre-diabetic. And, sadly, 1.4 million people a year are being newly diagnosed.

What is the link between Diabetes and Non-Alcoholic Fatty Liver and Linoleic Acid (LA)?

Linoleic acid (LA), an omega-6 fat, is a toxic and harmful ingredient in the modern diet. Excessive LA intake, in the form of industrial seed oils, is responsible for most chronic diseases, including obesity, cancer and heart disease. (*1)

Most health-minded experts still believe the primary cause for these trends is sugar, but Linoleic acid (LA) is far more dangerous than sugar, from a metabolic perspective. At this point, I believe it's really the excessive amounts of LA in our modern diet driving these metabolic diseases.

Rather than attempting to list everything you need to include in a healthy diet, it's far easier to identify and eliminate the dietary components that do the most harm.

Like sugar. Sugar, when consumed in excess over time will result in insulin resistance and metabolic inflexibility. However, if you cut out sugar, you can rather rapidly restore both your insulin sensitivity and metabolic flexibility, because your body can only store about a day's worth of glucose.

Not so with fat. Your body can store a lot of fat, for long periods of time. LA is literally incorporated into and stored in your cell membranes, where it can remain for up to seven years. Even if you go on a low LA diet, it'll take years to fully clear it out of your body. This also means you won't notice improvements in your health as quickly as you do when cutting out sugar.

(*1) https://www.hindawi.com/journals/jdr/2019/5267025/

The way sugar impacts the brain, and the way processed oils impacts the liver, we are not getting the nutrients the brain and the body require for living a healthy and vital life.

Is there a solution?

What if using a cooking oil alternative allows you to **"Give your body a break."** If you consider how much processed oil is consumed in a typical American's daily diet, along with the amount of sugars consumed in a typical day, the questions begging to be asked are, "How do I catch up with being healthy? How do I find homeostasis? And what happens if I don't?" These diabetes/fatty liver numbers are beyond alarming ... They reflect a silent epidemic! Without a strategy in place, what hope is there?

Suggestions often consist of:

~Reducing ingested animal proteins.

~Increasing carbohydrates in proportion with your protein.

~Eating a diet heavy in legumes, poultry and fish.

However, there is one suggestion that is rarely discussed.

~Decreasing the amount of oil and fat-based ingredients in your diet in order to lower the Linoleic Acid in the body. While it has been accepted by millions of diabetics to reduce their sugar, it has not been widely accepted to remove oils in support of a fatty liver.

The purpose here is "To Give Your Body a Break."

When your body has reached its toxic load, i.e., the point of developing disease, the only way to turn it around is to eliminate that which is creating the problem. And the healthiest step you can make is choosing to live an oil free and sugar free lifestyle. And taking your healing to that next level by incorporating Aquaschata™, as a Superfood, in your daily meals. Aquaschata™ For Life.

What is a Superfood?

A superfood is defined as "a food (such as salmon, broccoli, or blueberries) that is rich in compounds (such as antioxidants, fiber, or fatty acids) considered beneficial to a person's health," according to the Merriam-Webster Dictionary. Scientifically speaking, though, there is no official definition of a superfood, other than to say it is a food that offers high levels of desirable nutrients, linked to promoting personal health and wellness or preventing disease and sickness.

Food as Medicine is something that I have always spoken to. In fact, I go into detail on this subject in this Cookbook, *Epicurean Awakening*™. Food can either be medicine or it can be poison based on your toxic load and constitution. Each individual has a unique chemistry based on genetics, environment, diet and the foods you eat. A superfood falls into the category of "functional foods that provide benefits that can either reduce their risk of disease and/or promote good health."

How does Aquaschata™ fall into this category and provide the health benefits that will "Give your Body a Break?"

Aquaschata's™ key ingredients are Butternut squash and Turmeric.

- Butternut squash is packed with vitamins, minerals, fiber and antioxidants, lowering blood pressure and reducing your risk for stroke or heart disease. Its fiber helps with slowing the metabolism of the sugar in the squash making it low on the glycemic index and is an excellent healthy food for diabetics. The high antioxidant content may reduce heart disease, lung cancer and mental decline. And even has cholesterol and insulin-regulating properties.

- Turmeric, is another super potent anti-inflammatory and antioxidant. It may help improve symptoms of depression and arthritis. It has been scientifically proven to improve heart health and prevent Alzheimer's and cancer.

Again, it's time to "Give Your Body a Break."

The biggest concern people have regarding changing their way of eating comes down to... does it have any flavor? We hear this all of the time... "But it won't taste good ... "

That is just NOT true.

Meet Rebekah Kee Maya and my "one of a kind" cooking oil alternative, Aquaschata™. I have found a way to reinvent guilty pleasures without the guilt and bring in FULL flavor satisfaction. This cutting-edge cookbook, *Epicurean Awakening™*, is revolutionizing a new way of creating foods that deliver not only good health, it brings joy back to cooking, again.

Cook without the guilt of oil or sugars and transform your menu with this amazing, new, alternative to fatty cooking by using Aquaschata™. Your liver, your heart and your overall body will thank you.

Give your body a break.

What foods can you use Aquaschata™ in?

Aquaschata™ is used in both savory and sweet. It is used in salad dressings, BBQ sauce, stir-fries, breads, tortillas, pretzels, cakes, muffins, crackers, cookies and so much more. It is so versatile. It can be used cold or heated up. It literally replaces the oil in recipes. The only thing it doesn't work on, sadly, is popcorn. (But she is working on it!)

Rebekah's recipes are so creative and so delicious that you don't miss the sugar and oils. There is still fat, and there is still flavor. However, the body begins recognizing your lifestyle changes, and the weight begins to drop if you needed to lose some. Your energy comes back. Your life force begins to kick in as you support your body with the lifestyle change that's right for you.

You don't have to live with the story that is genetic. After all, we're talking chemistry here! You can change your diet and change your health. It's that simple. It's truly a choice.

Giving your body a break is what your body is asking for. If now is the time to try something new and different, then you've come to the right place.

Note - Aquaschata™ is in the process of having a Patent, and, even though the Patent is Pending, I am sharing as much of the recipe here, as I can. Someday, you will be able to buy it in the grocery store.

Aquaschata™ Recipe
Basic Recipe:
1/3 cup steamed Butternut Squash
1 cup Filtered water

Professional Grade Recipe:
1/3 cup steamed Butternut Squash
1 cup Filtered Water
1/4 tsp Turmeric
1/8 tsp Citric Acid
1 tsp Proprietary Blend
Dash of Salt

Let's get Started!

Where to begin? This is a process, remember? One step at a time ...
Going gluten-free ...
What do I eat now?
Becoming a vegan ... a whole new lifestyle change around food. Where do I start?
Becoming sugar-free ... no problem. I've got you covered. You won't feel deprived. I promise you that! What are the basic kitchen tools that will make this work for me?
Finally ... oil free ... ok, I crossed the line. That's just impossible!

No, it is not impossible.
You can actually live an oil-free life.
And not feel deprived?
Yes, and not feel deprived. Oil-free does not mean fat-free. It means you are giving your liver a break. It means your body can catch up to the toxic load you are carrying. If you have fatty liver disease or high inflammation or high cholesterol, changing how you eat is important. But even more important is how you live. Are you living with chronic stress? Is your environment toxic?

But I don't have any motivation to change ... I've been doing this for so long I don't know where to begin.

And that's where I come in. I was born to cook. I was born to bake! And I was born to create! However, more importantly, I was born to awaken the epicurean in me and the epicurean in you. Pleasure is a natural state of being. Just like good health. And if you are not having any pleasure, it is time to wake that up.

If you are here, reading this, you are looking for a change. You are looking to get out of pain. You are looking for a way to increase satisfaction! There is a whole new world of food satisfaction that I will be bringing you. Both in conversation and cooking instructions. I will show up for you and I ask that you show up for you. As of right now, you are choosing to make a commitment to yourself to allow greater pleasure and greater flexibility in your mind and in your body. Let's begin with "where do I start?"

Basic Starter Kit -

1 - Buy organic produce when possible.
2 - READ LABELS - avoid any packaged food that has hydrogenated oils or partially hydrogenated oils. If you are going oil-free, then zero oils.
3 - Avoid foods with corn syrup, fructose, glucose sucrose, etc.
4 - Avoid any food that contains red dye, blue dye, yellow dye, or any dye. These are cancer-causing. This includes shampoos, body lotions, etc. It may appear it is virtually in everything, but this is not so. Go deeper.
5 - Go through your food pantry and separate those foods that contain items from the above #2, #3, #4. Either donate them, place a 6-month limit on them for their use or throw them out. This may seem radical; however, you may be surprised at what is left that doesn't contain them.
6 - Spend the afternoon in a Natural Foods grocery store and learn what alternatives can replace what you have or want.
7 - Don't despair, it is a process. Allow small steps to be taken. You have plenty of time.

Vegetarian and Whole Foods are powerful for your health -

A Vegetarian menu or incorporating more natural and whole-grain foods is a powerful and pleasurable way to achieve good health. However, sometimes the food we put into our bodies isn't always the cause of poor health. Our thoughts and our environment are also influencing our bodies. One can eat the right foods and live in a toxic environment and still get sick.

The term vegetarian now a days can be confusing. That's why naming it "whole foods plant based" works. It defines the ingredients. You can be vegan and not eat healthy foods. I've seen a lot of people choose that. You can eat a whole food plant-based diet and include fish. Or eggs. I will get into the uniqueness of you later. For now, we will stick to the name whole foods plant-based diet to keep things simple.

Let's begin with -
Step 1 - Get 3 boxes. And mark on each box, throw away, keep and give away.
Step 2 - Go through your cabinets and pull out all of your food and set it on the counter. One cabinet at a time. Read the labels and place each item in one of the

boxes. What will you end up "keeping?" Have you had a box of food in your cupboards for 5 years? 10 years? dare I say, even longer? And what is it still doing in that cabinet? What are you attached to? Emptiness is a topic we will cover in this book, much later! It's time to throw it away. If you have food that is in good condition but doesn't fit your new lifestyle, place it in the giveaway box and offer it to a family that will enjoy it. If you have foods that are rotting in the fridge, if the salad dressing bottles are still there from 2 or 3 years ago ... it's time to LET THEM GO! You are about to learn what making space looks and feels like from the outside in. First in your kitchen, then in your body.

If you are going Gluten Free - wheat, barley, rye, couscous, triticale, farina, spelt, wheat germ, wheat berries, kamut, and white flour are put in the giveaway or throw-away box.

If you are going Sugar-Free - corn syrup, sugar, evaporated cane juice, sucrose, dextrose, any ingredient with "ose" at the end of the word is considered a sugar. This means all jams, jellies, cookies, candies, "that stash" for a splurge day, all go into the giveaway or throw-away box.

If you are going Oil Free - sunflower oil, olive oil, canola oil, safflower oil etc. Read what is in your extracts. Some have oils in them. Spaghetti sauce, oat milk, coconut milk, rice milk, cookies, breads, sauces, salad dressings, cans that have oil in them, soups ... read the labels. You will learn a lot!

If you are choosing a vegan/whole foods plant-based diet - If you see ingredients such as whey, dairy, casein, cheese, condensed milk, milk, or evaporated milk, in the boxes they go!

Extras - artificial flavored colors, autolyzed yeast, MSG, fried foods and preservatives.

Step 3 - What remains in your kitchen? Clean your refrigerator now. Wipe down the inside of your cabinets and let's start creating a shopping list. What do we get to fill your new pantry with?

Before we go shopping, here are some pointers if you are in the transition of changing your diet to a more healthier one.

1 - Think of 3 vegetarian meals that you already enjoy. Common ones are spaghetti with tomato sauce, vegetable soup and pasta primavera.

2 - Next, think of 3 recipes that you prepare regularly that can easily be adapted to a vegetarian meal. Examples of this are a favorite chili recipe, most ethnic foods and

many soups, stews and casseroles. With a few changes, you can have the healthier meal.

3 - Finally, check some vegetarian and whole foods cookbooks out of the library (magazines too) and experiment with the recipes for a week or so until you find three that you enjoy and can prepare easily.

4 – And sign up for my 3 month companion program, **Fearless in The Kitchen**, in order to see how *Epicurean Awakening*™ recipes are so easy to make. You'll also learn some fantastic new recipes! And, because you have already purchased this cookbook, you will receive a considerable discount. Check it out at EpicurianAwakening.com.

Health and Vitality

What does Health and Vitality mean to you? Is it just about food? Is it about your body? Is it your mind? Are you aware that your mind and your thoughts create your body? What do you think really matters? What your mind believes is what your body becomes. Are you carrying things that no longer support your body? Thoughts, feelings and emotions throughout your life have frequencies and they live inside your body. Each organ actually carries its own frequency. As does every cell in your body! And if you have a toxic load, you probably have some toxic thoughts. They sort of work hand in hand. Eliminating diets and detox diets (sort of like spring cleaning) are how we start to clear away the debris. Are you prepared for that? If not, it's something to consider. Even though it can develop into a thought like "eating healthier" makes you sick. Because there can be a 7 - 10 day period which may look like a cold starting when you start putting in the good stuff and removing the bad stuff. And when I say bad, it doesn't mean bad for everyone, just your body type. I will get into that later. For now, know that not everyone has a body that can handle juicing and raw foods.

This information is helping you build a foundation for your lifestyle change. And depending on where you are ... meaning in the beginning, in the middle or the end when it comes to eating right for your body type ... it's a process that keeps on keeping on.

So what do you value? Do you value your body? Do you value what you look like more than what you feel like? Do you value how you feel over what you believe others have to say about you?

Growing up, what did good health look like to you? Was it eating an apple a day keeps the doctor away? Or maybe eating your vegetables? There are some states in the

Midwest that believe iceberg lettuce is healthy. They believe that is what a salad is based on. In other cultures, eating cooked foods is what they consider healthy. A macrobiotic diet is based on all cooked foods and not raw foods. And yet, people believe that eating raw foods is healing to the body. Do you see the confusion this creates? Which is right? Which is wrong? Which will serve you?

Ultimately, it's about learning what works for you. Discovering what the different body types are is a subject that I cover for you later on in the book.

When we choose to live a life we love we are making a declaration in some way. Saying I choose to live a life with health, vitality and Well Being means that you are declaring this. However, it's not straightforward.

Wayne Dyer has a great story. It's about what's inside an orange. He asked an audience for people to answer this question. What's inside an orange? Well, it's orange juice of course! It cannot be pineapple juice or apple juice because it's an orange. It has to be what's inside and when it comes out you expect orange juice right? Well, this has the same effect on us. What's inside us? What comes out when we are squeezed? When we are under pressure.

Here we begin to see a bigger awakening to what this means. Is it love that comes out? Is it hatred that comes out? Is it sadness that comes out? You are filled with a lifetime of thoughts, feelings and emotions. And everywhere you have chosen a life that has been unhealthy, your body will show you the results of those choices. Unhealthy thoughts. Unhealthy actions. Unhealthy words. Unhealthy relationships (parents, family, children, primary, friends, work). All these defining moments create what's inside you. From the moment you are born all the way to today. And beyond!

If you have never done a detox, and are choosing it now, you are about to see what's inside your closets. Some closets are full of dust and cobwebs. We can't avoid this. The body will begin to break down one way or another if this isn't addressed. **Be sure to consult your physician before starting any cleanse or detoxification.**

So, what does choosing health, vitality and Well Being mean? It means that you begin the process of taking control of how you feel. How you wake up in your life. It means you are now in charge of the state of your being, by feeding your body and your thoughts something new and different. Bringing in new value, new awareness and new concepts as you have chosen a new lifestyle. Be prepared for it to not look like what you thought it might look like. And enjoy the journey, because that's what you are beginning. A new lifestyle change is the beginning of creating as you go.

Menu Planning

So what would you like to create? Let's start with Menu Planning. The ins and outs of it and why now is the time to do it.

Menu Planning helps your budget. You also don't waste food. How many times a week do you go to the grocery store? How many times do you go in for one or two things and come out with 25 or 40 things? Did you have a list? Did you buy things spontaneously? And when you do that, how much attention did you give things you thought you wanted but didn't use? Did they get thrown out? We waste time and energy buying things we aren't planning for.

Are you working full-time and don't have time to shop? Don't have time to prep foods and or don't have time to make things the way you want? Well, menu planning allows for some creativity and flow without the burden of "I don't have time." We are creatures of habit, yes? And when we don't have plans for dinner, the drive-through becomes the quick and easy route. But wait, you can't eat certain foods anymore, and now you have to behave ... so how long does that last? Well, if you understand where your weakness is, then perhaps menu planning will stop you from choosing the worst-case scenario.

Menu planning does a lot more than just saving money. When you menu plan, you are now able to adjust your recipes so you have a proper rotation diet. A rotation diet is allowing your body to receive the maximum amount of nutrients in a week without comprising your body by overloading it with the same food day after day. You can have a well-rounded diet now by rotating the foods you eat so your body is maximizing the nutrients it gets. This is a huge perk and many doctors suggest rotating our foods. 4 days is what is suggested here. In other words, if you eat a food today, wait 4 days before eating that same food again. Menu planning can really support this way of eating. Because frankly, it's easy to have leftovers every day. It's easy to not be creative in the kitchen. Again, we are discovering ways to expand.

The simplest way to start is to take out a piece of paper and make 7 columns. Put the day of the week at the top. And make three lines below for Breakfast, Lunch and Dinner. And start with your easiest one. Is it Breakfast or lunch? Do you go out to lunch daily for work? You know your schedule the best. So, start with the one that you have the most information about. Do you need snacks? Do you have an intermittent fast? Meaning you don't eat until noon and you stop eating at 5 or 6 pm? Do you have to eat every 3 or 4 hours with no snacks? We are all different. Your body is asking for fuel it can rely on. In Chinese medicine, there is Stomach Chi (this is the fuel the body uses). But when you skip a meal, now it has to rely on a different source of Chi. There are several types of Chi in the body. Your spiritual fuel and your food fuel are easy to understand. If you are skipping meals, is your body being sacrificed? Creating consistency is what your body will begin to trust you with. Skipping breakfast, skipping lunch, not remembering when you last ate, shopping for food while you are hungry and not having any plan is a total setup for burnout ... somewhere. Don't let that be you.

Embracing strategies for success is what builds confidence. When you run out of a food, add it to a list. Teach your kids to do it too. Structure may feel different to everyone. Some love it and some hate it. Now, if you were to ask your body this question, what do you think it would say? Would it be happy with the structure and routine you've given it? Do you exercise your body daily? Weekly? You haven't gotten around to starting yet? You started but then something stopped you and you haven't started again? Again, we live as creatures of habit. So what successful strategies are available so you feel you are gaining confidence in your new lifestyle change?

By the way, your call to action on this subject is to create a menu plan for 1 week. Try it and see what works, and what you like about it. What was frustrating about it? Did you stick to the plan? Or did you move them around? If your plans change, it's ok to move things around. You have leftovers? Great, you can freeze them and eat them on your "leftover" day. The more "leftover" days you have, the easier this menu planning gets, do you see that?

Comfort Foods

Alternative foods as comfort foods ... really? For most people, breads, pastas, chips, potatoes, sugar, salt, smooth, crunchy, hot, cold are the popular comfort food sensations. How about pizza? Ice cream? Cookies? Bacon? This is a fascinating topic that deserves to be addressed.

First, I'd like to ask you a question about emotional eating vs. comfort eating. Are they the same for you? For now, I am only addressing the comfort aspect. However, they can be confusing and mean the same thing for some.

The best way to start is by asking a simple question. "What are you filling yourself up with?" Similarly, "What are you hungry for?" When you begin to see the "signs" of what it is that is going on in your life, you will begin to see your patterns.

For now, a simple question, "What are you filling yourself up with?"

When you ask this, what do you hear?

Comfort is the gathering of evidence allowing you to create your "comfort zone." Maybe, asking yourself, "What am I uncomfortable with?" will begin the unraveling of what has contributed to what ails you. What is it you are avoiding? What are you needing?

This leads to the point of this book. What satisfaction level are you really seeking? Is it the crunchy foods? The creamy foods? The sugary foods? There's something that is triggering you that puts you in "need" to comfort yourself. With babies, it's more obvious, since they can't talk. Pacifying and swaddling babies are ways to help them feel safe. To help them self soothe. Foods are introduced in so many different ways. For some, it's bribing ... here's a cookie if you do x,y,z. Or here's ice cream as a reward. Food at a very early age is often used as a tool such as potty training ... you get rewarded with some kind of "treat" for performing. Because these patterns are instilled at such an early age, we have no idea, for the most part, why we do what we do. We only know that we do it.

Ready to break free from your limiting patterns? Stop seeing "change" as the problem and step out of your comfort zone? Then, here is a strategy to manage the changes with fun, creativity and delicious outcomes that may even surprise you. I'm also doing it in a way that isn't too much work. I know you are all busy and taking the time to take care of yourself may seem impossible to fit it into your already over-scheduled life. Remember, this is a lifestyle change. And that means finding time to make those changes. You're worth it.

This is why making it work for the whole family has value. Feeding your family these foods will support you in your quest for Well Being. And they might not find anything "missing." And embrace the idea of doing food differently. You can always offer "extra sides of what they also love" to what you have made them. And then everyone wins.

As part of my strategy for your success, I am visually "recreating" something familiar. Familiarity stimulates a level of comfort. As adults, there are a lot of situations that you might become "stressed out." It might be your home environment, your work environment, you might be taking care of a parent, you might have lost a job, your intimacy with your spouse has disappeared, and you have lost your connection to what lights you up and turns you on. Food is a REALLY easy way to fill those needs. And the unhealthier the food is, the quicker you might go into some kind of loop of self-punishment. We are looking to find what it is you're seeking to fill yourself up with. And if you can do it with healthier choices, you will most likely have a positive response to it.

Remember, we eat with our eyes first. If the eyes send a message that the food is "familiar," you have a better chance of self-soothing and feeling satisfied. And ultimately, satisfaction is what you are craving.

Taking these baby steps in practicing new choices, might undo some of the old wiring. And that may bring up resistance. It might even bring up some emotions. Stay on course and remember why you started this in the first place. What is your intention? Here is an exercise to get you started towards your new desire. A call to action.

Your Call to Action is to create a list of your own alternatives to your comfort foods. Have fun, be realistic and get creative!

Food Alignment - Food Frequencies

What does food alignment mean?

Let's consider the word alignment to also mean "harmony." When things are working in harmony, life seems to be working for you and not against you. The saying, "Path of least resistance" would fit into this concept of harmony. Not conflict or struggle. You can see how having a harmonious diet would set up success for a healthy body. Eating foods that are harmonious is supporting the choice you are making to value you and your body. To value you and your relationship to food and to the environment. Choosing to live a life of optimal health and vitality. In order to set you up in the correct mindset for Food Alignment, let's take a look at different aspects of your life and its environment to paint a picture of why this topic is so important for greater health.

Everything is a frequency. By definition, the simplest way to put this is the number of waves that pass a fixed place in a given amount of time. For example, an "A" note on a violin string vibrates at about 440 Hertz (440 vibrations per second). Our bodies are made up of mostly water. And water can be made up of crystals. As seen in Dr. Emoto's examples of different sounds, messages, and energies that are given to a single water crystal, resulting in images based on the "pure" or "toxic" messages in relationship to it. With this example, can you begin to understand that your body and its organs are living in a "pure" or "toxic" vibration, based on several factors. 1) The environment you live in now. 2) The environment you grew up in. 3) Foods you indulge in to nourish or deplete the body. When you discover that you are one big crystal formation, this concept of "food alignment" begins to take shape. Even the land the food grows in, contains its own frequencies. Some are supported in integrity and others are stripped of their integrity.

Farming is a big part of this conversation. The foods you eat. Are they organic? Are they local? Are they grown in your own garden, or bought at a supermarket delivered from other parts of the world even? This is a basic concept of how the ground is stripped of nutrition or how it's fed.

Farming practices are not all equal. Organic farmers take a lot of time giving back to the soil. With rotation crops and cover crops done over winter. Feeding the with nutrients allowing the plants to have a thriving, healthy and harmonious environment. Adding worms, and using compost tea, brings in the nematodes which feed the soil even greater. All of this is part of a harmonious cycle of growing foods that are going to give you the best nutritional bang for your buck.

Even companion planting allows for mutual respect in a garden. However, big farmers don't take the time for this. They plant the same crop year after year after year on the same land. Stripping it of nutrients. Stripping it of its integrity. And then using chemicals to keep the pests free and clear, adding fertilizer to create "perfect" crops and using GMO seeds to make a "better product" for the "consumer." In both of these examples, you can see where frequencies are not the same.

When integrity is compromised, you begin to see the bigger picture. That bigger picture now takes place in you and your body and your choices. Aligning with foods that are life-sustaining means choosing food grown in a harmonious manner.

Let's take another look with a different perspective. You may be that person who eats really healthy and is still finding you have food "issues" and or "gut health" issues.

The environment you grew up in … was it a loving home? Harmonious? Or was there a lot of fighting, conflict, yelling and absent parents? Did you have a happy childhood? Or did you suffer both emotionally and physically? Can you see how your body might thrive in a "healthy harmonious" environment and be nurtured better than the "toxic" environment? One that depletes and offers little emotional support? Frequencies are woven in and around the different types of environments you grew up in. You can do everything "right" eating wise, and still be sick, if your environment doesn't support you.

I'm going to take this a step further. Your constitution is also determined not only by genetics, it is also influenced by the health and well being of the mother, in utero. Were you welcomed? Were you considered a "mistake?" Were you the first born or the last born? The state of mind, the state of health and the joy or lack of joy your mother had while you were in utero defines the "frequency" imprint you start with and carry into your life. And you begin attracting like frequencies. Like frequencies attracts like frequencies. So if you were a victim growing up, being bullied, was your mother a victim? If you didn't have a lot of attention from your father, did you do things to be "seen?" Creating a way to get attention. Remember, negative attention is better than no attention. Again, setting up the "mind" and the family environment brings in "harmony" or "struggle/conflict."

Our thoughts create our reality. Our thoughts (if we buy into them) create the "form" of our bodies. Are you strong and healthy? Are you weak and anxious? Are you a positive person? Or do you grab the negative thoughts first? This complex system is then intertwined with what I call the "compensation system." And this compensation system is your "default" for how you live. It is your hard wiring. And that hard wiring is very inflexible when it comes to change.

What does this create then in the body? This question leads to a book of its own, so I will do my best to briefly cover this here. If you can, picture your body as a golden retriever following your mind around as a faithful puppy, looking to please its master. The non-meditative mind doesn't realize how toxic our thoughts can be. In fact, they believe they are right! That's the ego talking.

The mind also doesn't practice being present. It, too, strays to the past to "complain" or the "future" to complain and tends to never be satisfied with what is. Sending silent messages of "never being enough." This non-settled mind, this wandering mind, this unsatisfied mind, has spent a long, long time not being nourished and out of harmony.

Not being nourished means that what you see, what you take in, what you may or may not digest, sort, assimilate and process … your body has taken it on. These unharmonious "thoughts" are mirrored or reflected in your body. If your "go to" is struggle or conflict, it will be reflected in your state of health. If your go to is "gratitude and joy," it will be reflected in your health. If your relationships suffer, or are in complete denial and avoidance, the chances are, your state of health and body are also operating from "denial" and "avoidance" and you may experience physical pain.

What makes this even more complicated is whether or not you are an empath. Now you are taking on thoughts, feelings, and emotions of other people. Your spouse, your children, your work, your clients and any lack of boundaries creates confusion, dis-ease and "issues."

With all of this disharmony, you can see how the body might be depleted, undernourished and looking for "comfort" to fill you up. Looking for satisfaction, somewhere ... anywhere. Our constitution will also dictate where the weak link is. Is it the heart? The liver? The kidneys? Each one of these organs represent an emotional component. An emotional frequency. Creating another layer of frequencies.

This is where having an awareness of being stuck or stagnant may come into your mind. "I used to be able to do ... but I can't now." Blame it on aging. Is it really aging? Or is it the toxic load that has built up over your life based on a lifetime of choices? You are as old as you will ever be. And your choice of health and vitality is now your new "north star." Are you ready to choose harmony? Are you ready to "lighten" up? "Lighten your load?" Cleanse your toxic load?

Wayne Dyer once asked, "What's inside an orange?" The answer is of course, "orange juice." As simple as this question is, and how impossible for anything else to be inside an orange, such as grape juice or apple juice, the integrity of the orange will always be to contain *orange juice*.

Now let's apply this idea to you and your body? What's inside you? What's the integrity of you? Have you spent a life in gratitude? A life in joy and harmony? Or have you spent a life in struggle, a toxic environment and in anger? What's inside of you must come out. One way or another. Because each organ represents an aspect of the emotional component, an emotional "frequency," the body is now in or out of integrity with your health. According to Five Element Chinese Medicine, the heart is your fire, your passion, your love, your joy. The liver represents anger. The frequency of anger is a lot different than the frequency of hope. Or joy. The gallbladder is all about decision-making. Do you do that easily? Or are you frozen and overwhelmed when it comes to making decisions? The spleen represents your emotions. The pancreas, the sweetness of your life? Diabetics, has the sweetness of your life been taken? Is it even yours? The kidneys represent resentment and fear. Do you relate to this? Or are you fearless? The bladder is Faith. Do you have faith? Or does that word trigger you? Do you get a lot of UTI's? The lungs are about self-worth and expansion. The stomach is about digestion, the small intestines are about sorting. Do you get what I'm saying? Each organ has a function that mirrors an emotion. An emotional frequency as well as a physiological function. And your mind controls this. And your environment controls this. And your emptions controls this.

The wonderful thing about all of this, is, you are the one that gets to make a new choice. So, what would you like to choose now? And are you willing to receive it? Are you worthy? This is where the nutrition comes in. This is where supporting your body in the best, harmonious way possible comes in. And it can be done simply. The question is, are you ready?

Choosing You

"The emotional life is like a mighty river, flowing inside us all. When we dam up a river, the water can't circulate: It stagnates and seeks other routes to escape. A dam creates the potential for great destruction; just so, repression of feelings can turn emotions into a damaging force. However, since feelings are moving energy, they can never be destroyed, they can only be expressed, transformed or repressed. Living in the present means feelings aren't repressed, desires aren't perverted; all are accepted and then either fulfilled or transmuted."
Anonymous

What does choosing for you mean?

Do you tend to be a giver? Do you like being generous ... with others? Do you feel you have to do everything yourself because that's the only way it will get done? Let's go back to understanding the natural order of the four seasons and choices we make on a daily basis.

Seasons are always changing. Within each season, there is also a transition from one season to another, giving into an interdependent connection between these changes.

If we live our life separated from our inner being, and everything is outside of ourselves, we are not "connected" to those interdependent connections. I'm not referring to enmeshment. I'm referring to the natural order of existence. I'm not going into metaphysical terms here, just an understanding that everything has two sides to it. It's not just a one-way street. If you are giving, are you receiving? If you are doing, are you being? If you are forcing, are you surrendering? In each of these examples lies the mechanism within ourselves to allow or deny the makings of a greater possibility.

Choosing for yourself unselfishly, as in self-care, self-love and self-awareness, feeds the cycle of changing seasons. It brings clarity to what you need to do for yourself during these transitional times, so you may be prepared in the coming new season. Some seasons are meant to go within, and other seasons are meant to grow and reach upwards.

The cycle of daylight/moonlight within the year changes daily, gradually. We are surrounded by change. *And if we don't choose/receive the change, then what will happen to you and your body?*

If we don't adhere to natural principles, there is a tendency to fight, defend, blame, shame and attack anything and anyone that dares to change us. This resistance is the very nature of pain and suffering. When stress or other factors, like genetics and constitution, etc. … are considered, the body develops weaker links. Therefore, in these weaker links, you may develop symptoms and conditions creating "dis-ease."

I'm going to share several aspects of understanding this natural law of how our bodies can work in harmony with the environment.

In Five Element Chinese Medicine there is a flow from one element to another. Fire creates Earth, Earth creates metal, Metal creates water, Water creates wood and Wood creates Fire. This amazing cycle of life's elements is built into our bodies.

The fire is represented as the heart and triple heater. The Earth is represented as the stomach, spleen and body as a whole. Metal is represented as the lungs and large intestines. Water is represented in the fluids of the body, the kidneys and bladder. Wood is represented in the liver and gall bladder. It's also considered the General of the body and dictates or commands the rest of your body.

We were also born into a season. That season is built into your constitution. How we nourish our bodies, mind and spirit is a huge part of the wholeness we be. In Chinese medicine, they see things in either deficiency or excess. There is no judgment. It's a fact of not enough or too much in your body. Not enough fire might mean you don't have a strong metabolism and you gain weight easily. Too much wood and you control everything around you. If your metal is out of balance, you may have self-worth issues and low self-esteem. These are very simple examples but very clear how it works.

When we don't get enough sleep, there's a tendency to grab "sugary foods" to give the energy the body needs to make it through the day. This sugar then causes an inflammation in the body and perpetuates a cycle of not enough rest. Over time, the body is taxed and depleted. To find your "balance" again, you must make a new choice. And that choice will depend on how you accept or reject change.

In Tibetan Medicine and Ayurvedic Medicine, they too have a system based on the body's constitution. Your body type is dictating more than you realize. Food allergies may not be what you think they are. They may be the clarity that keeps your body healthy in its correct constitution. As always food is either medicine or poison depending on what self-awareness you have.

In Ayurveda Medicine there are 3 body types that are called 'D*oshas*'. You may have heard of them. Vata, Pita and Kapha. Vata people have anxious minds, tend to be cold, type "A" personalities, drink a lot of coffee and skip meals. They may have poor sleep habits and they thrive on routine. Pita body types are fire body types. Lean, fast metabolism, strong desires, driven and don't get cold. Kapha body types tend to gain weight easily. They are relaxed personalities, not in a rush, tend to love food and don't care for exercise much. They often love spicy foods.

In Tibetan Medicine, diet is 80% of treatment. Instead of Doshas, they use *'humors'* And they are called Wind, Bile and Phlegm. Each are similar in nature to the Dosha body types. Wind is appropriately named as that is often what element is out of control. Creating the "symptoms." Bile is the fire. Again, appropriately named, as is phlegm. They have Tibetan names, but the English offers a clearer image. Phlegm is dense and not fast moving. Think about a bottle of olive oil. When you put it in the refrigerator, it hardens and loses fluidity. In order to bring that fluidity back, you take it out of the cold and bring it to room temperature. This then allows its natural fluidity to take place. If you can recognize yourself in any of these descriptions, then follow along with the next piece.

Food is "medicine" to these body types. When you are aware of the properties that food brings such as spicy, cold, sweet, sour, salty or bitter, you now are tapping into food quality that will be medicine or poison to your body. If you tend to be a hot body and eat foods that create more heat, can you see how this might work against you? And cause "allergy symptoms."

If you are cold and eat spicy foods, can you see how this "warming up" allows the body to move and be more fluid? Also, sour helps cut through phlegm. This clear understanding of what foods support and work for and or against the body type could greatly increase your success to a healthier you. Choosing for you means you are choosing for your body type.

Understanding the seasons and how they create "primary and secondary" symptoms really turns you into your own doctor. When winter ends and you are in transition to the spring season, there is generally a 5 week period (between all seasons). This "thawing of cold" is like taking something out of the refrigerator and letting it warm up and become fluid again.

In this transition time, there can be uncomfortable symptoms. Like colds, runny noses, or blurry eyesight. Sour is the perfect medicine at this time. And taking something as simple as 2 T of unsweetened pomegranate juice in hot water will cut through that phlegm making the transition easier. Now if this phlegm is in your constitution, it might be your medicine year round.

If you tend to be anxious or nervous with high anxiety, don't sleep well and are cold a lot, then, avoiding foods like goat products (which are cooling) or bitter foods (which are cooling), can be that simple. And then, increase the warming foods that nourish and support you, like nutmeg and cardamom which are excellent for creating rest and calming the body and the winds of the mind.

There are times when you are in your "seasons" in life. Childhood can tend to be the phlegm season, puberty to menopause, in general, is the fire season and the "elderly" years can be the wind season.

Knowing this sets you up for greater success for your diet. As you can see, you are always changing and if you continue to eat the same foods that are antagonists, or don't nourish the correct body type, you may get frustrated and feel like things don't work. On the contrary, they do work when you live in that harmonious place of the outer world balancing out with the inner world.

Here is a list of foods that you should avoid or foods which benefit for each body type. To learn what your body type is, you will need to seek out a professional that treats the body, as a whole, in whichever system you are called to. No one is ever just one type. Usually, we have a combination of two. Since we are a combination, it helps to know what they are.

At times we just "know" which one we are. The qualities or the "properties" encourage and nourish or agitate and antagonize the body.

Here is a very descriptive list from Nashalla Nyinda, Tibetan doctor.

Vata/ Wind

Benefit: Asparagus, avocado, salt, fish, butter and ghee, bouillon and bone broth, garlic, coconut (on occasion) red cabbage, molasses, nuts, eggs, banana, apricot, grapes, nettle tea and soup, good quality soy sauce, radish, ginger, nutmeg, caraway, cardamom, cumin, warm and easily cooked foods.

Avoid: Buckwheat, caffeine from any source, chili spices, MSG, chips, rice cakes, chocolate, coffee and soft drinks, distilled vinegar, grilled foods, goat cheese, sour yogurt, old cheese, mint (especially peppermint tea) puffed rice, refined sugars, rye, celery, lemon and excessive sour foods, raw vegetables and salads, endive and bell peppers.

Pita/ Bile

Benefit: Bitter greens and vegetables, kale, collards, cabbage, dandelion greens, chicory, endive, artichoke, watercress, lotus root, fennel greens, spinach, Chinese cabbage, bok choy, beets, lettuce, celery, corn, cauliflower, pumpkin, squash, mushrooms, peas, eggplant, okra, melons and cucumbers, grapes, raisins, bamboo shoots (good for heat and inflammation in the lungs), berries of all varieties, apples (not sour), papaya, mint, fenugreek seeds, mallow, plantain, cumin, parsley, anise, saffron, coconut (fruit and water not oil), low fat white fish meat (no shellfish), goat, liver (especially from goat), buffalo meat, turkey and chicken (moderation), lentils (no red lentils), legumes, soybeans, rice, couscous, quinoa, freshly made yogurt, freshly made butter, fruit juices (low in sugar), previously boiled water and cooled.

Avoid: All alcoholic drinks (increase bile conditions), strong or excessive use of black and green tea, coffee and caffeine drinks should be reduced or completely eliminated, clarified butter, sheep milk, sheep and meat products, oily and fried and fatty foods, flax seed products, mango, pomegranate, pears, sour apples, sour oranges, grapefruit, avocados, lemon, lime, radish, cooked tomatoes, turnips, leeks, mustard seeds and greens, spinach, hot chili peppers, salty foods, ginger, garlic, onions, chives, garam masala, cumin, coriander, nutmeg, cinnamon, black onions seed, green or black cardamom, black pepper, turmeric, sesame seed products (tahini), nuts and nut butters (all), sour and fermented foods, excessive use of eggs, molasses and honey.

Kapha/ Phlegm

Benefit: moderate use of alcohol, fish, salty fish, beef, ginger, salt, black salt, turmeric, black pepper, cumin, cardamom, honey, hot boiled water, millet, mint, pomegranate, mango, radish, chicken, seaweed, yogurt, garlic, onions, strawberries, hot peppers, spinach, red Bhutanese rice, warm and well cooked, easy to digest foods, soups.

Avoid: Bell peppers, cold liquids and chilled foods, cooked foods eaten cold and at room temperature, leftover foods, eggplant, goat meat, milk products, pork, raw tomatoes, refined sugar, turnip, yams and potatoes, unripe fruit, carrots, bananas, apples, peaches, oranges grapefruit, coconut, lettuce and red cabbage, nuts, ice cream, tofu, excessive soy products, soy sauce, mushrooms, peas, excessive breads, heavy oily or rich foods.

Personal Accountability

"Stop Waiting ... for Friday, for summer, for someone to fall in love with you, for life. Happiness is achieved when you stop waiting for it and make the most of the moment you are in right now."
Anonymous

What does Personal Accountability mean?

Personal Accountability, in terms of a healthy, functioning and pain free body, means it's what you require to remain in alignment with your Well Being. We've talked about food frequencies and food alignment. So, it would make sense to continue this conversation as it pertains to Personal Alignment. This time, it's about what's beyond food. It's about the choices you make. It's about spoken contracts made ... to avoid whatever created the pain. Whatever created the disconnect. The super intense, challenging "too much" thing created from a choice that you made or, more often than not, the choice you didn't make.

Aha! What does this have to do with health? What does this have to do with personal accountability? Does it seem like I'm far afield from what the point of anything to do with cooking, eating or health is? Maybe ... Allow me to connect the dots.

I'm about to show you how close you are to learning a universal truth.

First, does your inner being need any lessons? No!

When you are connected to Source and celebrating life from your light, are you looking for lessons? Again, No!

Are you looking for answers? Of course not!

You are fully aware in the present moment ... enjoying the freedom of choice. Enjoying the freedom of ease and playfulness. Dare I even say fun?

Remember when you were a kid? When fun was your go to? And for what reason?   There is no reason!   You were present, connected and lit up by that favorite toy, that favorite friend, that favorite walk in the woods, that favorite swimming hole ...

You were CONNECTED. You were celebrating being alive. You were being you. You were choosing fun.

AND THEN ... what happened? ... life happened! Too busy! Too tired! Not enough time, not enough money, not enough ... not enough ... not enough ...

Well, enough is enough, I say.

Enough of this story you have been telling yourself.

Did it come before or after you signed a contract with your house, your car, your family, your marriage, your job, the devil?

When you make anything significant ... you have signed "YOU" over to that thing, that person, that house, that car, that relationship, that whatever outside of you. You have joined the NOT FUN side. You have joined the "have to's," the "should's," the don't want to, the commitment to the commitment, the not enough ... again, not enough. The lack. The empty place. The place that says, "I'm not enough," "I am not happy," "I am not who I used to be."

How does accountability play into this?   Well, let's go back to my earlier definition. It's what your body requires to stay in alignment with Well Being. What does that mean? Getting physical adjustments to make you feel better? Well, it can be that ... and beyond!

It means that your thoughts have integrity. What you say has integrity. Your actions have integrity. And realizing your body is a reflection of your thoughts, your words and your actions. Being accountable means, you begin by taking a look at how out of alignment you really are. It means assessing what happens to your body when you ARE out of alignment.

Do you complain about having back pain. Or how you're tired or exhausted. What happens when you keep going when exhausted? When do you flip out of it? How do you flip out of it?   What is even required to flip out of it? Wait for it ... wait for it ...

Forgiveness.

It begins with forgiveness. It begins with finding where all the leaks are? What do you mean by leaks? Leaks are the little places where you are out of integrity with what you say and what you do. What action did you take to align with what you spoke. Such as," I'm going to commit to walking every day."   And two weeks go by and you've walked once ... maybe twice. Or, I'm going to eat more vegetables ... and so once a week you eat more vegetables. Or I'm going to cook more at home, but you are too tired and forget and go through the drive through or eat out at a restaurant. Americans eat out on average 5 days a week. What happened to the family meal? Where is the family connection? Where is YOUR connection ... to your true self, your authentic self? Are you looking inwards at your inner being, your inner light, for some rest, relaxation? Or are you still running, avoiding or worse ... WAITING ...

Waiting for the sign that says, start here. Start today. Start ... when? Pick a starting point. The results are the same. You end up waiting. This idea of waiting. This idea that we need permission to choose ... for ourselves. If you are always giving, when do you give back to yourself? When is it time for you? When is it time to find your integrity? Your Well Being?

Integrity has tension. And tension has structure. And structure has a foundation. And a foundation is what we are building this new lifestyle change upon. Without that foundation, you will have a lot of leaks. Leaky gut, leaky relationships, leaky finances. Money is being drained. Your health is being drained. Your relationships are being drained. You are being drained. And when this happens, you find yourself in the NOT FUN drudgery lifestyle. You aren't lit up. You aren't turned on. You aren't creating from something generative. You are creating from lack. And that lack perpetuates "problems" or "issues" in your life. Struggle becomes a constant. Opposite of the uplifted, generative world, where fun, happiness and Well Being are the dominant experiences.

So how do you go from lack to abundance? From poor health to abundant health? From "problems" to thriving? What if I told you in one word how it's done? Would you believe me? Would you choose it? Are you truly done with the struggle? I know you say you are done ... And are you convincing me or are you convincing yourself? So what would your life be like without the struggle? Can you integrate FUN into your life so you can celebrate living? Can you choose FUN so you can create more playfulness?

These contracts and vows you have made for yourself, created openly and conscious or hidden and unconscious, are literally what is driving your life. Creating your life. We are creation machines, after all.

So, what is it you are creating and how do you make the changes you are asking for? What are the steps to this change? What must I change in order to change?

The word that frees you. Frees the struggle. That word is Forgiveness. When you can forgive the parts of you that is leaking. That part of you that is out of integrity. Out of alignment. That part of you that was created out of desperation.

Think about how intense your life has been to get you where you are today. Think about the choices made and the karma created. Think about the story you bought and sold to everyone... including yourself. Think about how out of integrity you are and how desperate you were when you made the choice, the contract, the vow you made. Think about what and who you were choosing for? If it was coming from lack, it wasn't coming from Source or your inner being. It wasn't coming as a gift to yourself. It was ultimately coming from a part of you that needed ... "<u>fill in the blank</u>."

Because avoidance temporarily removes the pain, you move on ... yes? We feel fulfilled ... yes? Or do we?

Or did we buy into an illusion? How old were you when you decided to stop living? How old were you when you decided you couldn't be the weight you really wanted to be. It's just too hard, too much work, not enough time, too many and too late. We are all carrying the "should" on our shoulders. We should have done this ... if only I did that. I should have known, how come I didn't see that? Again, who made the commitment? Who signed the contract? Was that person alive and thriving? Or weak and vulnerable and desperate.

How does forgiving change this? And what responsibility must you take to be in the integrity of your words so you may be in alignment and become accountable for your life? And what does this have to do with food?

For-giving ... is for giving the light back to you. For giving the light back to the other person. Forgiveness is a way of living life that creates space of being you without the hooks, without the aches and pains of attachments. Resistance to change is what creates the pain. By not forgiving yourself, you are staying in the chain of pain. The choice of pain. The struggle. The warped energy that keeps you out of alignment. Enslaved to your self fulfilled illusions.

Forgiveness is the way back to finding your way. Finding your way is growth. Growth is movement. Movement creates momentum towards lightening up. Lightening up starts cleansing the body. Cleansing the weight so you no longer are in the wait. Cleansing the blood. Sparking the liver. Reversing the stagnation in the liver and the brain.

Eating a no oil diet is part of setting yourself up for success. For lightening up. For cleaning your liver which cleans your mind. For-giving the light back to you. Your spark. Your joy. Your fun. Taking responsibility for your choices ... that is what being accountable means. Owning your part in the story. Not blaming. Not shaming. Not wronging the other person. Not wronging yourself.

Healing happens when you choose for you. Stop waiting to forgive yourself.

Allow yourself to finally be free.

Finally Free
Written by Rebekah Kee Maya
December 1st, 2020

A door looms in the darkened room.
Can I see who or what is behind the door?
Am I to open the door?
Or am I to push it away, living in fear of who or what's behind it?
What am I afraid of?
Who am I afraid of?
If being trapped for decades was the only thing stopping me, how will I know what being finally free feels like?
How does one escape that lifelong sentence?
Living behind the veil of darkness, forgetting that the light is one choice away ...
Would you grant yourself the gift of light?
Would you punish yourself for eternity?
And for whom would you be punishing yourself with?
And for what would you be punishing yourself with?
And why?
Who's punishment is it?
Is it the betrayal of a long lost prayer?
What projection and belief have you entertained?
Embellished?
Owned?
Keeping you from living out your God-given beauty?
Is this darkness a sign of good intentions gone bad?

With whom have you danced?
The devil?
The jester?
The poison you once drank as a dare?
What dance of the soul are you winking and flirting with under the full moon of despair?
 What abandonment of self and betrayal are you hanging out with tonight?
Under the full moon of denial?
Is despair a guise under the drunken state of stupidity?
What abandoned choices exist in the fearful and toxic
wasteland of your design?
Who's crippling choices are you living with?
Are you ready to be free?
Are you ready to live outside the lie?
Are you ready to wake up to a full moon of ecstasy?
In bliss?
Are you ready to be finally free?
Free to make a stand for yourself as the full moon illuminates your true brilliance?
Are you ready to see beyond the veil of darkness, and let the light shine?
What's it shining on?
How do you dust yourself off from the entangling cob webs?
Hear the whispers from the voices of silence.
How do you turn on when once, you were broken?
Are you ready to be free?
What would you choose to fill yourself up with, now?
What prayer to wholeness exists in the black hole?
What prayer of love can fill your empty cup?
What forgiveness is wiping your slate clean?
In the darkest hour is your greatest enlightenment.
Is that true?
Does one need to find the darkest hour to be finally free?
Can you claim forgiveness for the sake of being a deliberate creator?
Untying the knots of pain and suffering.
What does for-giving look like to you?

For giving the light back to yourself.

Pray it so.

Forgiving yourself as the embodied soul expression.

As the biggest fraud.

As the biggest impostor.

Forgive yourself.

Your soul.

Release your karmic debt.

Forgive yourself in the dark ... in the light ... in the fear ... in the shame ... and all the hatred.

Finally free is your song, your chant ... your love song for stepping into faith.

Faith that all is well.

And nothing more needs to be done.

You have lived it.

And now ...

You are Finally Free.

Photo by Frank Cone

Risk Taking ... Fearless in the Kitchen

"And the day came when the risk to remain tight in a bud was more painful than the risk it took to blossom."
Anais Min

This is one of my favorite quotes. When you truly get the core of it, you will see how it plays out everywhere in your life. In your relationships, including your relationship with food. Your relationship to yourself. Your relationship to Faith. And your relationship to risk taking.

We are designed for both contraction and expansion. That's what duality is all about. We are designed to see both sides. It's when we get frozen on one side and then judge it that creates the disharmony. And being stuck becomes a way of life. Animals in the wild freeze when they feel danger is near by. And when it passes, they shake it off and move on. They don't ask questions. They don't ask what it was. They don't "ask is it coming back?" They don't stay frozen, preventing themselves from coming back. They are present to their world. We are more evolved than animals and yet, the way we get frozen and stuck when something happens can be debilitating. The mind perceives and then it believes... each perception creates a pathway for another belief to be created. That's how the mind works. Your point of attention is what you are dialed in on. You can't get to a different channel if you aren't willing to receive another channel. EVEN IF the new channel would give you more pleasure. There's a part of the human design that is wired to continually live in this flight, fright or freeze. Without the presence of daily life threatening circumstances.

The expression, "Have you hit rock bottom?," is an interesting question. Have you had enough pain? There is NO such thing as rock bottom. The bottom is when you choose it. The bottom is when you've had enough. The bottom is when you respect yourself and your body to choose for you. The conversation about choosing you is really a pivot point. When you make that choice, everything in your "perspective" shifts. You get to have a new point of view. And when 'Shift Happens', your reality changes. Are you ready to change your perspective?

Are you ready to see life as an Adventure? Are you ready to have more Expansion? Are you ready to be present? Are you ready to let go of being scared of what has already happened? Not from the story of "when I did that, this happened."

How does this relate to food? To cooking healthier?

So much of life is processed through food. That's what emotional eating is. We have to process our thoughts, our environment, our feelings and then our food. But there isn't any separation or awareness of these energies.

Food carries frequencies. The frequency of the people that handle it. The farmers, the delivery trucks, the grocery store, and then you pick it up and cook it and feed it to your family. Do you see how many threads there are to ingest, assimilate, digest and process… then the sorting of what stays and what is rejected, begins. Does it support Well Being or not. That is the risk. So the question comes back to "How do you choose to live?" We've already talked about health and vitality. Now I am addressing the risk it takes to thrive. Living life as an adventure, with expansion as a great viewpoint. After all, we are looking at creating fun, right? Fun with food would be a great starting point!

So now, if you are truly choosing you, are you going to engage in adventure or are you going to live in fear. One point of view comes from abundance and the other one comes from lack. Your biggest risk then is about moving from contraction into expansion. Moving out of Lack and into Abundance. Creating a life of Fulfillment with little to no regrets. How does this translate in the kitchen? Well, that's easy. When was the last time you bought an unfamiliar, exotic or "new" ingredient? And how long before you actually used that ingredient? Did it sit on your shelf for 6 months? Is it still unopened?

"There are risks and costs to action. But they are far less than the Long-range risks of comfortable inaction."
John F. Kennedy.

When you begin to see that LIVING CAN BE FUN, life becomes an adventure. Or you can live seriously and not have fun or live safe and not have fun… becoming depressed and unfulfilled. You can make no choice at all, which is still a choice. No matter what, life always moves forward. Whether you are partaking in it or not. So the question really becomes how much fulfillment would you like? How satisfied would you like to be? It's kind of like investing money. You can go the safe route or the risky route. Or do nothing … all these set you up for a reward system that you will judge yourself accordingly.

"Until you change your thinking, you will always recycle your experiences."
Brian Weiner

Anticipation/ Catch the Wave ... establishing a new habit.

How do you establish a new habit then?

Anticipation is the fuel of desire. Are your desires lit up? Are you congruent with your desires? Risk Taking establishes a new habit. Risk Taking is breaking old habits. Trying new things. What feeds you to stay in the anticipation of your desires?

What sparks you? To sustain you? In your desires ... Do you choose things that are generative?

"When you take risks, you learn that there will be times when you succeed and there will be times when you fail, and both are equally important."
Ellen DeGeneres

"Where do you want to place your significance?"

Being **Fearless in the Kitchen** requires expansion. This means freely expressing yourself. It begins with choosing to have fun. It begins with seeing what you make and create as an experiment. When you are experimenting, do you know the outcome? Before you start, are you in the conclusion that it won't work? What value is there in approaching the kitchen (or anything) this way? Instead, make a game of it. Be playful. For instance, create a mystery box with your kids. Have *them* choose 10 ingredients and see what dish *you* can make.

Splurge! Buy that kitchen thing you've always desired. Have you desired it for a long time? ... is it really because you "can't afford it?" Would it have been paid off by now had you set aside money weekly for it? Can you give yourself permission to enjoy having it?

When we live in the "I can't have it," what does that create for you? "I can't have it" also includes food restrictions. I can't have dairy. I can't have eggs. I can't have almonds. I can't have oil, etc. Coming from the "I can't have," keeps you locked in as a victim to elements, thoughts and beliefs that are outside of you. And you are not a victim. You are learning how choosing for you creates a new perspective, opening the doors for living with greater health and vitality. A sense of Well Being. And that perspective shifts you into receiving more pleasure. You give yourself permission to enjoy what you can have. Focusing on the joy of foods you can eat. The list of foods you can eat is far greater than the list of foods you can't eat. It is out of habit that your limiting beliefs have haunted you into being afraid to try new things. It takes effort to change. That effort is about letting go and surrendering into the joy of being. The joy of living. The joy of food.

Taking a risk means choosing to go outside of your comfort zone. And the recipes in this book do just that! And as they may push you out of your comfort zone. I promise you, I won't take you somewhere that is a dead end. I will carry you through to something wonderful, delicious and fun! If you are used to having certain textures, high sugars and high fats in your diet, then getting used to clean eating may be a practice in both gratitude and patience. You are well on your way to creating your new lifestyle. It really is all about practicing. Showing up. Don't expect to get everything right the first time. I encourage you towards being **Fearless in the Kitchen,** even through an occasional flop.

Food Magic

"Food is not rational. Food is culture, habit, craving and identity."
Jonathan Safran Foer

What is food magic? For me, it's having fun with food. It's experimenting and getting excited about what else I can create. Expanding the mind… for instance… making an edible balloon. Finding ways to appreciate the value in food beyond your comfortable limited understanding. Trusting that these recipes are creating the health and vitality you require to bring Well Being to your gut, your liver or blood sugar balancing. Finding another way to live in the sweetness of life. Accessing the pleasure of food that creates food alignment and healthy food frequencies. Your time to reassess is now. What is your health priority in life? How healthy are you willing to be? How good are you willing to feel?

Are you willing to think outside of the box to be uncomfortable while learning a new lifestyle? Are you willing to take advantage of natural ingredients to achieve healthier results and enjoy the pleasure of the foods you no longer can eat? Let go of your story and find the fun in playing on a new playground. Making food is an art. For me, I think it began at 8 years old with mud pies and my easy bake oven. Now it's a whole new world of inventions. Get ready to see some pretty exciting new desserts, using Molecular Gastronomy, with meringues in the dessert section. Read through it and see what food magic looks like.

Alternatives A-Z

What's in your larder now?
Alternatives to foods you are familiar with, including eggs, dairy, oils, sugars and proteins. Here are some lesser known alternatives for you to experiment with, too.

Baking Powder 1 tsp - Divide tsp in fifths; use 2 parts cream of tartar, 1 part baking soda and 2 parts arrowroot powder.

Caramel - Date Nectar or 15 Medjool dates soaked in 1 cup hot water, 1/3 cup plus 1 T ground raw cashews, 3 T plus 1 tsp Oat milk, pinch of salt, ¼ tsp vanilla powder, 3 T Coconut Cream. Blend in blender or a seed grinder to whip. Use 1/2 cup to 1 cup of the date soaked water and 1 T of milk at a time to thin. Blend until smooth, with no more flecks. Store in fridge.

Cashews - Buy unsalted, raw Macadamia or Pili nuts and use 1 to 1 in any recipe calling for cashews. They have a similar creamy and smooth texture with a mild flavor making it an exceptional replacement.

Coffee substitutes - Chicory crystals, dandelion root tea, coffee extract flavoring.

Couscous - Substitute with **Riz Cous**. Unlike couscous, **Riz Cous** is gluten free. Once prepped, it's a quicker cooking time than regular rice. Great for camping or backpacking. To make your own. Grind long brown rice in a food processor making it just a little larger than grits. Spread on cookie sheet and bake for 30 minutes at 350 Degrees F. Stir rice every 7-10 minutes while roasting. Let it cool completely and then store in a tightly sealed container or use immediately. To cook Riz Cous - combine 1 cup **Riz Cous** to 2 parts hot liquid. Place water, Riz Cous and seasoning in a medium pot. Stir well to wet the Riz Cous. Bring to a boil. Reduce heat to low and cover. Cook for 15 minutes. Do not remove lid during cooking time. Remove from heat and let sit for 5 minutes. Remove lid and fluff with a fork.

Cornstarch 1 T -   Four options
1. Use 1 T Arrowroot powder
2. Use 1 T Kudzu Root
3. Apple Pectin, 1/2 of what is called for when using cornstarch
4. Agar Agar, 1/2 of what is called for when using cornstarch

Dairy Alternatives

Milk:
on cereal - Almond, Soy, Hemp, Oat, Rice, Cashew, Macadamia. Any grain can be turned into a milk by combining 1/4 cup nut or grain to 1 cup water and blend in blender. Pour into a nut bag and strain.

in baking 1 cup: Use 1 cup any nut milk or grain milk.

Sour cream: 1 cup raw cashew, 1/2 cup water, 1 T lemon juice, 3/4 tsp apple cider vinegar, (opt.) pinch of salt.

Buttermilk: 1 cup almond, oat milk or cashew milk with 1 T lemon juice.

Butter: Angel Butter, my exclusive butter substitute, can be made with this recipe. In a seed grinder, mix 2 tsp chia seeds, 2 T Coconut cream (refrigerate first), 1/8 tsp Turmeric and 1 T Aquaschata™. Add chives, basil or other herbs to flavor it. **Angel Butter** can be used in all of the following butter replacements:

in baking: 1 T: Use applesauce (up to 3/4 cup).

in mashed potatoes: nutritional yeast, ground flax seeds and lemon juice or 1 tsp light miso.

for sautéing: 1-2 T water at a time, 1 tsp yellow miso or white miso mixed with water, 1/2 tsp homemade veggie paste, vegetable broth or carrot juice.

Miso, Dark: 1/2 cup soaked sun-dried tomatoes in hot water.

Egg Replacements

In baking:
1. Use 1 T Defatted Soy flour or 1 T water with 1 T powdered soy lecithin.
2. Use egg replacer per package instructions.
3. Use 1/2 ripe banana.
4. Use 1/4 cup tofu or Pumfu.
5. Add 1 T flax seeds to 1/3 cup boiled water and soak 10 minutes.
6. Use 1 1/2 T ground flax seeds with 4 T hot water or 4 T hot Aquaschata™.
7. Use 1 1/2 T chia seeds and soak 4 T hot water or 4 T hot Aquaschata™.

8. Use one to one ratio of egg to apple sauce. One egg = 1/4 cup in volume.
9. Use 1 1/2 T tapioca flour, 1 tsp Baking powder, 1/4 tsp Xanthan gum, 1/8 tsp Cream of tartar and mix with hand mixer or seed grinder, frothing it.

Egg Wash:
1. Use liquid lecithin (warm and brush it on).
2. Aquaschata™ - 1/3 cup butternut squash blended with 1 cup water.

Binder:
1. Use 1 tsp nut butter with water or fruit juice to the consistency of a whipped egg.
2. 1 part soy flour and 2 parts water blended and heated, thickens as it cools.
3. 1 cup cold water and 2 T arrowroot powder.
4. Use 1 1/2 T chia seeds and soak in 4 T hot water or 4 T hot Aquaschata™.
5. Apple pectin.
6. Agar agar.
7. Kudzu root.
8. 1/4 cup Flax water with 4 T cooked butternut squash = 1 egg. Instructions for making Aquaflaxa, as well as alternative egg. 1/3 cup Flax seeds boiled in 1 cup water for 2 min, pour into a nut bag and strain. Save the liquid and you can reuse the flax seeds in another recipe. This is considered Aquaflaxa. In a blender, blend in 4 T cooked butternut squash for 5 seconds. Add extra baking powder to whatever you are making to give it extra lift.
9. Use 1 1/2 T tapioca flour, 1 tsp Baking powder, 1/4 tsp Xanthan gum, 1/8 tsp Cream of tartar 3 T warm water and mix with hand mixer or seed grinder frothing it.

Leavening:
1. 1 tsp baking powder substitute for omitting one egg from recipe.
2. Substitute 1/2 tsp arrowroot and 1/4 tsp baking soda for 1 egg.

Binder & Leavening: 4 T almond or cashew butter with 2 T lemon juice.

Egg whites: Flax water, see #5 on page 70, under "in baking."

Meringue -
1. Versawhip 600K™ - Modified Soy protein.
2. 1/2 cup Flax Water (Aquaflaxa), 1 tsp cream of tartar, 1 tsp vanilla powder, 1/4 tsp Liquid Stevia, 4 T Tapioca, 1 T xanthan gum, 1/4 - 1/2 cup Aquafaba.
3. Aquafaba.
4. Potatowhip (potato protein) by Sosa products.

Extracts

Essential Oils are a brilliant way to impact flavor. Most likely if the extracts don't have alcohol, they have sunflower oil in them. So instead, try using essential oils. Make sure they are food grade. DoTERRA® is a company that does make food grade essential oils. If it helps, I am a distributor.
Suggestions:
Lavender, Lemongrass, Lime, Oregano, Basil, Ginger, Orange, Clove, Peppermint and Cardamom to name a few. These can be used in desserts, ice creams, spaghetti sauces, baked goods and entrées.

Herbal Teas - Infusing flavor with herbal tea bags or loose teas is another way to get flavor. Drinks, ice cream, pana cotta and oatmeal to name a few. Using dehydrated orange peel or lemon peel, ginger tea, peppermint tea, mulling spices, chai tea, Earl Grey, green tea and chicory root crystals to name a few.

Freeze Dried Fruit - There are many, many freeze dried fruits. Passion fruit comes in a powder. The flavor is amazing. Raspberries, blackberries, mango, banana, etc. ... work great in a smoothie, ice cream, cannoli filling, cakes. By using freeze dried fruit, you have a very high vitality imbued into the food giving it not only excellent flavor, but it now has a high quality nutrition. Sometimes when a fruit is out of season, this will be an excellent choice.

Vanilla Powder and Vanilla Bean - Although pricey, it is worth it to invest in a high quality vanilla powder. They are not all equal. The cheaper they are, the less flavor they have. The higher the price, the more potent the product. Only 1/2 the amount is needed in a recipe as it is such a strong flavor.

Fresh Herbs - Basil, thyme, rosemary, peppermint (chocolate peppermint, spearmint, wintergreen, orange mint, and pineapple mint are a few you can grow) and winterberry. Using fresh mint in pesto, ice cream, or rosemary in bread or entrées brings another level of rich flavor that dried herbs don't carry. Also, fresh herbs have more life force.

Flours

I have always been fascinated by the chemistry of baking. I mill my own flours and I understand how to combine and blend them. And how to create a product that will bring you the end result you are looking for. Here is a list of properties of flours. When you know how they work individually, you can blend them together and substitute them out easily.

A note about Gluten - Many grains have a protein, generally called gluten. However, the majority of what people react to is gliadin and glutenin, found in wheat, barley, rye, spelt, triticale, kamut as well as brewers yeast.

The single most important factor, when using alternative flours, is understanding how to balance a dry flour with a moist flour. Too much of one or the other will make a very dry or very heavy product!!!

Flours that you can make in your own blender or seed grinder easily:
*Millet *Amaranth *Oat *Buckwheat * Teff (Golden & Brown).

Buying and Storing
Generally, these unusual flours can be found in most natural foods stores. Some are in bulk sections, while others are in prepackaged, 1-5 pound sacks. Milling your own grain provides the highest quality of freshness. In general, after 72 hours of milling, the oils in the flour tend to begin going rancid. So, in general, the flours found in the store probably have lost their nutritional quality. Some specialty flours will be found in the refrigerated sections. I recommend storing all of your flours in the freezer. If you are milling your own, maintaining quality will improve drastically when stored in the freezer. Unless you use them daily, then you won't have to be concerned.

When altering recipes, use a blend of grains for best results. For every cup of brown rice flour, combine it with another cup of 1 or more different flours. The exception to this rule is if the recipe has oily properties (i.e., nuts, dried fruit, applesauce, mashed bananas, - etc.) in which case it is not necessary to combine flours.

Properties and Types of Flours

1. Almond flour - *Can be substituted for regular flour at a 1:1 ratio for regular flour.* It is important to note that almond flour may require more support to bind the flour. Adding extra Xanthan Gum or an egg replacer.

2. Amaranth flour - A sweet flavor. Baked texture results in a smooth, crisp crust, moist fine crumb. It adds a very high nutritional value to the food, *in general, use up to 1/4 - 1/2 cup.*
However, there are recipes using as much as 1 cup. You can use the whole grain. Toasting it before milling gives it a nuttier flavor or use it whole in baking or in crackers.

3. Arrowroot powder - Arrowroot is a root vegetable often sold as a powder. It's used as a thickening agent and as a gluten-free flour. *General use is to replace up to a 1 cup of flour called for.* Many of its health benefits are associated with its starch content, which may promote weight loss, treat diarrhea, and stimulate your immune system. Great for baked goods such as cakes, pies, breads, pancakes and muffins. Soft in texture and similar to white pastry flour. This is a staple for any gluten free household. It can be used to thicken fruit compotes. *1-2 tsp per 1/4 cold water. Mix first in water then add to pot. It will clump if you pour it directly into anything hot. You can use this easily to replace tapioca flour.*

4. Sweet Brown Rice flour - A sweet flavor that when baked has a dry, fine crumb. Perfect for muffins, waffles, pancakes and can be replaced for regular brown rice flour if necessary. *Ratio is 1:1.*

5. Brown Rice flour - A sweet flavor. Baked texture results in a dry, fine crumb. Baking, pastas, pizza crusts, and crackers. *Ratio is 1:1.*

6. Buckwheat flour - A musty robust flavor. Has its own inherent binder that acts like having an egg. Baked texture results in a moist, fine crumb. Because of its strong flavor, it works well in a blend. *Ratio is 1:4.*

7. Coconut flour - Substitute coconut flour for all-purpose flour at a **1:4 ratio**, also, since you add 1 egg for every 1/4 cup coconut flour you will want the volume of liquid to match that of an egg. 1/4 cup liquid equals one egg *General use is 1/4 to 1/3 cup coconut flour for 1 cup of regular flour.* Due to its high absorbency, you'll also want to increase the liquid. It also tends to have a drying effect on baked goods, because it is so absorbent. The best way to counteract its drying effect is to use plenty of moisture like mashed bananas, zucchini or other "wet" or "moist" ingredients. when you're baking. The strong flavor of coconut can overpower delicate flavors. It's best used to complement other flavors.

8. Cassava flour - Made from Cassava root. It can be used in pasta, tortillas and pancakes. It's a very fine, sand like texture. And doesn't have to be blended with other flours. *Ratio is 1:1.*

9. Chickpea flour - Garbanzo bean flour is a protein. It is used to make hummus and falafel and can be added to breads and pastas. It has a distinct flavor so blending it with other flours will tone the flavor down. *Substitute 1/4 cup in a blend to keep the flavor toned down.*

10. Cornmeal - A slightly sweet flavor. Baked texture results in a grainy, slightly dry crumb. *Ratio is 3/4:1.*

11. Hazelnut flour - Is a meal from Hazelnuts (also known as Filberts). *You can replace with a 1:1 ratio with almond meal, which is a 1:1 ratio.*

12. Jerusalem Artichoke flour - Makes a great "binder" for brownies in baking. Use up to 1/4 cup. *Ratio is 1/4:1.*

13. Millet flour - A buttery, slightly sweet flavor. Baked texture results in a dry crumb. Best used with Brown rice flour. Great in breads, crackers and pizza crusts. *Use up to 1 cup in a blend, best used with a flour like sweet brown rice or brown rice. Ratio is 1:1.* It is a soft grain to mill in blender or seed grinder. You can also use it whole (toast on medium to high heat for a nuttier flavor) and add to bread recipes.

14. Oat flour - A sweet nutty flavor. Baked texture results in a coarse, large crumb, firm crust. Oat flour, like oats, has a binding property that results in a denser, gelatinous texture. *Up to 1/2 cup mixed with Brown Rice flour rice or sorghum works well. Ratio is 1 1/3:1.*

15. Pecan flour - This is easily done in your blender or seed grinder. Overdoing it will make pecan butter. This is good to use in place of breadcrumbs. *It can be substituted for regular flour at a 1:1 ratio.*

16. Potato flour - Potato flour is not the same as potato protein that is used in meringues. Potato flour, like potato starch, starts with whole potatoes, but this is where their similarities end. The potatoes are cooked, dried, and ground into a fine powder. The result is a powder that's more beige in color, similar in appearance to whole-wheat flour. *Use on a 1:1 ratio, but not more than 1/4 cup, every 3 cups of flour.*

17. Quinoa flour - Bitter in flavor. Best in a blend. It is high in protein, calcium and iron. Use this delicate flour when baking. *You can substitute this flour on a 1:2 ratio.*

18. Sorghum flour - Sorghum is an incredible whole grain replacement for whole wheat flour. In fact, it's my favorite. It's robust and moist in nature. Rich in Potassium and Phosphorus, it is very high in calcium, fiber and protein making it one of the healthier options for gluten intolerant people. It's easy to work with and has a **1:1 ratio**. This grain is perfect in all baked goods and makes a great blend with brown rice flour and arrowroot powder.

19. Soy flour - Has a slightly bitter flavor. Baked texture results in a moist, fine crumb spongy crust. *Use as an "additive," with a ratio of 3/4:1 and no more than 1/4 cup in baked goods.*

20. Brown Teff flour - This is a staple in Ethiopia. The brown has higher iron than the golden. Teff has an earthy, nutty flavor. *Use in blend up to 1 cup. Ratio of 3/4:1.* Using it by itself is an acquired taste. It goes great in pancakes, breads, crackers and pie shells.

21. Golden Teff flour - This is similar to cracked wheat. It has a milder flavor that children love. It's easy to make in a blender or seed grinder. *Use in blend up to 1 cup. Ratio of 1:1.* It goes great in pancakes, breads, crackers and pie shells.

22. Tapioca flour - Tapioca is a starch extracted from the storage roots of the cassava plant, a species native to the North and Northeast regions of Brazil, but whose use is now spread throughout South America. If you have a recipe that uses all-purpose flour for thickening (think sauces, stews, gravy, etc.), *replace with tapioca flour at a 1:1 ratio. If using in baked goods, in general, you can use up to 1/2 cup. Or use arrowroot powder.* The texture of foods used to thicken tapioca and even baked goods can have a slippery or "slimy" texture that is particularly known to tapioca. Because of this, I prefer arrowroot powder. However, tapioca flour works perfectly in the meringue recipe and royal icing recipe.

23. White Bean flour - made by grinding white, navy beans or baby lima beans into a fine powder. White beans and Navy beans tend to be high allergens, so baby lima beans work best for this. Beans combined with grain form a complete protein which is exceptionally efficient nutrition for the body. You can whisk in white bean flour to chicken stock, vegetable stock or milk as a base for a fast, hearty soup. *Use up to 1 cup in a flour blend. Ratio of 1:1.* It is flavorless and replaces white or whole wheat flour beautifully. Great for pizza crusts, pies, cakes, breads, crackers and pancakes. Because it is a bean, it will spoil quicker than any grain flours, so use it and eat it.

I find that combining smaller amounts of the more exotic flours with larger quantities of sorghum and brown rice flours work best.
Remember to write down what you've done so you know if it worked or not . (A tape recorder works well for those that can't seem to get into the writing habit.)

Extras

*****Corn flour -** In the UK, it is the same as cornstarch in the US. *Ratio is 1:1.*

*Kudzu root - *General Use: Dissolve 1 T in 1 cup of cold water.* The edible root of the Pueraria genus of plants. It is a vine that is considered invasive in the US. You can cook and eat kudzu root as you would other tuber vegetables, such as potatoes. It has many health benefits for your kidneys. Kudzu is used in Chinese medicine to **treat alcoholism, heart disease, menopausal symptoms, diabetes, fever, the common cold and neck or eye pain**. It is sometimes used in combination with other herbs. Lab studies suggest that kudzu has anti-inflammatory and neuroprotective properties. Avoid using if on a blood thinner. *In baking, replace up to 1/2 cup of flour with Kudzu Root.*

*Apple Pectin - *1 T of bulk pectin powder gels 4 cups of fruit. Use 2 T per 8 cups of fruit.* The standard jam recipe is 8 cups of fruit, 6 to 8 cups of sugar, 1/4 cup lemon juice. You can also make your own. Use 2 quarts apples, cores and peels, or whole unpeeled apples, chopped into 1-inch chunks. In a pot with 1 gallon water. Bring to a boil until apples soften, about 1 hour. Turn off heat and pour into a large bowl lined with layers of cheesecloth.

*Xanthan Gum - It is an effective thickening agent and stabilizer to prevent ingredients from separating. *General use is 3/4 - 1 tsp in baked goods.*

*Guar Gum - Extracted from **guar beans**, it is used as a thickening and stabilizing agent in food. The guar seeds are mechanically husked, hydrated, milled and screened according to application. It is typically produced as an off-white powder. Since it is gluten-free, it is used as an additive to replace wheat flour in baked goods. *Use 1 tsp in recipes to stabilize with a "gluten" texture.* It also has been shown to reduce serum cholesterol and lower blood glucose levels.

*Citrus Fiber powder - 1 tsp - 1 T in general. Moistens, and when used with xanthan gum stabilizes and has emulsifying properties. Ideal in confectionery and sauces to substitute fats, texture enhancer, provides the sensation of pulp in the mouth and is a perfect thickener for cakes and batters. Aids in the creaminess of non - dairy ice creams. Thickens to make mayonnaise textures as well.
- Purchase at https://supplies.gusta.ca/

*Agar Agar - is a gelling agent extracted from red algae, which is mainly used for setting jellies and another popular thickening agent. **1 tsp agar agar powder is equivalent to 8 tsp gelatin powder**. Because gelatin is made from animal collagen, agar agar makes a viable vegetarian alternative. It still resembles seaweed when sold in strips. Be sure to mix with water before adding to other ingredients.

*Potato starch - a starch extracted from potatoes. The cells of the root tubers of the potato plant contain leucoplasts. To extract the starch, the potatoes are crushed, and the starch grains are released from the destroyed cells. The starch is then washed out and dried to powder.

*Psyllium husks/powder - Is the common name used for several members of the plant genus Plantago whose seeds are used commercially for the production of mucilage. Psyllium is mainly used as a dietary fiber to relieve symptoms of both constipation and mild diarrhea, and occasionally as a food thickener. *It is excellent in making gluten free bread products. Generally, when using the Husks, it is 2 – 6 T for each recipe. Powder only requires 1 – 3 T per recipe. Greater amounts means greater elasticity.*

*Purple Yam Flour - Also known as Ube, it is commonly used to add color to sweet pastries, cakes and other baked goods. It is an edible root from the Philippines and is found in Asian markets, as it is used in many Asian cuisines. Made from dried, ground yam roots, it is also available freeze dried. Either way, it is packed with fiber, energy and several immune boosters, including anthocyanins. It is considered low on the glycemic index. Use a quarter cup with every 2 cups of flour.

Food Coloring -
Yellow - Turmeric
Blue - Freeze dried Blue Pea flower.
Purple - Freeze dried Blackberry.
Green - Dried Spirulina, liquid chlorophyll or freeze dried Pandan leaves or paste.
Black - Food Grade Activated Charcoal.
Magenta - Freeze Dried Blueberry.
Pink - Freeze dried Dragon fruit

Fruit - dehydrated and Freeze Dried.

Gelatin dessert, 1 T -
1. Use 1 T granulated Agar Agar and 3 1/2 cups liquid.
2. Use 1 tsp Agar Agar powder to 1 T flakes.
3. Apple Pectin.
4. Use 1 T to 1/4 cup Kudzu root.

Potato – Taro root, Parsnip, Rutabaga, Celery Root and Lima Beans.

Salt - Low Iodine Diets means, no SEA SALT. Desert Salt works in its place. There is a Desert smoked salt as well. Herbamare® has Kelp in it. So again, if you are on a low Iodine diet, Herbamare® won't work for you. If you are looking for salt substitutions and can have sea salt, Herbamare® is great.

Spaghetti Noodles - Grain Free Options - Chickpea, Red lentils, Cassava, Kelp, Shirataki (Konjac), Yam or Sweet Potato. Spaghetti squash cooked or dehydrated. Make your own spiral noodles - Zucchini, carrots, potato, beets.

Sweeteners

The list of alternative sweeteners below are the ones I commit to in this cookbook. There are dozens of other kinds of sugar alternatives, but for the sake of those really needing to be completely sugar free, these are the alternatives used in this book.

Bananas - Adds both volume and a natural sweetness to cakes, muffins and breads. It also helps to brown baked items.

Date nectar - You can easily make your own date paste with 15 Medjool dates soaked in 1 cup hot water. Works well to activate yeast for bread. Refrigerate up to 2 weeks. Freeze if you have leftovers.

Maple syrup - Derived from the Maple tree sap. It's a very concentrated sugar, high on the glycemic index. Activate yeast for baking with 1/2 tsp. Or, you can use 1/2 tsp of Date Nectar.

Inulin - Inulins are a group of naturally occurring polysaccharides produced by many types of plants, such as onions, garlic, Jerusalem artichokes, chicory root and agave plants. Industries most often use the inulin extract from chicory root. The inulins belong to a class of pre-dietary fibers known as fructans. Inulin is used by some plants as a means of storing energy and is typically found in roots or rhizomes. When the roots are prepared, a juice can be made from them and then made into a powder. This powder is used in baking, ice creams, and candy, such as "gummy" candies. Depending on the chain of polysaccharides (short vs long) determines whether it's used as a fat replacer or a sugar replacer. It can be used in both hot or cold applications. And there are different products just for each one of those. You can buy them as hot inulin or cold inulin. In general, 1 - 4 T is added to use as both a sweetener and fat replacer. I use this in many recipes.

Benefits of Inulin -
The gut microbiota is the population of bacteria and other microbes that live in the gut. This community is highly complex and contains both good and bad bacteria.

Having the right balance of bacteria is essential for keeping the gut healthy and protecting the body from disease, Inulin can help promote this balance. Studies have shown that inulin can help stimulate the growth of beneficial bacteria.

Increasing the amounts of healthy bacteria can help improve digestion, immunity, and overall health.

It can also relieve constipation, promote weight loss, and most importantly it can control type 2 diabetes. It also improves mineral absorption and bone health. There are so many other benefits including preventing colon cancer and IBD. You can see why it's worth mentioning.

Pure Monk Fruit Sweetener -
General use - 1/32 tsp equals 2 tsp of white sugar. A little goes a LONG way!!! It is great to use in smoothies, tea, oatmeal, etc. This fruit is naturally very sweet. It's almost 200 times sweeter than sugar. The sweetness comes from antioxidants in the fruit itself.

Monk fruit has been grown in southern China for hundreds of years. It's a small, melon-like fruit, and gets its name from the Buddhist monks who originally grew it centuries ago. It is known as Swingle fruit (Siraitia grosvenorii) or lo han guo . It is from the same food family as gourds like pumpkin and melon. It's been used for medicinal purposes in eastern countries to treat intestinal problems and the common cold. Its use as a sweetener is fairly new. It reduces calories. Because monk fruit sugar is metabolized differently than regular sugar, you can reduce your caloric intake. Most sweeteners come with an aftertaste. Although taste is subjective to each person, monk fruit sugar has reportedly little to no aftertaste.

It comes with its own set of benefits as well. These include, but aren't limited to:
- *It doesn't affect blood sugar. Monk fruit sugar doesn't affect your blood sugar levels and can improve your glycemic control.*
- *It's anti-inflammatory. The sweetener in monk fruit sugar, also known as mogrosides, has anti-inflammatory effects.*
- *It can help fight cancer. Mogrosides can help your body fight cancer.*
- *It doesn't cause cavities. Since there's no actual sugar inside monk fruit sugar, you don't need to worry about it causing cavities.*
- *Since it's 150 - 200 times sweeter than sugar, you only need a pinch.*

Monk fruit sugar is made in four general steps:
The fruit is crushed, releasing the juice. It is then mixed with hot water and filtered to reveal the fruit infusion. The sweet infusion is dried to create a powder known as pure monk fruit sugar. *The recipes in this book use Monk fruit in its pure form, not with fillers.* Most companies sell them with corn alcohol called erythritol. If you prefer to use that, you may need to make some adjustments in some recipes.

Xylitol -

Use in Baking - 1:1 in recipes. 1/2 cup sugar equals 1/2 cup xylitol. When used in baking or, if melted, the weird flavor is not present. That only occurs when used raw. Can be made into a simple syrup (Page 372)

General Use - Start with 1 T and adjust as you need more. Best when used with citrus. Xylitol (pronounced Zy-Li-Tall) is a type of carbohydrate called a sugar alcohol, or polyol. They are water-soluble compounds that occur naturally in many fruits and vegetables. Xylitol is also commercially produced from birch bark and corn cob for use as a sweetener to replace calories from carbohydrates and sugars. Xylitol has been approved for use in food by the Food and Drug Administration (FDA) since 1963.

The name Xylitol comes from the word "xylose" or "wood sugar" because it was first made from birch trees. It has a cooling sensation in the mouth when consumed. As a result, xylitol is a preferred ingredient in sugar-free chewing gum and other oral health products like breath mints, mouthwash and toothpaste. When used in cooked food it is almost indiscernible, though, some people are able to tell when it is present. Though it's not my first choice, used correctly in certain desserts, it is brilliant. There are people that say it doesn't sit in their stomach well. I think consuming small amounts, if tolerated, is a healthy way to achieve sweetness. I don't believe it's meant to be consumed in quantity.

Conversion Table - Sugar to Stevia

Granulated Sugar	Green Stevia Powder	White Stevia	Liquid Stevia
1 tsp	1/8 tsp	Small dash	2-4 drops
1 T	3/8 tsp	1/2 pinch-1/4 tsp	6-9 drops
1/4 cup	1 1/2 tsp	Up to 2 1/2 tsp	1/4 tsp
1/2 cup	1 T	Up to 1 1/2 T	1/2 tsp
1 cup	2 T	Up to 3 T	1 tsp

Stevia -
This is also known as "sweet herb." It is a South American sweetening leaf. It is totally non-caloric, and approximately 25 times sweeter than sugar when made as a concentrated infusion of 1 tsp leaves to 1 cupful of water. Two drops equal 1 teaspoon of sugar in sweetness. In baking, use the conversion chart above to determine how much Stevia to use. It comes in both liquid drops and powder. Some stevia powder has a 1:1 ratio with sugar, so be sure to check the packaging. And speaking of checking the package, all of my recipes call for pure stevia. **Be aware that many stevia products have added sugars like dextrose or eurythritol.** Read the label and stay away from these products. Then there are brands that flavor the liquid drops, such as hazelnut, berry, vanilla, English Toffee, peppermint, pumpkin spice etc. ... and have zero calories. Clinical studies indicate that stevia is safe to use even in cases of severe sugar imbalance.

Important notes about baking with stevia.

1. Baked goods with stevia do not brown. Regular sugars create the caramelizing effect which allows for a baked item to brown. One way around this, I have found, is to use things to "trick" what you see. Such as chocolate zucchini cake. Another trick I use are roasted beet puree. The color will start off pink and turn "brown" after baked. You can also use a pastry brush and use Aquaschata™. Paint it on top of the cake, the bread, muffins (since it's acting like an oil or egg wash) and it will have a darker color from the natural sugars in the butternut squash. And gives it a golden cooked color. Also, if you would like to have your baked goods browned throughout, steep chicory crystals and use as a replacement for a Tablespoon of the required liquids.

2. Since you will be using a lot less Stevia than you would sugar, there will be an adjustment you need to make with the volume ratio of sugar in a recipe. By adding other ingredients to increase the bulk of your baked goods you will find it works well. Start with about 1/3 cup of liquid for every one cup of sugar replaced by Stevia. Applesauce, squash, roasted beets, apple butter and fruit purees are a few good options to replace the lost volume the white sugar would have occupied. **It's important to not skip this step so your baked goods will not collapse in the final product.**

3. If one of the ingredients is already being used in the recipe, just increase that ingredient. Such as mashed bananas or applesauce. Simply increase the amount by 1/3 cup more in the recipe.

4. Sugar makes cakes lighter. When going sugar free, your finished cake will be denser and potentially doughy. However, using whole grains may also vary the results. You can counter this by adding a little more baking powder than the recipe calls for, or, adding vinegar.

Oils

Aquaschata™ - 1/3 cup steamed butternut squash, 1/4 tsp turmeric, 1 tsp Proprietary blend, 1 cup Filtered Water.

Apple sauce - Generally **1:1 ratio.**

Red Wine

1. Option: 1/2 cup soaked, sun-dried tomatoes in hot water. Strain and use liquid.
2. Option: Add roasted, ground walnuts to a stock, giving tomato sauce depth and richness.
3. Option: Boil 1 large, shredded beet in 2 - 3 quarts of water for 20-30 min. Use as stock for the base of any dish.

Equipment

There is an infinite amount of "toys" that we often dream into, desire or wish we had. The truth is, there are many basics that work quite well. Without having all the fancy things. It's fun to have them, but not necessary. At my website, EpicurianAwakening.com, on the Epicurean Awakening™ Cooking Program link, I share a standard list of equipment that you can use within this book or cooking alongside with me in my program. Breaking it down this way makes it far less overwhelming. Starting can be one of the hardest steps to take. Just like anything, you have to start where you are at. In this case, you may already have the basic list. If that is the case, you are ready to begin. I try to make all my recipes user friendly, for everyone.

The Basic list is:
Measuring Cups and Spoons
Mixing Bowls
Silpat Mat
Silicone Molds
Parchment paper
Blender
Food Processor
Rolling Pin
Nut Bags
Mesh Strainer
Seed/Spice grinder
Cheesecloth (reusable - durable)
Non stick griddle
Stand Mixer or hand mixer
Non stick Mini Muffin Tins (silicone molds work great)
Non stick Muffin pan (silicone molds work great)
Pastry bag and piping tip

The "Would be nice" list is:
Grain mill
Instant Pot
Juicer
Pasta attachment/ pasta roller
Ravioli cutter
Double Sided rings cookie cutter (multiple sizes)

Kitchen Aid Stand Mixer
And, the "Just for fun" list includes:
Spiral Slicer
Sheet Slicer
Sprouting Jars/lids
Ice cream maker
Whipping cream canister
Mini Waffle maker
Non stick Donut Pan

Slow Cooker or Instant Pot?

Which is better? Crockpots or Instant Pots?

Crockpots have their place as do Instant Pots. One is not "better" than the other, one is different than the other. Rice cookers are for cooking rice or whole grains. Crockpots are usually used for making soup overnight. There are small crockpots that are ideal for steel cut oats. Instant pots vary. There are some that are fast cook and are pretty simple. There are others that dehydrate, air fry, sauté, pressure cook, steam, bake and broil. The fancy ones may intimidate you but rest assured, they are easy to use. Once you get a taste of all they can do, you will wonder how you lived without it. Artichokes for example, take only 15 minutes in the pressure cooker as opposed to an hour on the stove top, steaming away. And they are consistent, creamy and packed full of flavor. You can cook "one pot wonders" in them, also. You can rise bread in them AND bake the bread. If you have never had freshly made pressure cooked garbanzo beans, you are in for a treat. Far superior to the canned. Once you know what your "needs" are in the kitchen, you will choose accordingly. They make 6 qt and 8 qt sizes, depending on your family size, and it does make a big difference. No oil cooking means that you can use the air fryer without oil and eat foods that you love without the guilt and without the lack of not having. This IS a game changer.

Quick Reference Guide, At a Glance

Having a quick reference guide can help you navigate through this cookbook easier. With so many new alternatives, it may be hard to know which is best. Some recipes will offer which egg replacer is best. Or other alternatives that you might not know about. Here is a quick and easy list for you.

Egg Replacer

Mix with a hand mixer or seed grinder, frothing it.

1 egg
1 1/2 T tapioca flour
1 tsp Baking powder
1/4 tsp Xanthan gum
1/8 tsp Cream of tartar
3 T warm water

2 eggs
3 T tapioca flour
2 tsp Baking powder
1/2 tsp Xanthan gum
1/4 tsp Cream of tartar
1/4 cup +2 T warm water

3 eggs
4 1/2 T tapioca flour
3 tsp Baking powder
3/4 tsp Xanthan gum
1/2 tsp Cream of tartar
1/2 cup + 1 T warm water

4 eggs
1/4 cup + 2 T tapioca flour
4 tsp Baking powder
1 tsp Xanthan gum
3/4 tsp Cream of tartar
3/4 cup warm water

Angel Butter - Vegan Butter Replacement
1/4 cup = 2 T Coconut cream, 1 T Aquaschata™, 2 tsp ground chia seeds, 1/8 tsp Turmeric

1/2 cup = 4 T Coconut cream, 2 T Aquaschata™, 4 tsp ground chia seeds, 1/4 tsp Turmeric

3/4 cup = 6 T Coconut cream, 3 T Aquaschata™, 2 T ground chia seeds, 1/3 tsp Turmeric

1 cup = 1/2 cup Coconut cream, 1/4 cup Aquaschata™, 2 T + 2 tsp ground chia seeds, 1/2 tsp Turmeric

Flax Egg for Pasta

Single recipe
3 T Flax meal
1/2 cup + 2 T Aquaschata™ + 1 T water (heated)

Double Recipe
1/4 cup + 2 T Flax meal
1 cup + 1/4 cup Aquaschata™ + 2 T water (heated)

Walnut Pastry Dough for
Single recipe
1/2 cup toasted Walnuts*
1/2 cup Sweet Brown Rice flour
1/2 cup Sorghum flour
2 1/2 T ground Flaxseeds
2 T Arrowroot flour
1/2 cup Aquaschata™
1/4 tsp Liquid Stevia
1 tsp Vanilla Powder
1/2 tsp Salt

Double recipe
1 cup toasted Walnuts*
1 cup Sweet Brown Rice flour
1 cup Sorghum flour
1/4 cup + 1 T ground Flaxseeds
1/4 cup Arrowroot flour
1 cup Aquaschata™
1/2 tsp Liquid Stevia
2 tsp Vanilla Powder
1 tsp Salt

Sugar = Liquid Stevia
The simple rule of thumb.
1/4 cup = 1/4 tsp
1/2 cup = 1/2 tsp
3/4 cup = 3/4 tsp
1 cup = 1 tsp

Five Star Feature
☆☆☆☆☆

Another quick reference feature of this cookbook is the ☆☆☆☆☆ near the name of each recipe. Take advantage of this special feature by using a highlighter to indicate just how much you loved each recipe…

  Great   Good   Like   Ok   Not so much

Rate the recipes that you and your family love, indicating at a glance, what recipes you've tried and liked or tried and didn't like. If you see one without a highlighted star, you'll know you haven't tried it yet.

Resources

Hard-to-Find Supplies at your fingertips …

The internet will be your best friend and in many cases, my Amazon Affiliate link will help you locate the high quality kitchen items you are looking for. Access your dreams with the Epicurean Awakening™ QR code.

Here is your portal for most of the hard to find as well as regular ingredients used in the Epicurean Awakening™ recipes throughout this cookbook.

Kitchen Alchemy has never been easier. This QR code will link you to the most recent Molecular Gastronomy ingredients, bringing your taste buds into the 21st century.

Juices & Smoothies

Juicing. It does a body good.

The benefits of juicing are not really understood until one actually tries it. The juice bypasses digestion and gets assimilated immediately, therefore the results are noticed quickly. In addition, the raw foods are packed with enzymes and rich in vitamins. Mental clarity, physical endurance and nourishing the cells of the body (as a cleaner and fuel) are ways that juicing impacts the human body. Whether it's a hot day and you just want to cool off or your needing the nutrients to support an illness, the benefits are there for everyone to reach out and experience.

I will introduce two categories (Vegetables and then fruits). Organic foods will greatly enhance the value of the quality of juice you make. Not only does it support your own body, but it supports the environment and the organic farmers. The quality of organic produce surpasses conventional produce as it is rich in vitamins, enzymes and flavor. And more importantly, without the chemicals, because juicing concentrates whatever is going into your juicer or blender. Including the pesticides, herbicides etc.

Our bodies have an enzyme bank, however, if we do not continuously support and replenish it, we will deplete it quickly. We can only get enzymes from raw foods!

Vegetable juicing can be an acquired taste for some and very enjoyable for others. Once you see the benefits from this, you will be inspired to juice more often than not.

Vegetables and herbs commonly used:
Carrots, Celery, Beets, Cucumbers, Fennel, Ginger, Spinach, Parsley, Tomatoes.

Vegetables uncommonly used:
Alfalfa sprouts, Cabbage, Dandelion leaves, Endive, Kale, Mustard Greens, Parsnip, Potato, Radish.

The combinations work in their own special way. Depending on what you're wanting to nourish, determines what you use. An example would be eyesight: carrots, spinach and endive would be very nourishing for the optic nerve.
An apple is considered both a vegetable and a fruit in juicing terms. It sweetens many vegetable combinations making it more palatable.

Fruits worth Juicing:
Pineapple (skin has lots of vitamins), Strawberries, Blueberries, Raspberries, Blackberries, Apple, Pear, Black Cherry, Orange, Grapefruit, Watermelon and Grapes.

Fruits that are not ideal for juicing and are best used in smoothies:
Papaya, Coconut, Banana, Honeydew, Cantaloupe, Peach, Plum/Prunes, Apricot, Avocado and Mango.

Additives:
Spirulina, Wheat Grass, Barley Green, Royal Jelly, Flax seeds, Slippery Elm, Lecithin, Garlic, Mint, Cinnamon, Horseradish Root, Lemon, Fennel.

Juicing has had a lot of feedback over the decades about it being the end all, be all for healing the body from cancer and other diseases. When recovering from a surgery or illness, juicing plays an incredible role in your healing. Feeding your body the nutrients in a way that doesn't "tax" the body is very important. The body is thirsty for a speedy recovery and is looking for support, as the body naturally heals. And if we adhere to the natural laws and allow the body to heal without interference, then that is what it will do.

However, if you tend to be a "cold" person, juicing may not be for you ... yet. If you tend to be an anxious person, "juicing may not be for you …yet. For a majority of us, getting nutrients is a thing. If people eat the SAD diet, then juicing will no doubt have its perks. Vegetables are better juiced than fruits. Fruits can be high in sugar. However, carrots and beets are also high in sugar. And if you are diabetic, it may not be the right thing for you at this time. Smoothies can also soften the glucose glycemic index spike because of the fiber. If you have wanted to buy a juicer and haven't, there are things to know about which juicer is the best to buy ... Do your research.

What is your budget? That will also drive your choice of what to buy? However, you can always get a used juicer. You'd be surprised at how many people sell them.

Remember to save your vegetable scraps!!! Place them in a container that goes in the freezer. NOTHING is wasted!! Very important to remember that. If you have a recipe using fruit, juice the vegetables first and set the veggie scraps aside and then juice the fruit. You will use these to make your veggie paste; fully explained in my next cookbook, Epicurean Delights. Sorry, I can only fit so much into one cookbook!

Juice Machines - What to Look For.

If you don't have a juicer yet, it would be very beneficial for you to understand the difference and which one would be best suited for you. For example, if you travel a lot, perhaps having a lighter weight unit would be easier to carry.

Ease: This is the most important requirement because the easier a juicer is to use and clean up, the more often you will use it. None of the other criteria matter if you don't use it.

Yield: This is the amount of juice extracted from the fruit or vegetable. It is important that you maximize the amount of the juice extracted. An efficient juicer can get as much as 40% more juice. Juicers that eject the pulp outside the machine yield about 30% less juice than those that keep the pulp in the basket. 30% less juice is equivalent to throwing 1 glass of juice down the drain for every 3 glasses you drink.

Reliability: A good juicer is built to last many years, even decades. They usually come with a 5 or 10 year warranty. An inexpensive juicer lacks reliability and is typically warrantied for 90 days to 1 year. Most inexpensive juicers were not built for daily use. The cutting blade usually wears out after 2 - 4 months and the motor burns out after your warranty expires.

Power: A powerful motor will allow you to juice harder produce quicker without straining the motor and overheating. Power is measured by the watts and not RPM's. RPM's measure the number of rotations per minute. Lower RPM's are better. The higher the RPM, the quicker the nutrients can be destroyed from the heat and oxidation.

Replacement Parts: Finding replacement parts for unknown juicers can be a nightmare. Getting replacement parts from some manufacturers can take 4 - 8 weeks. Once you get into juicing daily, 1 week can feel like it's too long to go without a juicer. Imagine not having a toothbrush for 4 - 8 weeks! Yikes ... Just saying.

Types of Juicers:
Centrifugal, Masticating and Hydraulic Press are the 3 types of juicers available. A Blender is not considered juicing as it doesn't separate out the pulp. There are many people that enjoy keeping the fiber, however the purpose of juicers is to extract the

fiber. The Masticating juicers have additional uses that the other two types don't have as well. Let's take a closer look.

Champion Juicer: Mastication. Pulp extractor. Stainless steel internally in juicing section. Grinds nuts and seeds into nut butters. Makes frozen fruit sherbet. Grates vegetables (separate attachment). Attachment available for grinding grains and making flours as well. Weighs 25lbs. Heavy duty 1/3 hp motor, 1725 RPM's. 5 year warranty. Made in USA. Price available anywhere from $199.00 to $250.00. Used juicers are available.

Omega: Centrifugal. All stainless steel bowl, basket and blade. 2 quart capacity. 3600 RPM's. 11 lbs. 1/3 hp GE motor rated 200 watts. 10 year warranty. Made in USA. Citrus attachment available. List price is $109 - $500.

Breville: Centrifugal. Warranty 1 year. 1000 watts. Stainless steel. 13,000 RPM's to give you up to 30% more juice. Prices available $150 - $450.

Sana: Masticating. Stainless steel drum cap blade system and auger to achieve the higher yield. Weighs 21.7 lbs. 15 year warranty covers all parts and labor. BLDC Brushless DC Motor. The motor is lighter weight and more durable, longer operating time, lower power consumption, quiet operation and more precise variable speed control. Speed settings are for 40, 65, 90 and 120 RPM's. This minimizes foam and oxidation and are best with soft or fibrous produce. Prices available from $600 - $700.00

Green Power: Masticating. Pulp extractor. Juices all vegetables, fruits, sprouted grains, wheat grass. 110 RPM's. Very quiet machine. Twin blade, and removes pesticides on the blades. Made in Korea. 12 year warranty. Price $650.

Norwalk: Two part machine in one. Masticator and hydraulic press. All interior and exterior surfaces are stainless steel. Unlimited capacity. Heavy duty 1/3 hp motor. 54 lbs. Price $1800.

Note: *With the world being what it is, all prices are subject to current reality.*

Smoothies -
Is making a juice in the blender then considered a smoothie?

That's a great question. Smoothies tend to have other ingredients in them like milk, yogurt, oats, protein powders or other supplemental supports for fortifying. Juicing or blending your vegetables in a blender is not a smoothie. The intent of a smoothie in general has many other ingredients supporting it more as a meal or protein dense drink.

If you are going to use your blender for your vegetable juicing, the fiber has its own controversy. Digesting the fiber does help slow down and prevent any spikes in your blood sugars. Juicing bypasses digestion and goes straight to your bloodstream. Which is why it's so good for your Well Being. Your body is already taxed from the recovery process. If you are going to blend your vegetables, spinach is one of those ingredients that people tend to blend in whole and drink.

Smoothie recipes tend to have frozen bananas, frozen berries or frozen mangoes ... they also can be blended with nuts. You can make a nut milk or you can add the whole nut and drink. Almonds tend to scratch your throat, so straining them is best. Cashews, walnuts and pecans blend really well. Sunflower seeds, pumpkin seeds and hemp seeds make really good nutritional smoothies. Grains like cooked teff, cooked amaranth, cooked quinoa and even rice make grain milks. Again, 1/4 cup of cooked grain to a cup of milk. Blend and strain. Unless you want the grain in it to make it more filling.

Since fruits are higher in sugars, the berries (blueberries, blackberries, raspberries and marionberries) are a good choice for a low glycemic fruit. The anthrocyanins are extremely beneficial for the body as well. Vegetables that make really good smoothies are butternut squash, pumpkin, roasted beet, cucumber, and avocado. Frozen bananas are a good source of sweet. Liquid stevia and flavored stevia (like chocolate or hazelnut) are also great additions without adding extra fat, calories or sugar and keeping to your diet.

You can add fortifiers if you desire. Such as Bee pollen, flax or chia seeds, slippery elm powder, psyllium husk powder, wheat grass or Spirulina powders and lecithin granules. Lots of options here.

Vanilla powder, mint leaves, cilantro leaves add extra flavors to your sweet or savory drink. In addition, lemon or lime juice, fresh ginger, horseradish and cinnamon and nutmeg make excellent additions. Orange and lemon peel, dehydrated, add flavors as well as many freeze dried fruit powders. A little goes a long way and you aren't eating excessive fruits.

You may also like adding tahini, hazelnut butter, cashew butter, walnut butter, almond butter, sunflower seed butter, pumpkin seed butter and can be added to give the fat and fill you up to last longer.

Some of my favorite simple smoothie recipes:

Blueberry Smoothie
1/4 cup Oats
3/4 cup frozen Blueberries (or 1 heaping T freeze dried Blueberry powder)
plant based milk
1 - 2 tsp Cinnamon
5 - 9 Liquid Stevia drops to taste

Banana Maple Pecan
2 frozen Banana
1/4 cup Pecans
1 cup water
Maple flavored stevia (or a drop or two of maple syrup)

Oat Nogg (very warming, perfect for a cold day)
1 cup Oat milk (if you use your own, it will have to be finely strained or it will thicken the oats when heated).
1/2 cup Hot water
1 1/2 cups cooked Butternut squash (heated not cold)
1/2 tsp Nutmeg (grate your own for freshest flavor)
1 tsp Vanilla powder
1 small ripe Banana (about 1/2 cup)
pinch of Sea salt
Pinch of Turmeric
pinch of Cardamom
pinch of powdered Ginger or fresh grated

Maple Pecan Banana Swirl serves 2
To me this tastes just like pancakes, but with a lot less work.
I use frozen bananas but it is optional. Enjoy. It is one of my favorites. You can use English Toffee Stevia for an even more delicious flavor.

2 frozen Bananas
1/4 - 1/3 cup fresh Pecans
1 T Flaxseed (optional)
9 drops liquid Stevia
1/4 tsp Maple flavoring (optional)
1 cup Water (adjust as needed)

Cooking Instructions:
1. In advance, peel fresh ripe bananas and freeze until hard.
2. In the blender, add pecans and flax seeds. Blend until there is a fine meal. Break bananas into small chunks and combine with water, flax, nuts and sweetener. Blend on high until smooth and creamy.

Flax Seed Shake
3 T Flax seeds
1 - 2 T papaya dried or 1/2 fresh papaya
1/2 T grated ginger
Liquid Stevia to sweeten
1 cup water

- Mix flax seeds with water overnight.
  In a blender mix water and flax seeds on high for 3 - 4 minutes.

Variations for flavors:
*1/4 - 1/3 frozen blueberries, 1 - 2 T dried papaya, and 1 - 2 tsp powdered ginger, sweeten with Liquid Stevia.

* 2 - 3 T Carob powder & 1 tsp 1/4 cup fresh mint leaves or Mint stevia.

*1/2 fresh Mango, 1 tsp of dried orange peel & fresh peach, pinch of nutmeg, 1/4 - 1/2 tsp cinnamon, and 1/2 tsp coriander (Sweeten with liquid stevia if it needs it).

*2 T cacao, 1 T Chicory crystals (steeped in 1/4 cup boiling water), 1/2 tsp vanilla powder, liquid stevia to sweeten. Use Hazelnut Stevia flavor for a nutty flavor.

*1 1/2 oranges, 1 - 2 T grated fresh ginger, 1 - 3 T dried papaya.

Juicing Combinations for Well Being

Improves eyesight: Carrots, Spinach, Endive, Parsley

Aids in Digestion: Carrot, Celery, Apple, Fennel
Carrot, Celery, Spinach, Fennel, Ginger
Carrot, Beet, Spinach
Carrot, Beet, Ginger

PMS/ menstruation: Carrot, Spinach
Carrot, Fennel
Carrot, Parsley
Carrot, Celery, Parsley, Spinach
Carrot, Beet, Cucumber

Acne: Carrot, Lettuce, Spinach

Allergy: Carrot, Beet, Cucumber
Carrot, Spinach

Backache: Carrot, Celery, Parsley, Spinach
Carrot, Beet, Cucumber
Carrot, Spinach

Bronchitis: Carrot, Spinach
Carrot, Dandelion
Carrot, Celery, Radish

Colds: Carrot, Lemon, Ginger, Cayenne Pepper

Coughing: Carrot, Beet, Cucumber
Carrot, Spinach

Diabetes: Carrot, Asparagus, Lettuce
Carrot, Brussel Sprouts, String Beans
Carrot, Celery, Parsley
Carrot, Spinach
Carrots, Lettuce, Brussel Sprouts, String Beans

Eczema:	Carrot, Spinach
	Carrot, Celery, Parsley, Spinach
	Carrot, Beet, Cucumber
Fatigue:	Carrot, Spinach
	Carrot, Beet, Cucumber
Gout:	Carrot, Spinach
	Carrot, Celery, Parsley, Spinach (Black cherry juice as well)
	Carrot, Beet, Cucumber
Headaches:	Carrot, Spinach
	Carrot, Celery, Parsley, Spinach
	Carrot, Beet, Cucumber
Heart:	Carrot, Beet, Cucumber
	Carrot, Spinach
	Carrot, Celery, Parsley, Spinach
Hemorrhoids:	Carrot, Spinach, Turnips, Watercress
	Carrot, Celery, Parsley, Spinach
	Carrot, Beet, Cucumber
Indigestion:	Lemon taken in hot water
	Carrot, Spinach
	Carrot, Beet, Cucumber
Insomnia:	Carrot, Spinach
	Carrot, Celery
	Carrot, Beet, Cucumber
Laryngitis:	Carrot, Spinach
	Carrot, Beet, Cucumber
Menopause:	Carrot, Spinach
	Carrot, Beet, Spinach, Turnip
	Carrot, Beet, Pomegranate (Unsweetened)
	Carrot, Beet, Cucumber

Pregnancy:	Carrot, Beet, Cucumber
	Carrot, Spinach
	Carrot, Dandelion, Turnip
	Carrot, Beet Lettuce, Turnip
Prostrate:	Lemon
	Carrot, Beet, Cucumber
	Carrot, Spinach
	Carrot, Asparagus, Lettuce
Sinus Trouble:	Fenugreek Tea (1 T in pot of boiling water)
	Boil for 5 min. Reuse up to 3X.
	Lemon Juice 1 whole lemon to
	1/4 tsp ground horseradish
	Carrot, Spinach
	Carrot, Beet, Cucumber
Varicose Veins:	Carrot, Spinach
	Carrot, Celery, Parsley, Spinach
	Carrot, Spinach, Turnip, Watercress

Now for some fun juices ...

Pineapple, orange, banana - This juice is full of enzymes. Juice the first two and then add it to a blender with the banana. Preferably a frozen one. Add mint leaves for an extra burst of yum! If you omit the banana, it's still very creamy.

Apple, pear, celery - This is a very creamy juice. It is excellent for quenching your thirst and balancing your sodium/potassium levels. Omit the pear and it's just as good.

Strawberry juice - When strawberries are at their peak and you can't eat all of them, juice as many as you want and put in ice cube trays. Then store in a zip lock bag in the freezer. Use them in a glass of water and let them melt or use in a smoothie.

Symptoms of Healing that may take place ...

Often there can be symptoms that appear just when we start cleansing. This is natural and appropriate. When closets get cleaned out, we have to remove everything, then clean it before we put anything back. Then make new choices about what goes into the closet. Do we love it, use it or is it time to get rid of it? Are you on a kidney cleanse? A liver detox? Are you removing the top 10 allergens? When we make a new choice to "clean house" the body finally gets a break. And what does that break look like? Here's a list of things that the body may go through in order to rid the body of it's toxic load. There's no room for judgment. There's only gratitude for what was inside of you is now coming out of you. That's the true healing.

Headache	Dizziness	Diarrhea	Hot Flashes	Acne
Eczema	Stuffy nose	Nausea	Muscle Aches	Fever
Asthma	Faintness	Bronchitis	Running nose	Rash
Weakness	Irritability	Bad Breath	Irregular Heartbeat	Fatigue

*These symptoms may be more noticeable if you are on a fast or cleansing program.

Dairy Alternatives:
Butter, Cheese, Sour Cream, Aioli, Cream Cheeses, & more

Riced Cauliflower……………………………...106

Angel Butter…………………………………107

    Basic……………………………………107

    Herb……………………………………107

    Sundried Tomato……………………..108

Vegan Sour Cream…………………………….108

Macadamia Cauliflower Ricotta Cheese……...109

Dairy Alternatives:
Butter, Cheese, Sour Cream, Aioli, Cream Cheeses, & more
Continued ...

Basic Cream Cheese………………………………...110

    Cashew…………………………………………..110

Flavored Cream Cheese……………………………...110

    Pumfu…………………………………………...111

    Chive……………………………………………111

    Basil…………………………………………...112

    Hazelnut………………………………………..112

    Faux Lox………………………………………...112

Mayonnaise…………………………………………113

Aioli………………………………………………..114

    Cilantro Garlic…………………………………..114

    Basil…………………………………………...115

    Roasted Red Pepper/Smoked Paprika
    Basil/Artichoke………………………………...115

All things Dairy Alternatives

This section does not include desserts. You will find those starting on page 282.

These Dairy Alternative recipes include vegan butter, sour cream, cream cheese, ricotta and pestos. For even more ideas and recipes refer to the beginning of the book on Alternatives A-Z. There you will find a very thorough "what do I use instead?" There are times we can't eat something while other times we run out and want to use something to replace it without having to run to the store every time we are missing an ingredient. Having a stocked freezer and pantry of some basics as to eliminate this from happening will support the ease and flow in your daily life as well as your creative outlet.

◆ *A side note: Citric Acid is helpful to keep things fresher longer. It can be an allergen for some people. Rare as it may be, make sure you know you won't be affected by it. It makes a huge difference in how long Aquaschata™ and salad dressings can stay fresh in the refrigerator before spoiling.*

A note about Cashews - Cashews do tend to be avoided by some people. If you are one of them, look into alternatives such as Macadamia or Pili Nuts. They are an excellent replacement for cashews. Buy unsalted and use 1 to 1 in any recipe calling for cashews. They have a similar creamy and smooth texture with a mild flavor making them an exceptional replacement.

Included in this section is prepping Riced Cauliflower. It's such a versatile food that having this here makes the most sense. As most of the recipes in this book use it as a dairy alternative.

Cauliflower, Riced ☆☆☆☆☆

Riced Cauliflower is absolutely amazing. It virtually has no flavor and will add the "bulk" of the filling without adding the calories to your waist as most dairy can. Let's look at the basic recipe of what you need for this transformation to take place.

1 head Cauliflower any color
Food processor
Pot/skillet/wok - anything to cook 6 cups in
Large Sieve or Drum Strainer
Large Plastic scraper that has flexibility
Nut milk bag or cheesecloth – bag that has a string and allows for hanging.
Large shallow Tupperware or 9x13 baking dish – that fits in freezer to cool cauliflower off quickly.

Cooking Instructions:

1. To prepare the cauliflower, using a food processor, rice 1 head of cauliflower (equivalent to 6 cups). Pulse until you get the texture of rice. Depending on the size of the cauliflower head, you may have to do this in more than one batch.
2. Place in a bowl and rinse with water removing any large pieces.
3. Using a large skillet or wok, add the riced cauliflower and cover with water. Remove any large pieces. Bring to a boil and cook on medium - high heat for 5 min. It will get foamy and frothy. Next, using a large sieve or a drum strainer, strain water out pressing out all the water with the large plastic scraper. At this point, you can use a nut bag to squeeze out the remaining water. It is hot still, so be careful to not burn yourself. If you don't have a nut milk bag, a clean kitchen towel will work also, but it is harder to get all the pieces out. A wooden spoon will also push all the water out but the large scraper is best. Once you feel all the water has been removed, place the cauliflower in a large tray or container and set it in the freezer for 10 minutes to cool off.
4. It is now available to be used in the recipe. The recipes in this book call for the amounts before it's been cooked. One head is roughly 6 cups. So, half would be 3 cups. However, the amount it yields after it is cooked is much less. So don't be alarmed. That has been taken into consideration when developing the recipes.

Notes: Use this in both savory or sweet. You can blend fresh fruit in a blender with it. You can use it in pestos and make it savory. The versatility of this is spectacular.

Angel Butter *makes 1/4 cup* ☆☆☆☆☆

Angel Butter is a name I have created combining Chia seeds, Aquaschata™ and Coconut Milk. The combination makes a beautiful "butter" alternative to use in many of the recipes in this book. This nondairy butter alternative is good for baking. Use in recipes calling for butter in baking.

Basic recipe:
2 tsp ground Chia Seeds
2 T Coconut cream
1 T Aquaschata™
1/8 tsp Turmeric

- In a seed grinder, add all ingredients and mix. It will be very creamy. Refrigerate it to harden. Or use it for baking wherever it is called for in the recipes.

Herb Angel Butter *makes 1/4 cup* ☆☆☆☆☆

Another variation of this nondairy butter alternative for homemade bread or bagels.

2 tsp ground Chia Seeds
2 T Coconut Cream
1 T Aquaschata™
2 T Chives, Basil, or Dill
Dash of salt

Sour cream - *Add lemon juice to turn it into sour cream.*

- In a seed grinder, add all ingredients and mix. It will be very creamy. You can put it into a Silpat candy mold for fun shapes. Refrigerate to harden. Use for mashed potatoes, baked potatoes or veggies.

Sun-dried Tomato Basil Angel Butter *makes 1/4 cup* ☆☆☆☆☆
Another variation for adding to a pasta cream sauce. Or fresh pasta.

2 tsp ground Chia seeds
2 T Coconut Cream
1 T Aquaschata™
2 T fresh Basil
1/2 T chopped Sun Dried Tomatoes soaked in water.
3 chopped Olives (optional)
Dash of salt

- In a seed grinder, add all ingredients and mix. It will be very creamy. You can put into Silpat candy mold for fun shapes. Refrigerate to harden. Use this as a spread on bread or crackers.

Vegan Sour Cream *makes 1 cup* ☆☆☆☆☆
3/4 cup Oat milk
1 cup Raw Cashews (Or Macadamia/Pili nut)
1 1/2 tsp Apple Cider Vinegar or Lemon Juice

- To make the Sour Cream, blend the oat milk and cashews until smooth and creamy. Add more nuts if necessary. Then blend in the vinegar or lemon juice.

Vegan Buttermilk *makes 1 cup* ☆☆☆☆☆
1 cup almond* or cashew milk
1 T lemon juice

- To make buttermilk, blend the almonds or Cashews until smooth and creamy. Add more nuts if necessary. Then blend in the vinegar or lemon juice.
  *Almonds tend to be gritty, however, if you are baking, it's up to you whether you strain it or not.

Macadamia Cauliflower Ricotta Cheese *makes 3 1/2 cups* ☆☆☆☆☆

Macadamia nut allergies are rare. Less than 5 % of the population have them, so, PLEASE enjoy this amazing recipe! The cauliflower creams this beautifully and keeps it light and not rich. So you can enjoy this without the heaviness or richness of dairy. Use this recipe as the base for both sweet or savory ricotta recipes.

- *Basic Recipe:*
  1/2 Cauliflower riced (Page 106),(Cooked) = 1 head of Cauliflower Raw
  1 cup Macadamia nuts ground into a meal
  1/4 cup Nutritional yeast
  Salt to taste

- *Savory Version:*
  Add 1 cup of pesto to this base and use as the filling for Cannelloni, Shells, Manicotti or Lasagna.

- *Sweet Version:*
  Cut recipe in half and remove Nutritional yeast.
  Add fruit coulis, like raspberry, blueberry, chocolate, ginger, orange or lemon zest.
  Use cacao powder to replace the nutritional yeast.
  1/2 tsp Liquid Stevia (Flavored Stevia works well here if you have a specific flavor in mind)
  1 1/2 tsp Vanilla powder

Basic Cream Cheese Recipe ☆☆☆☆☆

This section has two basic cream cheese recipes. One with Cashews and one with Pumfu (pumpkin seed tofu). Each are equally exciting and provides a lot of flexibility. If you avoid Cashews, then making the pumpkin seed one will be satisfying. If you can't have any nuts or seeds, make it with Riced cauliflower. If you can't have coconut cream, try it with white miso. This book is all about inspiration and thinking outside of the box. Being **Fearless in the Kitchen** *is about challenging yourself to find the satisfaction factor, not the deprivation factor.*

Ingredients
3/4 cup ground Raw Cashews**
3 1/2 T Coconut Cream only
1/4 cup Filtered Water
1/2 T lemon juice
Salt to taste

- Blend in seed grinder and refrigerate.

Variations with other flavors:
- Cream Cheese with Chives - Add 3 - 4 T chopped fresh Chives.
- Cinnamon Cream Cheese - Add 1 T Cinnamon powder,
- Hazelnut Cream Cheese - 1 1/2 T Cacao Powder and 1/8 tsp - 1/4 tsp Hazelnut Stevia.
- Herb Cream Cheese - Add 3 - 4 T chopped Dill, Basil, Chives or any combination.
- Roasted Red pepper Cream Cheese - Add roasted red pepper and blend.
- Jalapeno Cream Cheese - dice Jalapeno into it.
- Strawberry Cream Cheese - Blend 4 or 5 fresh strawberries or 1 - 2 T Freeze. Dried Strawberry powder.
- Garlic or Onion Cream Cheese - Add 1/2 tsp Garlic powder and or 1 tsp Onion powder or both.

** Replace with Macadamia or Pili nuts if you are avoiding Cashews.

Pumfu (Pumpkin Seed Tofu)

Pumpkin seeds make an exceptional replacement in many of the dairy alternatives and desserts in this book. As a cream cheese, there is a slight bitterness that comes through when not using onion powder or cacao powder. It seems these two powders are the magic to minimize the bitterness. There are so many possible recipes here, simply try them or come up with your own combinations. You can use them on sandwiches, fresh bread by itself, inside raviolis, even in desserts, the cacao pinwheels use the hazelnut cream cheese recipe below. It's extremely versatile, a gorgeous color and fun! Since soy is an allergen to many, pumfu is an exceptional replacement.

- **Cooking Instructions:** Blend in a seed grinder and refrigerate in an air tight container.

Cream Cheese with Chives ☆☆☆☆☆
4 ounces Pumfu
3 1/2 T Coconut Cream
3 T Filtered Water
2 T Lemon Juice
1/4 cup Chives
1/4 tsp + 1/8 tsp Onion Powder
Salt

Cream Cheese with Fresh Basil leaves ☆☆☆☆☆
4 ounces Pumfu
3 1/2 T Coconut Cream
3 T Filtered Water
2 T Lemon Juice
1/4 cup Chives
1/4 tsp + 1/8 tsp Onion Powder
1/8 tsp Garlic Powder
Salt

Cream Cheese with Fresh Cilantro ☆☆☆☆☆

4 ounces Pumfu
3 1/2 T Coconut Cream
3 T Filtered Water
2 T Lime Juice
1/4 cup Cilantro
1/4 tsp + 1/8 tsp Onion Powder
1/8 tsp Garlic Powder
1/2 tsp Cumin Powder
Salt

Hazelnut Cream Cheese ☆☆☆☆☆

4 ounces Pumfu
3 1/2 T Coconut Cream
3 T Filtered Water
1 1/2 T Cacao Powder
1/8 tsp - 1/4 tsp Hazelnut Stevia
Salt

Faux Lox Cream Cheese ☆☆☆☆☆

4 ounces Pumfu
3 1/2 T Coconut Cream
3 T Filtered Water
2 T Lemon Juice
1 T dry Dill Weed
1/2 tsp Onion Powder
1/8 tsp Garlic Powder
1/4 tsp Smoked Salt

Basic Mayonnaise Recipe

☆☆☆☆☆

This can be made with any tofu, cashews, pumpkin seeds or cooked lima beans. Pumfu, made from Pumpkin, seeds give it a beautiful light green color. This recipe is mild and can be adapted to make any kind of aioli. Use black salt (also known as kala namak) found in Indian stores. It has a sulfur like smell, and flavor and is actually used medicinally to treat bloating symptoms. Use it in any recipe that calls for eggs, and it transports you to believe it has eggs in it. A very small amount is all that's needed because it's very strong. Sprinkle it in or use the monk fruit 1/32nd scoop. Making it with herbs like cilantro, basil or parsley keeps the questions and answers more acceptable when it comes to kids....as in why is it green?

Ingredients
1 package of Pumfu - 8 ounces
1 1/2 lemons, around 2 1/2 T to 3 T
1 T Aquaschata™
2 tsp Dijon mustard or 2 tsp Natur Emul
3/4 tsp Onion powder
1/2 tsp Garlic powder
3/4 tsp Salt
1/32 tsp Black salt, Kala Namak
1/2 cup - 3/4 cup Filtered water, to your
  desired thickness

- Combine - in a food processor, blend all the ingredients until creamy. Taste and adjust.

Cilantro Garlic Aioli

☆☆☆☆☆

Ingredients
1 package of Pumfu - 8 ounces
1 1/2 lemons, around 2 1/2 T to 3 T
1 T Aquaschata™
1/3 cup Fresh Cilantro leaves (not the stems)
1 raw Garlic clove
2 tsp Dijon mustard or 2 tsp Natur Emul
1 tsp Onion powder
3/4 tsp Garlic powder
3/4 tsp Salt
1/32 tsp + sprinkle to taste Black salt, Kala Namak
1/2 cup - 3/4 cup Filtered water, to your desired thickness

variations: Fresh Rosemary, Fresh Garlic, Fresh Thyme

Garlic Aioli

☆☆☆☆☆
add 1 - 1 1/2 cloves raw garlic

Basil Aioli

☆☆☆☆☆
add 2 cups Fresh Packed Basil leaves

Roasted Red Pepper and Smoked Paprika Aioli

☆☆☆☆☆

Ingredients

1 package of Pumfu - 8 ounces
1 Red Bell Pepper, roasted
1 1/2 lemons, around 2 1/2 T to 3 T
1 T Aquaschata™
2 tsp Dijon mustard or 2 tsp Natur Emul
3/4 tsp Onion powder
1/2 tsp Garlic powder
1/4 tsp Smoked Paprika (or smoked salt)
3/4 tsp Salt (or 1/2 tsp if using smoked salt)
1/32 tsp Black salt, Kala Namak
1/2 cup - 3/4 cup Filtered water, to your desired thickness.

Basil Artichoke Aioli *makes 1/2 cup*

☆☆☆☆☆

Serve this either hot or cold. Try it as a dipping sauce, a salad dressing or on fresh pasta. This makes an excellent base for other savory variations.

1 can Artichoke Hearts
1/4 cup Fresh Basil (packed)
3 T Coconut Cream
1 tsp Roasted Garlic powder
1/2 Lemon, juiced
2 tsp Nutritional Yeast
1/8 tsp Onion powder
1/4 tsp Salt
White pepper

Aioli Preparation Instructions:
- For all Aioli recipes, combine ingredients in a seed grinder or food processor, blend all the ingredients until creamy smooth.

Herbs for Cooking & Baking

Pate Seasoning Blend..................................120

Korma Seasonings..121

Garam Masala Blend......................................121

Taco Seasoning Blend....................................121

Italian Seasoning Blend……………………..122

Herb Salt..122

Chai Spice Mix..123

Everything Seasoning Blend..........................123

Sauces & Salsa

BBQ Sauce..124

Pico de Gallo Salsa....................................124

Mango Salsa...124

Green Salsa...125

Dark Cherry BBQ sauce............................125

Herbs for Savory Cooking:

Marinades: Basil, bay, coriander seed & leaves, cumin, dill, fennel, garlic, juniper berries, lemon balm, lovage, mint, onion greens & bulbs, parsley stems, rosemary and tarragon.

Casseroles: Borage, bay, chicory, chives, coriander seed, dill seed, fennel, garlic, lemon balm, lovage, marjoram, mint, oregano, parsley, sage, savory, and thyme.

Salads: Alexanders, angelica, arugula, basil, borage leaves, caraway, chervil, chicory, Chinese chives, chives, coriander leaves, dill, fennel, lemon balm, lovage, marjoram, mint, mustard seedlings, nasturtium leaves, orach, parsley, purslane, salad burnet, savory, sorrel, sweet cicely, tarragon, thyme, watercress.
Edible Flowers: bergamot, borage, calendula, chives, marigold, nasturtium, pansy, primrose, rose petals, sweet rocket, violet.

Herbs for Sweets:
General: Angelica, aniseed, elderflower, lemon balm, lemon verbena, pineapple sage, rosemary, saffron, sweet cicely leaves and green seeds.

Custards: Bay, lemon thyme, mint, rose petals, scented geraniums.

Fruit Salad: Aniseed, lemon balm, mints, rosemary, sweet cicely leaves and green seeds.

Fruit Compote: Dill, mint, aniseed, caraway, coriander, dill with apples, savory with quinces; angelica, sweet cicely with acidic fruits.

Spices for Sweets: Cinnamon, Cardamom, All Spice, Ginger, Cloves, Fennel.

Herbs for Bread:
Aniseed, basil, caraway, chives, dill, fennel, garlic & onion powder, lovage seed, poppy seed, rosemary, sunflower seed, thyme.

Herbs for Soup:
General: Chervil, garlic, juniper berries, lemon balm, lovage leaf and seed, marjoram, mints, onion (green and bulb), parsley leaf, stem and root, rosemary,

savory, sorrel, tarragon, thyme.
Minestrone: Basil, rosemary, thyme.
Pea: Basil, borage, dill, marjoram, mint, parsley, rosemary, savory, thyme.
Potato: Bay, caraway, garlic, onion, parsley.
Tomato: Basil, dill, marjoram, oregano, thyme.

Seasoning Blends
What is a seasoning blend?
Flavor is one way to make our taste buds happy. Food that tastes good is essential to the Epicurean novice. Making your own seasoning blends allows you to control the sodium levels, makes it super fresh, therefore, enhancing your pleasurable experience. And be aware, many seasoning blends have MSG in them. Making your own eliminates that as well. This is an easy way to impress your family and your dinner guests.

Using fresh blends brings a whole other level of vitality to your cooking. The vibrant colors are brilliant. Fresh is best! The vibrant flavors keep for 1 month before fading. Store in air tight jars or spice bottles.

Pate Seasoning Blend ☆☆☆☆☆
1 T white Pepper
1 T black Pepper
1 T Paprika
1 T whole dried Thyme
1 T Marjoram
1 T Nutmeg
1 T Ginger powder
1 T dried Basil
1 T Allspice
1 T Garlic powder
1/2 T Clove powder

- Place all ingredients in a seed grinder and blend. Transfer into a spice bottle and store at a cool room temperature. The mixture will lose its vitality after a month. Cut the recipe in half if you won't use it all in a month's time.

Korma Seasonings (Curry) ☆☆☆☆☆

1 T Whole Coriander seeds
1 T Whole Cumin seeds
1 T Whole Fennel seeds
1 T Whole Fenugreek seeds
1 T Cardamom seeds
1 T Poppy seeds
1 T Ground Cinnamon
1 T Ground Ginger
1 T Ground Turmeric
1 tsp ground cloves

- Place all ingredients in a seed grinder and blend. Transfer into a spice bottle and store at a cool room temperature. The mixture loses its vitality after a month. Cut recipe in half if you won't use it all within 4 weeks.

Garam Masala Blend ☆☆☆☆☆

1/3 cup Coriander seeds
1/4 cup Cumin seeds
10 black Cardamom pods, peeled (found in Indian stores)
15 green Cardamom pods, peeled (found in most stores)
25 Cloves
2 Cinnamon sticks broken up
1 tsp black Peppercorns
1/4 tsp fresh Nutmeg (For fresher flavor, buy whole nutmeg and grate it.)

- Mix together and grind finely, but not to a powder, using a coffee/seed grinder, spice grinder, mortar and pestle, rolling pin or food processor. Store in an airtight jar.
- *Note: This is a very warming blend if you tend to be a cold person. It will help calm the mind of anxieties.*

Taco Seasonings ☆☆☆☆☆

3 T Chili powder
1 T Onion powder
1 T Smoked Paprika

2 1/2 tsp Cumin
1 tsp Oregano
1 tsp Garlic powder
1 - 3 tsp crushed Red peppers (chipotle or cayenne pepper)

- Mix everything together and store in an airtight container. Use within a month.

Italian Seasoning blend ☆☆☆☆☆

1 T dried Basil
1 T dried Oregano
1 T dried Rosemary
1 T dried Thyme
1 T dried Marjoram
1 T Fennel seeds
1 tsp minced, dried Garlic (optional)

- Mix together and store in a seal jar.

Herb Salt ☆☆☆☆☆

This herb blend allows you to use less salt with greater flavor. If you are on a low salt diet, you can cut the salt in half.

4 T Salt
1 T dried Basil
1 T dried Thyme
1 T dried Marjoram
1 T dried Mint
1 T dried Rosemary
1 T dried Sage
9 Whole dried Bay Leaves

- Grind ingredients into a fine powder using a seed grinder. Store in an airtight container.

Chai Spice Mix ☆☆☆☆☆
1/2 tsp Anise
2 tsp Cinnamon
1 tsp ground Ginger
1/4 - 1/2 tsp Grated nutmeg (use whole nutmeg)
1/2 tsp Cardamom
1/4 tsp ground Cloves

- Grind all of the ingredients into a fine powder using a seed grinder. Store in an airtight container.

Everything Seasoning Blend ☆☆☆☆☆
Ideal for bagels, breads and crackers. Makes 3 Tablespoons:
2 tsp White Sesame Seeds
1 1/2 tsp Black Sesame Seeds
1 tsp Dried Minced Garlic
1 1/2 tsp Dried Minced Onion
1/2 tsp Poppy Seeds
1 tsp Sea Salt Flakes

makes 3/4 cups:
2 T + 2 tsp White Sesame Seeds
2 T Black Sesame Seeds
1 1/2 T Dried Minced Garlic
2 T Dried Minced Onion
1 1/2 T Dried Minced Garlic
2 tsp Poppy Seeds
4 tsp Sea Salt Flakes

makes 3 cups:
1/2 cup + 3 T White Sesame Seeds
1/2 cup Black Sesame Seeds
1/2 cup Dried Minced Garlic
1/2 cup Dried Minced Onion
2 T + 2 tsp Poppy Seeds
5 T + 1 tsp Sea Salt Flakes

Mix the ingredients together in a small jar or bowl. Store in an airtight container. Perfect for topping on bagels, crackers and bread.

BBQ Sauce *makes 1/2 cup* ☆☆☆☆☆
4 T Tomato paste
2 1/2 T Chicory tea (1 1/2 T Chicory crystals steeped in 1/2 cup hot water)
1 T Aquaschata™
1/4 tsp Liquid Stevia
1/2 tsp Onion powder
1/4 + 1/8 tsp roasted Garlic powder (it clumps less)
1/2 tsp Lemon juice
1/8 tsp smoked Paprika or smoked salt
1/8 tsp Chili powder (optional)
1/4 tsp Salt (omit if using smoked salt)

Cooking Instructions:
1. Steep the chicory crystals in hot water for 3 - 4 minutes. The longer it steeps the more bitter it gets, so steep less to make it less bitter.
2. In a bowl, add the tomato paste, Aquaschata™, and Chicory tea. Mix until well blended. Add in the remaining ingredients. Taste and adjust seasonings. Store in airtight container in refrigerator or use immediately.

Pico de Gallo Salsa *makes 2 cups* ☆☆☆☆☆
1 medium Onion (white or red) diced
2 large Tomatoes, chopped (*Use Tomatillos if Histamine Sensitive*)
2 - 3 T Green chili peppers or 1 jalapeño diced

- Mix all together in bowl.

Mango Salsa *makes 1 cup* ☆☆☆☆☆
1 Mango, peeled and chopped (*Use peach if Histamine Sensitive*)
1/2 tsp finely chopped Green chili
1 clove Garlic, diced (or 1/2 tsp dried)
1 T Lime juice
2 T chopped fresh Cilantro or 1 T cumin seeds
1 T chopped fresh Parsley

- Dry Roast the cumin seeds in a skillet over low medium heat until the fragrance is released. Stir the remaining ingredients in a bowl and add the cumin seeds. Mix, cover and refrigerate until serving time.

Green Salsa *makes 2 1/4 cups*
☆☆☆☆☆
1 lb. Tomatillos
1 small Onion, chopped
2 cloves fresh Garlic
1 Anaheim Green chili (or 2 Jalapeños seeded and diced)
1 T Lime juice
1/2 cup Fresh Cilantro leaves
Salt to taste

Cooking Instructions:
1. In a saucepan, add the tomatillos, onion and garlic. Bring to a boil and simmer for 10 minutes.
2. Add to a blender with the remaining ingredients and blend. Store in airtight container in refrigerator.

Dark Cherry BBQ Sauce *(low Histamine) makes about 2 cups*
☆☆☆☆☆
2 cups Dark Cherries, pitted
2 tsp dehydrated Orange peels
1/4 cup Aquaschata™
3 T Date Nectar
1 T Onion powder
1 tsp Ginger powder
2 1/2 cloves Garlic
1/4 cup ground, roasted Walnuts
1/2 tsp Smoked Salt
1/2 tsp Cacao powder
20 drops Chocolate Stevia
2 T Xylitol

Cooking Instructions:
1. Prepare 24 hours ahead for a full flavor.
2. Roast Walnuts at 325 degrees F for 10 min. Cool and grind in a food processor.

3. Add all ingredients into a blender and blend until silky smooth. Refrigerate 24 hours to get the flavors to blend together.

Happytizers
Hors d'œuvres to make you smile

Pizza Bites..129

Mini Pizzas on English Muffins........................130

Artichoke Sun-dried Tomato Basil Dip..................131

White Bean Dip...132

Beet or Butternut Squash Hummus.........................134

Roasted Red Pepper Hummus...................................134

Sun-dried Tomato Hummus......................................135

Kalamata Hummus..135

Artichoke Spinach Jalapeno dip..............................136

Phyllo Stuffed Mushrooms.....................................137

Sun-dried Tomato, Basil and Mushroom filling wrapped in Phyllo like dough..................138

Tortilla Pinwheels with Cream Cheese Filling......139

Pesto Dips with Crackers & Macadamia Cheese Dip..140

Guacamole served with Baked Homemade Tortilla Chips or Tostadas...141

Happytizers - Hors d'oeuvres

Pizza Bites
☆☆☆☆☆

These are my kids' favorite snack. They love the surprising flavor inside. Serve with a roasted tomato dipping sauce or simply enjoy them by themselves.

Ingredients
1 Profiterole Recipe, depending on servings desired, double it. (Page 300)

Pizza Filling Ingredients
1 can Artichoke hearts in water, drained and rinsed
1 tsp roasted Garlic powder
2/3 cup Fresh Basil, packed
2 T Sun-dried Tomatoes, soaked in hot water to soften
1/2 Lemon juiced
2 tsp Nutritional yeast
3 T Coconut Cream
1/8 tsp Onion powder
1 T Dried Oregano
Salt to taste
Black pepper

Cooking Instructions:
1. Soak the Sun-dried tomatoes for 10 - 15 min. Strain. Keep the water.
2. Place everything into a food processor and process until creamy.
3. Set aside Pizza filling.
4. Make Profiteroles. (Page 300)
5. Once the Profiteroles have cooled down, poke a hole in the side or bottom of the profiterole. Place the filling in a piping bag. Push the piping bag tip into the hole, and squeeze the filling until you feel the sides of the profiterole bulge. Fill all the profiteroles.
6. If you make a dipping sauce, fire roast the tomatoes on a gas stove burner.
    Notes: *The amount this makes depends on the size of the profiterole you pipe. One bite makes for a good Happytizer.*

Quick Dipping sauce
1 6 oz. can Tomato Paste
2 - 3 Tomatoes Fire Roasted or 1 can Fire Roasted diced.
1 tsp Garlic powder or 1 clove fresh Garlic
1 T *Italian seasoning* (Page 122)
Salt
1/2 cup Filtered Water

- Blend all ingredients in a blender. Simmer on the stovetop for 30 min.

Mini Pizzas on English Muffins
☆☆☆☆☆

Here's another fun way to upscale a pizza.
Ingredients
1 Recipe English Muffins (Page 185)
1 Recipe Sun-dried Tomato, Roasted Garlic Pesto on (Page 157)
1/2 cup black Olives, diced small

Cooking Instructions
1. Prepare the Sun-dried tomato pesto and while it's chilling, begin making the English Muffins.
2. Instead of using a 3 inch round cookie cutter, change it to either a 1 inch round cookie cutter or a 2 inch round. Depending on the size you are looking for. Bite sized is generally a finger food and 2 bites is completely acceptable.
3. After the English Muffins have cooled a little, cut them in half. Next, place them on a cookie sheet and put in a 300 degree F oven to slightly toast them. If you would like to add flavor to them, take 1 or 2 cloves of roasted garlic and make a paste. Mix it well with 1 or 2 T of Aquaschata™. Using a pastry brush, brush each top of the English muffin before going into the oven and bake for 3 - 5 minutes warming it.
4. Fill a pastry bag with a large round piping tip and starting at the top of an English muffin, on the outside piping left, spiral once around while moving towards the inside, and spiraling into another circle. This creates a pretty spiral. Sprinkle with black olives that are diced finely.

Artichoke Sun-dried Tomato Basil Dip *makes 1/2 cup*
☆☆☆☆☆

This nut free, allergy friendly dip may just become one of your favorites. This savory dip, as my son puts it, is a "party in your mouth." The pizza flavor this delivers creates the perfect filling for savory profiteroles. It is also perfect to eat with breadsticks.

1 can Artichoke Hearts
2 T soaked sun-dried Tomatoes
3 T Coconut Cream
1/2 Juiced Lemon
1/3 cup Fresh Basil leaves (packed)
3 tsp Nutritional Yeast
1 tsp Roasted Garlic powder
1/8 tsp Onion powder
1 T Dried Oregano
Salt to taste
Black Pepper

- **Cooking Instructions**

  In a seed grinder or food processor, blend all the ingredients until creamy smooth.

White Bean Dip *makes 12 servings*
☆ ☆ ☆ ☆ ☆

This is an exceptionally flavored dip. Use it on crackers, bread, cucumbers, carrots or stuff inside mushrooms and bake. You can also stuff it inside cherry tomatoes for a wonderful Happytizer.

Pate Seasoning Blend
1 T White pepper
1 T Black pepper
1 T Paprika
1 T whole dried Thyme
1 T Marjoram
1 T Nutmeg
1 T Ginger powder
1 T dried Basil
1 T Allspice
1 T Garlic powder
1/2 T Clove powder

Ingredients
1 cup roasted Walnuts
2 - 3 Water for sautéing
2 cups diced Shallots
2 cups chopped Mushrooms
4 tsp Pate Seasoning blend (above)
1 1/2 tsp Sea salt
2 cups cooked Baby Lima beans (use chickpeas optional)
~~4 tsp Seasoning Blend~~

(40 minutes preparation and 1 hour chill time)

Cooking Instructions:
1. To make the Seasoning blend, combine all the ingredients in a seed grinder, blend and transfer to a covered container.
2. Preheat oven to 325 degrees F.
3. Spread walnuts on a baking sheet and roast for about 15 minutes or until lightly browned and fragrant.

4. Remove from oven and transfer walnuts to a container to cool slightly.
5. In a 10 inch frying pan, add 2 - 3 T water to sauté the shallots, mushrooms, seasoning blend and salt over med heat for 10 min. Remove from heat.
6. Coarsely chop walnuts.
7. In a food processor, combine all ingredients and process until smooth.
8. Refrigerate in a covered container for 1 hour or until chilled through. Serve cold or at room temp.
9. The seasoning blend can be used with many other dishes. Add 1 tsp of the blend per pound of protein.
10. Navy beans tend to be a high allergen bean, using baby lima beans are a great substitution for them. Garbanzo Beans also work fantastic in this Both ways are absolutely delicious.

Beet or Butternut Squash Hummus ☆☆☆☆☆

The color of Beet Hummus is exquisite. Vibrant Rich Reds to Bright Pinks.
Pipe it inside a cucumber or in a falafel waffle bowl for added fun. Kids love this.

2 cups Garbanzo Beans cooked (1 cup dry, cooked in a pressure cooker)
1 Lemon juiced
1 - 2 tsp Garlic powder
1/2 – 1 tsp Cumin
Salt to taste
1 T Tahini
2 T Roasted Beet puree or 3 T cooked Butternut Squash (or both)
1/2 cup Water

Cooking Instructions:

- Place all ingredients in a blender or food processor, and process or blend until you get the desired texture. Eat immediately or refrigerate.

Note: You can substitute Roasted beet with raw beet. Add 1/4 cup of raw.
It will have less sugar as the roasting brings out the sugar more.

Roasted Red Pepper Hummus ☆☆☆☆☆

2 cups Garbanzo Beans cooked
1 Lemon juiced
1 - 2 tsp Garlic powder
1/2 – 1 tsp Cumin
Salt to taste
1 T Tahini
1 Red bell pepper
1/2 cup Water

Cooking Instructions:

- Roast a red bell pepper on top of a gas flame or inside an oven at 450 Degrees F until blackened. Peel the red pepper and place all the remaining ingredients in blender or food processor, and process or blend until you get the desired texture. Eat immediately or refrigerate.

Sun-dried Tomato Hummus

☆☆☆☆☆

2 cups Garbanzo Beans cooked (1 cup dry, cooked in pressure cooker)

1 Lemon juiced

1 - 2 tsp Garlic powder

1/2 – 1 tsp Cumin

Salt to taste

1 T Tahini

1/2 cup Water

2 T softened diced Sun-dried Tomatoes (Soak in hot water for 15 minutes prior)

Cooking Instructions:
- Place all ingredients except the sundried tomatoes in blender or food processor, and process or blend until you get the desired texture. Mix by hand the sun-dried tomatoes. Eat immediately or refrigerate.

Kalamata Hummus

☆☆☆☆☆

2 cups Garbanzo Beans cooked (1 cup dry cook in pressure cooker)

1 Lemon juiced

1 - 2 tsp Garlic powder

1/2 – 1 tsp Cumin

Salt to taste

1 T Tahini

1/2 cup Water

4 Kalamata Olives (diced)

Cooking Instructions:
- Place all ingredients except the Kalamata olives in blender or food processor, and process or blend until you get the desired texture. Add olives and mix by hand. Eat immediately or refrigerate.

Artichoke Spinach Jalapeño Dip

☆☆☆☆☆

This is an incredibly creamy dip. Your family and friends will have a hard time believing it doesn't have any dairy in it. It is rich and delicious. It's perfect for a potluck or if you are looking to freeze leftovers. It freezes great.

Ingredients
1 1/2 cups Raw Cashews (soaked 4 - 6 hours, or ground up in seed grinder)
4 cloves Garlic or 1 1/2 T Garlic powder
1 small Onion, chopped
1 1/2 cup unsweetened plant based Milk (almond, oat or coconut)
1/4 cup Nutritional Yeast
1 - 2 T Jalapeños, diced
4 cups Spinach
2 cans Artichoke hearts, in water, drained and rinsed (save the liquid)
1 - 2 T Lemon juice
1 1/2 tsp Salt

Cooking Instructions:

1. Preheat the oven to 425 degrees F.
2. In a blender, add cashews, plant based milk, nutritional yeast, lemon juice, salt and blend until really creamy. Set aside.
3. In the food processor, add Jalapeños, onions, garlic, and artichoke and pulse until chunky. Pour into a medium or large bowl.
4. Next, add the spinach to the food processor by itself and process to chop, not puree.
5. Mix the spinach into the artichoke mix until well blended.
6. Next, pour in the milk that was blended into the spinach and artichoke mix. Feel free to add onion powder if you prefer a stronger onion flavor. 1 tsp works well. Taste to make sure there's enough salt.
7. Pour into a deep dish baking dish. Bake until warm, bubbly and browned on top. Start with 20 - 40 minutes as ovens vary. It will have a golden brown crust when done. The longer it cooks, the dryer it will become. It's your preference, dry or moist.
8. Dip with crackers and bread.

Phyllo Stuffed Mushrooms

☆☆☆☆☆

This Happytizer is a spin off of my award winning recipe from the magazine, Vegetarian Times, recipe contest. This is the filling that went inside the portabella mushroom wrapped in phyllo dough. Though I had used this filling inside the whole mushroom, I found it tastes 1,000 times better when putting it directly into the dough. This little morsel of goodness will put a smile on your face any day of the week. Perfect for bite sized finger foods.

Ingredients
1/2 Recipe Phyllo-Like Dough (unless you would like leftovers) (Page 365)

Filling
10 - 14 Cremini Mushrooms
2 cloves Garlic
1 Green Scallion
1/4 cup raw Pecans

Cooking Instructions: Preheat oven to 400 degrees F

1. Prep the filling by placing all the ingredients into a food processor and process. Set aside.
2. Prep the Phyllo-Like Dough. If you are using a pasta machine, make thin to #6 or #7. And cut a square that you can stack 3 layers or you can roll it three layers. Whichever is easiest for you. Place the filling at the top or center and tuck, fold and roll. Tuck it under, fold the sides in and roll. Place seam side down on a parchment paper lined cookie sheet.
3. Bake at 400 Degrees F for 12 minutes or until golden brown.

Packed with flavor, these bite sized nuggets freeze wonderfully.

Sun-dried Tomato, Basil and Mushroom Filling Wrapped in Phyllo-Like Dough

☆☆☆☆☆

This filling is also used inside Ravioli. It's another taste bud teaser.

Ingredients
1/2 Recipe Phyllo-Like Dough (unless you would like a ton of these)

Filling
1/4 cup Sun-dried Tomatoes
1/4 cup boiling Water
1/2 cup Pecans (roasted optional)
2 cups Cremini Mushrooms (chopped)
1 - 2 T minced Garlic
1/3 cup fresh Basil leaves (packed)
2 T Olives, diced (optional)
1/4 tsp Salt
Pepper to taste

Cooking Instructions:

1. Soak the Sun-dried tomatoes in hot water for 10 - 15 min. Preheat oven to 400 degrees F.
2. Sauté garlic and mushrooms in water.
3. Add all ingredients (including the liquid from the sun-dried tomatoes) into a blender or food processor and blend until it has a smooth texture.
4. Prep the Phyllo-Like Dough. If you are using a pasta machine, make thin to #6 or #7. Cut a square that you can stack 3 layers or you can roll it three layers. Whichever is easiest for you. Place the filling at the top or center and tuck, fold and roll. Tuck it under, fold the sides in and roll. Place on a parchment paper lined cookie sheet, seam side down.
5. Bake at 400 degrees F for 12 minutes or until golden brown.

Tortilla Pinwheels with Cream Cheese Filling
☆☆☆☆☆

Another perfect finger food that is fast and easy but completely satisfying.

Ingredients
1 Recipe Tortilla Wraps (Page 229)
1 Recipe of one or more of the following: (Page 110)
Herb Cream cheese, Sun-dried Tomato Cream cheese,
Roasted Red Pepper Cream Cheese or Jalapeño Cream Cheese

Garnished toppings
Fresh Dill, Fresh Basil or Fresh Chives
Golden and red cherry tomatoes cut in half. (Optional)

Cooking Instructions:
1. Prepare tortillas and set them aside.
2. Prepare Cream Cheeses. I recommend several flavors for variety.
3. Prepare the garnished toppings for adding something extra special.
4. With a frosting spatula, spread the cream cheese onto the tortilla. Generously apply a thick layer of Cream Cheese. Next, roll it up. The size of the tortilla will depend on the size of the Happytizer you desire. Small ones will be small bites.
5. Cut them 3/4 inch to 1 inch in width with a sharp knife. Place on tray and garnish with a variety of toppings. These add color to the platter,

Pesto Dips with Crackers
☆☆☆☆☆

Anything pesto is a big hit as a Happytizer. And there are so many cracker recipes available that it are easy to create a win - win combination.

Ingredients
1 Recipe Crackers: (Page 170)
1 or 2 Pesto Dip Recipes: (Page 144)

Cooking Instructions:
- Prepare pesto ahead of time. Bake your favorite cracker recipe fresh for same day enjoyment.

Macadamia Cheese Dip; Plain or Basil Collard Pesto
☆☆☆☆☆

Ingredients
Basil & Collard Green pesto
1 cup Fresh Basil leaves
2 large leaves Collar Greens
2 cloves Garlic
1/3 cup Artichoke hearts

Macadamia nut and Cauliflower Ricotta cheese
1/2 Cauliflower riced (Cooked) = 1 head of Cauliflower, Raw
1/2 cup ground Macadamia nut
2 T Nutritional Yeast

Cooking Instructions:
1. Prepare Basil and Collard Green Pesto in a food processor.
2. Prepare Cauliflower on page 106.
3. Combine together and eat fresh. Or freeze remainder.

Guacamole *makes 3 cups*
Serve with Baked Homemade Tortilla Chips or Tostadas
☆☆☆☆☆

Make double the amount of chips, they seem to disappear into thin air.

Ingredients
2 Green Onions
4 ripe Avocados
½ tsp Chili powder
1 large Garlic Clove, diced (or 1/2 tsp dried garlic powder)
2 - 3 Plum Tomatoes
1 T Fresh Lemon Juice
½ cup fresh Parsley
1 tsp ground Cumin
1 tsp dried Oregano
salt and pepper to taste

1 Recipe Baked Corn Chips (Page 232)
1 Recipe Pico de Gallo (Page 124)

Cooking Instructions:
1. In a mixing bowl or food processor, mash avocados.
2. Dice tomatoes and add to avocados with the remaining ingredients.
3. Set aside and make the Baked corn chips:

Variations: *Roast tomatoes for added flavor. Add Jalapeños or roasted Jalapeños for added flavor.*

Salads, Salad Dressings, Pesto & Soups

Salads

Carrot Beet Salad…..146

Rainbow Avocado Raisin Salad................................147

Pistachio-Apple Macaroni Salad................................148

Tofuna Salad..149

Broccoli with Mint Pesto Sauce.........................150

Rebekah's Famous Pasta Salad..................................151

Salad Dressings

Caesar Salad Dressing...152

Spicy Mango, Lime Mango Poppyseed Dressing....153

Mustard Dill Salad Dressing.......................................153

Creamy Ranch Dressing..153

Avocado Cucumber Mint/Basil Dressing..................154

Creamy Cucumber Dill Dressing........................…...154

Creamy Dijon Dressing...155

Sesame Garlic Dressing..155

Sesame Cream Dressing..156

Salads, Salad Dressings, Pesto & Soups

Continued...

Pesto

Dill Pesto………………………………………..156

Lemon Mint Pistachio Pesto…………………….157

Sun-dried Tomato & Roasted Garlic Pesto …...157

Lemon Macadamia Basil Pesto…………….....158

Artichoke Pesto……………………………....158

Basil Collard Pesto……………………….......159

Soups

Lentil Quinoa Vegetable Soup……………..........161

Cream of Asparagus Soup..……………………..162

Corn Chowder…………………………………...163

Carrot Soup………………………………….....164

Pirate Stew…………………………………...165

Fall Harvest Soup……………………………...166

Kale and Sweet Potato Soup……………………167

Orange Dal Soup……………………….........168

Simple Moong Dal Soup……………………......169

Salads & Salad Dressings

What makes a salad great? I'm going to say it has to be both visually satisfying, and the textures are in harmony with one another. But, what pulls it all together is the salad dressing. So, what makes a good salad dressing, and how can you create your own oil free versions?

The basic make up of a salad dressing is 5 parts...
An emulsifier, fat, oil, acid and sweetener.

So, we need to know what each role has and what replaces it best. What is an emulsifier? It's the thing that makes it creamy. In this case it's coming from mustard. But if you can't have mustard, it can be made with other ingredients. Soy or Sunflower lecithin granules make things extremely creamy. Citrus Fiber acts as an emulsifier. Eggs act as one as well, but since we are making this plant based and eggs are a high allergen, we are looking for alternatives. Xanthan gum acts as a stabilizer so that should be considered as a support as well.
Next, high fat ... well, here's where you get to control it. Hemp seeds make a good option. Avocado adds a healthy fat and creaminess. Cashews blend beautifully as well. You get to choose. And put in as little or as much as your body allows.

Acid means vinegar. However, not everyone likes vinegar or eats vinegar or can have vinegar. So the next best thing to replace it is with lemon or lime juice. Any citrus. Grapefruit juice or orange juice works as well.

And finally, a sweetener. Mango's are super creamy and sweet. Papaya works beautifully as well. Dates if you can handle them. If not, liquid stevia is the next best option. You can make a delicious creamy salad dressing and not feel deprived any longer. Enjoy your fresh greens with these wonderful dressings. Here are a few that I love.

If you can't have nuts, have no fear! You can use silken tofu or Pumfu (pumpkin seed tofu) for super creaminess. If you aren't eating soy, baby lima beans and butter beans work fantastic. They have zero flavor pretty much. You can get your protein from the dressing and have a great meal.

Edible flowers - Flowers offer stunning colors and flavors.

*Nasturtiums are both vibrant in color, easy to grow and add a peppery flavor to any salad. Both the leaves and the flowers are edible.

*Borage flowers are a gorgeous blue

*Rose petals

*Marigold petals - gorgeous orange petals.

*Squash Blossoms - beautiful orange

*Pansies and Violets - Array of purples, yellows and oranges

*Day Lilies

Salads

Carrot Beet Salad

☆☆☆☆☆

This salad is not only vibrant, your palate will burst with many flavors in your mouth.

Ingredients
2 cups Shredded Carrots
1 1/2 cup Shredded Red Beets
2 - 3 T Black dried Currants
1/4 - 1/3 cup Roasted Walnuts (crush lightly, keep chunky)
4 T Lemon juice
1 T dehydrated Orange Peels
1 Green onions, diced
1/4 cup Curly Parsley, chopped finely
Salt to taste

Cooking Instructions:

1. Roast walnuts at 325 degrees F for 10 - 15 min. Chop loosely.
2. Using a food processor, shred the beets and carrots. Place them in a large mixing bowl.
3. In a seed grinder or by hand finely chop the parsley.
4. Add the remaining ingredients. Adjust the lemon juice and salt to your taste.

Rainbow Avocado Raisin Salad *serves 4 - 6*

☆☆☆☆☆

Ingredients
1 Sweet Red Bell Pepper, cut into thin strips
1 cup Cabbage, shredded
1 medium bunch Broccoli, steamed & cut into pieces.
1 medium Avocado, quartered & thinly sliced
1/4 cup Raisins or Currants (optional)
1/4 cup Sunflower Seeds (or roasted Walnuts)

Dressing
4 ounces Pumfu (Pumpkin seed tofu)
1/2 Lemon, juiced
1/2 tsp dried Dill
1/2 tsp dry Mustard
1/2 tsp Onion powder
1/4 cup of Brine water from a can of Artichoke hearts

Cooking Instructions:
- Prepare Vegetables. Prepare Dressing and refrigerate. Toss together and serve.

Pistachio - Apple Macaroni Salad

☆☆☆☆☆

This dish is very similar to a Waldorf salad and can be enjoyed for picnics, buffets or luncheons. The pistachios add a different and exciting new flavor. The dressing will soak up quickly in this dish so add it just before serving.

Ingredients
3 med. tart Apples, cored & sliced
1/4 cup dried Currants, Raisins, or Black Mission Figs (optional)
1/4 cup unsalted raw Pistachios, coarsely chopped
    (or raw almonds, pecans, or walnuts)
1 med. celery stalk, diced

Dressing:
1/2 cup pureed soft Tofu (or Pumfu, or lima beans)
1 T Aquaschata™
6 - 9 drops Liquid Stevia
2 T fresh Mint (1/2 tsp dried)
1/4 tsp Cinnamon

1 Box elbow, penne or rotini gluten free pasta
Dark green lettuce leaves or spinach leaves

Cooking Instructions:
1. In a blender or food processor add dressing ingredients in the order given.
2. In a medium sized saucepan, cook the pasta.
3. In the meantime, cut the apples (leave skin on if desired), grind the nuts and chop the celery. Add this to the cooked pasta. Mix in the Dried Fruit, pour the dressing over the pasta and combine it all together with a spoon. Serve over a bed of lettuce or spinach and garnish with slivers of apple and a sprig of mint.

Tofuna Salad *serves 6*

☆☆☆☆☆

I ate tuna fish just about every day when I was in college. The cafeteria food was terrible and it seemed like tuna was all I could tolerate. I never grew tired of it, but when I stopped eating meat I did miss the idea of a tuna fish sandwich. This tofu mixture satisfied my longing for what was once my daily ritual. The kelp powder in it gives it the fishy flavor and has a lot of nutritional value. This substitution for tuna fish is loved by all, especially children. It makes for a nice nutritious school lunch. This is a great way to hide tofu and let the nutritional value benefit everyone. Serve it on bread, in a pita, in a green or as a pasta salad.

Ingredients
8 oz. firm Tofu* or 8 oz Pumfu (pumpkin seed tofu) or Lima beans**
1 large Celery stalk, diced
1 green Onion, minced
1 Carrot, shredded (opt.)
1/2 cup Caesar salad dressing (Page.152)
2 T Bragg® Liquid Aminos (optional)
1 T Lemon juice
1 tsp powdered Kelp
1 1/2 tsp dried Dill

Cooking Instructions:
1. Drain the tofu and cut into thin strips. Wrap in a kitchen towel for 30 minutes. This will remove moisture and give it more texture. If you like a chewy consistency, you can freeze it, then thaw.
2. Crumble into small pieces in a bowl. Add celery, carrot and green onion. In a separate bowl, combine Caesar salad dressing, Bragg® Liquid Aminos, lemon juice, kelp powder and dill. Add to tofu mixture and mix well.

Soybeans are one of most popular grains grown, corn being in the lead. Because it is so cultivated, it is heavily sprayed with pesticides and herbicides to control the insects and disease that may cause damage. If you are not buying organically grown tofu you are not only putting unnecessary toxins in your body, you are also supporting industry in continuing this habitual destructive pattern to our planet.
*** 1 1/2 cup cooked Lima beans mashed with a fork and add 1 T psyllium powder to absorb moisture.*

Broccoli with Mint Pesto Sauce

☆☆☆☆☆

Ingredients
4 cloves Garlic
1 cup fresh Basil leaves
1 cup fresh Mint leaves
2 Heaping T Pine nuts
2 - 4 T Aquaschata™
3 cups steamed Broccoli
1 lb. gluten free Spaghetti

Cooking Instructions:

1. Rinse basil and mint leaves. In a food processor blend garlic, basil and mint together. Then add pine nuts. Slowly, through the top, add 2 T Aquaschata™, and 1 T at a time thereafter until you get the saucy consistency you desire (*Refrigerate if not using immediately*).
2. Cook spaghetti.
3. Steam broccoli.
4. Set aside 1/4 to 1/2 cup of water from broccoli.
5. In a small saucepan, add water and pesto. Heat through but do not boil.
6. Pour over steamed broccoli and spaghetti.

Rebekah's Famous Pasta Salad
☆☆☆☆☆

I have to thank my college roommate Heather Langton for giving me this idea. In fact, she was one of my inspirational friends on how to creatively cook without limitations and expectations of the end result. Never did I think you could throw as many herbs together without measuring and have it come out as good as it does. So, there's really nothing that could go wrong with this dish.

Ingredients
1/2 - 1 pound GF rotini (Brown rice, Quinoa, Red Lentil or Chickpea)
1 red Bell pepper
1 green Bell pepper
1 Carrot chopped into 1/4" rounds
1/2 cup Broccoli florets
1/2 cup Celery diced
3 plum Tomato's
2 T Aquaschata™
1/4 cup Brine of Artichoke hearts soaked in water (Use artichoke hearts in the salad if you choose)
1 Lemon juiced

Herbs: (1 1/2 T equal amounts of each)
Garlic powder or 1 - 2 cloves fresh, minced
Oregano
Thyme
Basil
Dill
Dried parsley or 1/4 cup fresh, chopped
ground Black Pepper

Cooking Instructions:
1. In a saucepan bring water to a boil and cook noodles till done. Rinse under cold water.
2. Add vegetables and mix.
3. Add Aquaschata™, artichoke brine water and lemon juice.
4. Finally, add all the herbs and mix. If it appears too dry, add more brine water. Taste and adjust as needed. The brine water and lemon juice balance each other

out so a 2:1 ratio is desired. If it sits for too long, the noodles will soak up all of the moisture, therefore, combine ingredients just before serving. If it sits overnight, you may need to add more liquid before serving.

Salad Dressings

Caesar
☆☆☆☆☆

This is a very popular recipe. Finally, a salad dressing that really dresses up your salad! Works perfectly as a Falafel dressing too. It's delicious!

1/2 cup Artichoke Brine from a can of artichokes soaked in water only
4 T Lemon Juice
4 - 6 T Filtered water
2 T Dijon Mustard (or 1 tsp Natur Emul)
1 cup Raw Cashews (soaked overnight)
1/2 tsp Garlic powder
1/2 tsp ground Black Pepper
1/3 - 1/2 tsp Salt

Cooking Instructions:
- Add all the ingredients into a blender and blend on high for a minute or two. Chill for several hours.

Note: *There are many recipes in this book that use artichoke hearts. This recipe doesn't need mustard if you are avoiding it. The Natur Emul works great! Substitute Macadamia or Pili Nuts if you are avoiding cashews.*

Spicy Mango or Lime Mango Poppyseed ☆☆☆☆☆
1 large ripe Mango (cut into cubes or slices) about 2 cups
1 clove Garlic
1/4 cup Apple Cider Vinegar (or 1 - 2 oranges juiced or ¼ cup lime juice)
2 T Filtered Water
1/2 tsp Red Pepper Flakes
pinch of salt

Cooking Instructions:
- Add all the ingredients into a blender and blend on high for a minute or two Chill for several hours.

Mustard Dill Salad Dressing ☆☆☆☆☆
4 ounces Pumfu (Pumpkin seed tofu)
1/2 Lemon, juiced
1/2 tsp dried Dill
1/2 tsp dry Mustard
1/2 tsp Onion powder
1/4 cup of Brine water from a can of Artichoke hearts

- Combine all ingredients in a seed grinder or high powered blender and mix. Double

Sweet Version - Add 9 - 15 drops of Liquid Stevia

Creamy Ranch Dressing ☆☆☆☆☆
1 1/2 cup Baby Lima Beans, cooked
2 T Filtered water or Aquaschata™
1 Garlic clove (or 2 tsp granular powder)
1 round tsp Onion powder
1 tsp Salt
1 ½ T Lemon Juice
1 T Nutritional Yeast
1 - 2 T fresh Dill, Oregano, Parsley or Cilantro or blend.
Fresh ground pepper; add at end (optional)

Cooking Instructions:
- Add all the ingredients into a blender and blend on high for a minute or two. Chill for several hours.

Avocado Cucumber Mint or Avocado Cucumber Basil Dressing
☆☆☆☆☆
2 ripe Avocados
1/4 tsp Garlic powder
1/4 tsp salt
5 T Lemon Juice
1/2 English Cucumber chopped
1/2 tsp Citrus fiber (Natur Emul)
1/2 tsp Xanthan gum
(1 - 2 T Dijon Mustard instead of citrus fiber and xanthan gum)
1/2 cup Mint leaves or 1/2 cup Fresh Basil loosely packed
1/2 cup fresh Parsley
4 green onions (both white and green parts)

Cooking Instructions:
- Add all the ingredients into a blender and blend on high for a minute or two. Chill for several hours. *Serve on baked potatoes, tacos or salads.*

Creamy Cucumber - Dill Salad Dressing *makes 1 cup*
☆☆☆☆☆
2 T Lemon Juice
3 T Coconut Cream
1 T Aquaschata™
1 (4 inch segment) Cucumber, peeled
1/8 to 1/4 tsp Dry Mustard
2 T Fresh Dill or 2 tsp dried dill
1 small Garlic clove
Salt (optional)

Cooking Instructions:
- Add all the ingredients into a blender and blend on high for a minute or two. Chill for several hours.

Creamy Dijon Dressing *makes 1 1/2 cups*
☆☆☆☆☆
1/4 cup (4 oz.) Firm tofu (or Pumfu)
2 T Aquaschata™
2 T Coconut Cream
1 med. Garlic clove
1 small Tomato
2 tsp Bragg® Liquid Aminos *(optional)*
3 T Water
1/2 tsp Dijon style Mustard
2 1/4 T rice Vinegar *(optional)*
3 T Lemon juice
1 T apple cider vinegar
1 (1-inch) Onion, diced
1 1/2 T Fresh dill or 2 tsp dried
1/4 tsp salt

Cooking Instructions:
- Add all the ingredients into a blender and blend on high for a minute or two. Chill for several hours.

Sesame Garlic Dressing *makes 1/2 cup*
☆☆☆☆☆
2 T Aquaschata™
2 T Coconut Cream
1 Garlic clove
2 T Lemon Juice
1 heaping T Tahini
2 T Filtered water
1/2 tsp dried Oregano
1/2 tsp dried Chervil
1/4 tsp Salt
Pepper to taste.

Cooking Instructions:
- Add all the ingredients into a blender and blend on high for a minute or two. Chill for several hours.

Sesame Cream *makes 1 1/4 cup*
☆☆☆☆☆

This is great with falafels, pita sandwiches, salad dressing or garden burgers.

1 Garlic clove
1/2 cup raw Sesame Tahini
1/4 to 1/2 cup Filtered water
1/3 to 1/2 cup Lemon juice, according to taste
Salt to taste

Cooking Instructions:
- Add the garlic, tahini, and 1/4 cup water in a blender. Blend on high to turn into a paste for a minute or so.
- Add lemon juice, which will thin the paste. Add more water to thicken to desired consistency, then blend in desired seasonings.
- Chill for several hours.

Pesto Plus

Dill Pesto *makes 3/4 cup*
☆☆☆☆☆

1 1/2 cup fresh Dill
1/2 cup Parsley
2 T Pine Nuts
2 large Garlic cloves
3 T Coconut Cream
4 T Filtered water
2 T Nutritional Yeast

Cooking Instructions:
- Add all the ingredients into a blender and blend on high for a minute or two. Chill for several hours before serving.

Lemon Mint Pistachio Pesto *makes 1 cup*
☆☆☆☆☆
1/2 cup unsalted Pistachio nuts
2 cups fresh Mint leaves, packed
1/3 cup Oat milk
1/4 cup Lemon juiced

Cooking Instructions:
- Add all the ingredients into a blender and blend on high for a minute or two. Chill for several hours.

Sun-dried Tomato & Roasted Garlic Pesto
☆☆☆☆☆
This pesto is perfect as a pizza sauce. It is versatile and can be used on pasta, inside ravioli, and eaten with bread sticks. Divide in half for less or freeze the excess.

2 cups Sun-dried Tomatoes, softened and minced (Soaked in hot water)
1 - 2 cloves Garlic, roasted and peeled
3 - 6 Pasilla chilies (rehydrated, deseeded and minced)
4 Greens Onions
1/4 cup minced Parsley
1/4 cup Pine Nuts, toasted (Or use Walnuts, Sunflower seeds, or Almonds)
1 6 oz. jar of Artichoke hearts, drained and diced
2 T Aquaschata™
1/3 cup Filtered water
3/4 cup Pumfu tofu
Extras: Rosemary leaves, Fresh Basil leaves, fresh ground pepper, hot pepper sauce, fresh lemon or lime juice

Cooking Instructions:
1. Bake garlic in foil in a 400 degrees F oven for 25 - 30 minutes.
2. Combine remaining ingredients and mix in a blender.
3. This can be frozen for up to 6 months.

Lemon Macadamia Basil Pesto *makes 1 cup*

☆☆☆☆☆

1/2 cup Macadamia Nuts
1 cup Fresh Basil leaves (packed)
3 T Lemon juice
2 T Nutritional yeast
1/2 tsp fresh grated Nutmeg
3 T Shallots (diced)
1 T Aquaschata™
1/4 tsp Salt
White Pepper

Cooking Instructions:

1. In a seed grinder, grind the Macadamia nuts until fine.
2. Add all the remaining ingredients in the seed grinder and blend until creamy.
   Note: Macadamia nuts will have grit in the pesto (especially in ravioli it will be noticeable) if you don't cream it completely. Test to make sure there are no pieces.

Artichoke Pesto *makes 1/2 cup*

☆☆☆☆☆

This is a flavorful, light and airy pesto for crackers, pasta and veggies. You can use this as a base for other pestos as well, but this doesn't work inside a savory Profiterole. It's too light. By using it as a base, you get to enjoy the flavor while building on the lightness of it.

1 can Artichoke hearts in water, drained and rinsed (*save the brine*)
1 tsp roasted Garlic powder
1/4 cup Fresh Basil, packed
1/2 Lemon juiced
2 tsp Nutritional yeast
3 T Coconut Cream
1/8 tsp Onion powder
Salt to taste
White pepper

Cooking Instructions:

- Place everything into a food processor and process until creamy.

Basil Collard Pesto *makes 1 1/2 cups*

☆☆☆☆☆

Ingredients

2 cups Fresh Basil leaves
2 large Collard Green leaves, stems removed
5 cloves Garlic
1/2 cup Artichoke hearts (1/2 can)

Cooking Instructions:

- Add all the ingredients into a blender and blend on high for a minute or two. Chill for several hours. Enjoy!

Soup's On

**Experiment #1
Lentils and Quinoa - it works!
AKA - Veggie Broth**

What is an experiment? In science class, do you remember lab? Do you remember doing experiments where you mix one color of something with another? One element with another ...
You don't know what's going to happen. You are open minded and curious. Were you afraid? Did you have any expectations? And were you worried about doing it wrong? How could you? It was an experiment.

Playing in the kitchen is very much the same thing. It's chemistry. Mixing flours, mixing flavors, understanding the properties of food ingredients is nothing more than chemistry. And I have found myself experimenting a lot. Finding courage to experiment in the kitchen is very healthy. Losing attachments to the outcome, being curious and finding the gratitude when it works. This is the joy of cooking. This is being **Fearless in the Kitchen.**

When I had to start an oil free, vegan, Whole Foods, plant based life style again (for health reasons) after years of eating meat, I knew I had to let go of my agenda and attachments to food. Again. This isn't the first time. So rather than having a pity party over all the great foods I can't eat anymore, I jumped in with experiment #1. *The crock pot.* I made a soup that I would never, ever, have made. And, to my surprise, it worked. And not only did it work, it became the soup stock base of many dishes. It had a strong enough flavor that I use it as a veggie broth for cooking. Because it has lentils and quinoa in it, it's not just a veggie broth. It is protein based, an added bonus. It makes a lot, so freeze it in smaller amounts and take out what's needed. It's great as a cup of soup or a base in stir fries and soup stock. The first time I made it, I threw everything in the crock pot over night. Walked away and the next morning opened it and saw nothing cooked. I had turned the time on but forgot to hit the power button. These mistakes happen. I thought I would wake up to the amazing smells of cooked soup. Experiment #1 taught me many lessons. **Don't be attached ...** to my surprise, this soup packs a powerful punch in the kitchen.

Fearless in the Kitchen means not being attached to the outcome and being brave with new ingredients. This allows you to have fun. Same goes for kitchen equipment. The Ninja 8 qt instant pot has 9 in 1 cooking possibilities. It is a pressure cooker, dehydrator, bake, broil, air fryer, sauté, steam, grill and rice cooker. How can you NOT be intimidated by this? I have never pressure cooked food before. To me that was scary. After watching some videos on YouTube, I was comfortable I would not hurt myself. And then I was brave enough to try making 1 cup of chickpeas. If you never start, your success rate doesn't exist yet. If you take the steps from the place of "it's just an experiment," then there's no failure. The judgment is removed. And let's face it, judgment is the only reason why we don't start.

Experimenting in the kitchen opens the door to gratitude. And I have learned gratitude and judgment cannot coexist.

Experiment #1 - Lentils and Quinoa Soup.

☆☆☆☆☆

Ingredients
1 cup Lentils
1/2 cup Quinoa
Half a bunch Kale chopped
1 Onion chopped
3 - 4 garlic Cloves
3 Carrots chopped
2 Celery stalks chopped
1 T dried Thyme
1 T dried Rosemary
4 - 6 Bay leaves
2 T Poultry seasonings
Black pepper
Salt to taste (add after it's cooked)

Cooking Instructions:

1. In a Crockpot set for overnight, add all the ingredients.
2. Set crock pot on high for 10 - 12 hours. Once cooked, add soup to blender, remove bay leaves first, (also, not all at once, it won't fit), add salt and blend.
3. Add back in pot, bowl or crock pot. Store in smaller quart containers in freezer and use as a cup of soup or to season stir fries or other dishes that need a base.

Cream of Asparagus Soup *serves 6*

☆☆☆☆☆

This soup is creamy, delicious and quick to make. Serve it with a Green Salad and freshly made Multi grain bread (Page 196) and herb cream cheese (Page 110).

Ingredients
6 cups Water
1 bunch Asparagus, chopped into 1 inch slices (3 cups)
3/4 cup - 1 cup Shallots
3 - 4 cloves Garlic
1/3 - 1/2 cup Oat milk
Salt/pepper

Cooking Instructions:
1. In a medium pot boil the water and cook the asparagus.
2. In blender add 3 cups of water with asparagus.
3. In a small skillet, with 2 T of water, sauté shallots and garlic. Add oat milk and heat. Pour into blender with pureed asparagus and blend until creamy.

Corn Chowder *serves 4 - 6*

☆☆☆☆☆

This soup has a superb flavor and it doesn't matter that it's dairy free.

Ingredients
2 cups Onion, chopped
3/4 cup Red Bell Pepper, finely diced
1/4 cup Green Bell Pepper, finely diced
3 - 4 cloves Garlic
1 cup whole Corn Kernels (fresh or frozen)
1 tsp ground Cumin
1/2 tsp dried Thyme (1 tsp fresh)
1/2 tsp Curry powder
1/4 tsp Veggie Paste (optional)
1 T chopped Parsley or Scallions for garnish
1 tsp Salt and Pepper to taste
1/4 cup Water

Cooking Instructions:
1. Heat water in a large saucepan. Sauté the onion, bell pepper, garlic and 1/2 cup of the corn for about 5 minutes. Add the salt, cumin, pepper, thyme, curry powder, and soup base. Sauté for another 5 minutes.
2. Steam or boil the remaining corn until it is soft and sweet to the taste (5 to 10 Minutes). Drain the corn, reserving 1 cup of the cooking liquid. Blend the corn with the liquid and add this puree to the sautéed vegetables. Mix all the ingredients, heat through, and serve. Garnish with chopped parsley or scallions.

Carrot Soup

☆☆☆☆☆

A wonderfully soothing comfort food. Serve with green fresh salad or Pumpernickel bread (Page 198) with herb cream cheese (Page 110).

Ingredients
5 med - large Carrots, chopped
1 med Onion
4 cups Water
1 T Vegetable Broth
1 T Celery seed or 2 stalks of Celery, chopped
2 - 4 T Nutritional Yeast
3 cloves Garlic, crushed
2 - 3 Bay Leaves
2 tsp dried Chervil
1 tsp dried Ginger
2 T fresh Parsley
Salt and Pepper to taste

variations:
Carrot - Fennel (add 1/2 fresh Fennel bulb, thinly sliced)
Carrot - Leek (1 Leek, diced)
Carrot - Basil (1 cup fresh Basil, minced)

Cooking Instructions:

1. In a 4 qt. Pot, sauté onions and garlic in 2 T water for 5 minutes. Add carrots and continue to sauté about 4 - 5 minutes. Add nutritional yeast and mix. Add more water if necessary and add the remaining seasonings.
2. Add remaining water and vegetable broth and bring to a boil. Simmer 30 minutes. In blender, add 3/4 soup and blend. Add remaining 1/4 back and season to taste.

   Notes: *Garnish with a dollop of vegan sour cream & parsley.*

Pirate Stew

☆☆☆☆☆

This will warm anyone up on a cold winter's day. Enjoy with or without the beans. It is packed with flavor. Serve with Biscuits with Green Onion (Page 212) or any of the cracker recipes (Page 170).

Ingredients
2 cups Red Onion, chopped
3 cloves Garlic, crushed
3 cups organic Tomato Juice
2 tsp Soy Sauce, Bragg® Liquid Aminos or Coconut Aminos
1 cup Filtered Water
2 tsp Dill
1 tsp Allspice
lots of fresh Black Pepper
4 T dark Mustard or Dijon
9 - 15 drops Liquid Stevia
2 T fresh Lemon Juice
1 - 2 Carrots, diced
1 - 2 Celery stalks, minced
(optional : 1 tsp freshly grated Ginger)
3/4 tsp Salt (more to taste)

2 cups cooked Anasazi Beans, Butter Beans, Brown Rice or Noodles

Cooking Instructions:
1. If desired, add 2 cups cooked Butter beans or Anasazi beans or cooked brown rice, noodles or potatoes for variations.
2. In a large saucepan, sauté the onions and garlic in water. (About a 1/4 of an inch just to cover bottom of the saucepan, without drying up and burning, add more if necessary, throughout cooking time.) Sauté until onions are soft. (5 - 8 minutes)
3. Add all remaining ingredients, except the vegetables and your choice of beans, rice, noodles or potatoes for variation. Cover and simmer for about 30 minutes. Combine the vegetables and simmer another 15 - 20 minutes. Garnish: Top with vegan sour cream, green onion and parsley sprig.
   Notes: *The flavor will improve overnight as it is refrigerated.*

Fall Harvest Soup *serves 10 - 12*
☆ ☆ ☆ ☆ ☆

The list of ingredients may be a little intimidating but don't worry, if you only have some of the vegetables, it's still amazing. I grew a big garden this particular year and all that I could think of was to make a lot of soup. It's very tasty. Serve with Cornbread.

Ingredients
16 cups Water
5 - 6 Garlic cloves, diced
1 Potato, cubed
3 Carrots, sliced
2 Parsnips, sliced
2 cups Mushrooms, quartered
1 Red Onion, chopped
2 Rutabagas, cubed
1 1/2 cup Brussel Sprouts (whole or halved)
1 cup Delicata Squash, cubed
1 Zucchini, sliced
3 stalks Celery, chopped
1 16 oz. can Tomato Sauce
2 T Nutritional yeast
1 T Bragg® Liquid Aminos
1 T Lemon Juice
1 1/2 tsp Lemon Pepper
1 T Cumin
1 T Curry
1/2 T Basil
1 T Oregano
Garlic powder to taste
Salt and Pepper to taste
4 cups of cooked beans, lentils, or rice, Optional

Cooking Instructions:
1. In a large soup stock pot, bring the water to a boil and add all the vegetables. After 20 minutes add tomato juice, lemon, Bragg® Liquid Aminos, and seasonings.
2. Add any additional protein, or grain. Cornbread makes a nice accompaniment with it. This recipe freezes really well.

Kale and Sweet Potato Soup *serves 6 - 8*
☆☆☆☆☆

This is a very nourishing and warming soup, very good for a cold winter day. It's a great way to use your garden vegetables when it is time to harvest. Serve with your favorite fresh bread with an herb Angel Butter.

Ingredients
8 - 10 cups Water
1 tsp Veggie Paste
2 - 3 cups Kale (leave in small to medium pieces)
2 Sweet Potatoes, peeled & cubed
1 1/2 - 2 cups Leeks
1 1/2 cups Rutabagas, chopped
1 1/2 cups Mushrooms, sliced
2 T Ginger, minced
1 T Thyme
1 tsp Lemon Pepper
2 T Nutritional yeast
2 T Bragg® Liquid Aminos
3 tsp Garlic powder
2 T Lemon juice
1 1/2 tsp Spike seasoning
1 T Tahini (optional)

Cooking Instructions:
1. In soup pan, heat 1/2 cup water to sauté leeks over high heat. Allow them to soften 2 - 3 minutes.
2. Add thyme, mushrooms and ginger and heat another minute or 2.
3. Add water and bring to a boil. Add veggie broth, sweet potato, celery, kale and rutabagas. Cook 10 min. or until potatoes are done.
4. Add lemon pepper, yeast, garlic powder Bragg® Liquid Aminos, lemon juice and spike. Simmer another 10 minutes or so.
5. Adjust the seasonings as necessary.
   Flavor will develop more fully overnight.

Orange (Red) Dal Soup *serves 6 - 8*

☆☆☆☆☆

This comforting and nourishing soup is perfect for a cold wintery day. Packed full of flavor and simple to make. Serve with Farmhouse Bread (Page 193) or Dinner Rolls (Page 208).

Ingredients
3 Carrots, peeled and sliced
3 Sweet Potatoes, peeled and chopped
3/4 cup split Orange (Red) Lentils
1/2 tsp Veggie Paste (optional)
2 Plum Tomatoes
2 tsp ground Coriander
1/2 to 1 tsp ground Ginger
1/2 tsp Turmeric powder
1 tsp Garam Masala
1/4 tsp Cardamom seeds crushed
1/4 cup Fresh Cilantro
1/4 tsp Fresh Mustard seeds
10 to 12 cups Water
Salt to taste

Cooking Instructions:
1. Bring 10 -12 cups water to a boil and add the carrots, sweet potatoes, tomatoes, veggie paste and lentils. Cook for 30 minutes or until the lentils are cooked.
2. In a blender, add 4 cups of the liquid and all the lentils, and cooked veggies. Blend until creamy. You may need to do this in batches and pour the creamy soup into a large bowl until they are all blended. With the last batch blended and combined, add in the cilantro and remaining seasonings.
3. Pour back into soup pot and reheat if it has cooled off.
4. Garnish with green onion.

Simple Moong Dal Soup *serves 4*
☆☆☆☆☆

Don't let this simple recipe fool you. It's one of my household favorites. It's quick with simple ingredients and 100% satisfying. Serve it with homemade Naan or Breadsticks for a delicious lunch.

Ingredients
1 cup Moong Dal, uncooked
6 - 8 cups Filtered Water
2 - 3 Carrots, peeled & chopped
1 med Onion, chopped
1 tsp Garlic powder, optional
1 - 2 tsp Cumin
Salt and Pepper to taste

Cooking Instructions:
1. Bring the water to a boil and add moong dal, carrots and onion. Cook for 20 - 25 minutes until the moong dal is cooked through.
2. Place in blender along with seasonings. Blend on high power until creamy smooth.

variations: 1 tsp Chinese 5 Spice. Or, add 1 chopped Fennel bulb to the mix.

Crackers

Basic Cracker Recipe……………….…..…...172

Cracker recipe #1 - Onion cracker……………..172

Cracker recipe #2 - Protein cracker……………173

Cracker recipe #3 - Multi grain cracker………173

Cracker recipe #4 - Everything cracker……….174

Black Lentil Crackers with fresh herbs………175

Saltine Crackers - makes a lot of crackers…...177

Rebekah's Crackers - Pizza Flavor…………….178

Rebekah's Herb Crackers………………………180

All about Crackers

Making Crackers is surprisingly easy. The steps on this page are what you can use for all the cracker recipes, except Rebekah's Pizza and Herb flavored crackers. That's a different approach. In general, you need a Silpat mat, a frosting spatula, cookie sheets and parchment paper. The basic recipe can be done in a blender. After that, I elaborate with more ingredients and toppings.

Instructions For Making Crackers

1. Decide which recipe you will be making and gather the ingredients for it.
2. In a large mixing bowl, combine the flours and the liquid. The consistency you are looking for is pourable. Not watery but not thick. Spreading it with the spatula will give you an idea of what is too runny.
3. Place Silpat mat on top of a cookie sheet. Pour half the batter onto the mat and spread consistently and evenly with a thin, long, metal spatula (I use a cake decorating one). Spread as evenly as possible. The thinner they spread, the crispier they are.
4. Sprinkle "Everything Toppings" (Page 123) over the entire sheet. Or just white sesame seeds for contrast. Or any other toppings you might fancy.
5. Bake in a 400 degree F oven for 25 - 35 min. Ovens vary. This covers two whole cookie sheets. If there is overflow and you have a toaster oven, take a stoneware or small cookie sheet and line it with parchment paper and cook the remaining.
6. After 15 - 18 minutes when the crackers begin firming up, I take them out and score with a knife where to cut them. And rotate cookie sheets. When the edges begin to curl away a bit from the mat, I take a big, long knife and slide it underneath. You can also let them sit on the sheet for 5 minutes and be able to peel it off the mat completely. It varies on time. I usually pull the ones on the edges and remove the center ones (which are never done before the edges) and place them on stoneware and cook another 10 min. Sometimes just turning the oven off will dry them out. If you like softer (pita like) crackers you can take them out earlier. If you like them crunchy, keep them in there until crisp. Be careful not to overcook them as they will brown and all taste like that flavor.
7. Break up the ones that are all done and put on a plate or cooling rack to cool completely. Sometimes they get soft again and you can bake them a little longer. I store them in an airtight container or zip lock bag. Some may be soft the next day. I just re-bake them in the toaster oven for a few

minutes on 400 degrees F and they are perfect.
8. *Silpat mat verses Parchment paper.* If you are making small ones like 4 - 6 inches, parchment paper works fine. If you are covering the entire cookie sheet, Silpat works better. The wet will pull on the parchment paper, creating wrinkles. Stick to Silpat for large sheets. If you have small batches of leftover batter, then parchment paper in the toaster oven works great. They create different results, believe it or not.

Notes: You can store them in the freezer in an airtight container as well. Use the herb and spice blends in the book to flavor them. Lots of ideas to play with. Depending on where you live, summer vs winter, damp vs dry will influence the end result. See how they are the next day… dry, brittle, moist, pliable. Sometimes, the flexible ones are a lot like a pita and you can enjoy it that way. Experiment and have fun. Oil free crackers are super easy and everyone likes them. Kids included!

Basic Cracker Recipe -
☆☆☆☆☆
1 1/4 cup whole grain
1 cup water

- Combine in a blender, blend and pour on Silpat mat. Smooth with spatula and bake for 25 - 40 minutes at 350 degrees F. This is the simplest method. Any whole grain works. Add salt or toppings.

Cracker recipe #1 - Onion cracker
☆☆☆☆☆
1 cup GF flour, any variation
1/2 cup Oat flour
1/2 cup Chickpea flour
1 tsp Onion powder
1/2 tsp Baking powder
1/2 tsp Salt
1 T Tahini
1/2 - 3/4 cup warm water
See Instructions for Making Crackers (Page 171)

Cracker recipe #2 - Protein cracker

☆☆☆☆☆

1/4 cup Chickpea flour
1/4 cup toasted Amaranth (ground)
1/4 cup Teff flour
1/4 cup Sorghum flour
2 T Chia Seeds
2 T Pumpkin Seed Protein Powder (optional)
2 1/2 T Rosemary
1 T Tahini
1/2 - 3/4 cup warm water
1/4 tsp - 1/2 tsp Salt

See Instructions for Making Crackers (Page 171)

Cracker recipe #3 - Multi Grain cracker

☆☆☆☆☆

1/3 cup Chickpea flour
1/3 cup Teff flour
1/2 cup Millet flour
1/3 cup Sorghum flour
1/2 cup Buckwheat flour
1 T Rosemary
1 T Onion powder
1/2 tsp Baking powder
1/2 tsp Salt
1 cup Aquaschata™
1 T Tahini
2/3 cup water

See Instructions for Making Crackers (Page 171)

Cracker recipe #4 - Everything cracker

☆☆☆☆☆

1/4 cup Millet flour
1/4 cup Amaranth flour
1/4 cup Chickpea flour
1 T ground Chia Seeds
1 T Hemp Protein powder
3 T Pumpkin Seed protein powder
1 T Psyllium Husk Powder
2 T Rosemary, crushed
1 T Garlic powder or onion powder
1/2 tsp Salt
Add another cup of water
1/3 cup Butternut squash
1 T Tahini or Sunflower butter or Almond butter
1/2 - 3/4 warm water
1/3 cup Aquaschata™
Sprinkle Everything Toppings mix over crackers before baking.

See Instructions for Making Crackers (Page171)

Black Lentil Crackers with Fresh Herbs

☆☆☆☆☆

4 dozen large crackers

Ingredients
1 cup black Lentils
1/2 cup Forbidden Rice
1/2 tsp Fenugreek seeds
1/2 cup Water
1/2 cup cooked Butternut squash
1/4 cup packed fresh Basil leaves
1/4 cup fresh curly Parsley
1 T Onion powder
1 T Garlic powder
1 T dried Rosemary
1 cup Sorghum
1/4 cup Buckwheat flour
Salt

Cooking Instructions:

1. Overnight - Cover with water to soak, in large bowl, black lentils, forbidden rice and fenugreek seeds.
2. Next day - Rinse and strain mixture. Add to a blender and drop in basil leaves, parsley leaves, butternut squash and water. Blend and pour back into bowl.
3. Mix in onion powder, garlic powder, rosemary, sorghum, buckwheat and salt.
4. Place Silpat mat on top of a cookie sheet. Pour half the batter onto the mat and spread consistently and evenly with a thin long metal spatula (I use a cake decorating style). Spread as evenly as possible. The thinner they are the crispier they are.
5. Sprinkle Everything Toppings (Page 123), or just white sesame seeds on top.
6. Bake in a 400 degree F oven for 25 - 35 min. Ovens vary. This covers two whole cookie sheets. If there is overflow and you have a toaster oven, I take a stoneware or small cookie sheet and line it with parchment paper and cook the remaining.
7. After 15 - 18 minutes when the crackers begin firming up, I take them out and score with a knife where to cut them. Rotate the cookie sheets. When the edges begin to curl away from the mat, I take a big long knife and slide it underneath.

You can also let them sit on the sheet for 5 minutes and then peel it off the mat completely. It varies on time. I usually pull the ones on the edges and remove the center ones (which are never done before the edges) and place them on stoneware and cook another 10 min. Sometimes just turning the oven off will dry them out. If you like softer (pita like) crackers you can take them out earlier. If you like them crunchy, keep them in there until crisp. Be careful not to overcook them as they will brown and all taste like that flavor.

8. Break up the ones that are all done and put on a plate or cooling rack to cool completely. Sometimes they get soft again and you can bake them a little longer. I store them in an airtight container or zip lock bag. Some may be soft the next day. I just re bake them in the toaster oven for a few minutes on 400 degrees F and they are perfect.

Notes: *You can store them in the freezer in an airtight container as well.*
Silpat mats work best and parchment paper works second best.

Saltine Crackers - makes a lot of crackers

☆☆☆☆☆

Dry Ingredients
1 cup Sorghum flour
1 cup Brown Rice flour
1/2 cup Millet flour
1/2 cup Arrowroot flour
1/2 cup Buckwheat flour
1/2 cup Amaranth flour
2 T Rosemary
Salt

Wet Ingredients
1 cup Aquaschata™
1 T Tahini
1 cup water
1/2 cup - 3/4 cup more water

Cooking Instructions:

1. In a blender, mix 1 cup Aquaschata™ with 1 T Tahini.
2. In a bowl, mix all the flours together.
3. Mix the liquid together with the flour adding another cup of water.
4. Add additional water if necessary for desired texture. Not thick and not runny.
5. Follow the instructions on using Silpat Mat or parchment paper for making crackers (Page 171)

Topping suggestion: Everything Seasoning (Page 123)

Rebekah's Crackers - Pizza Flavor

☆☆☆☆☆

I'm crazy about crunch. I'm crazy about crackers. So it would make sense that I have lots and lots of cracker recipes. You can half the recipe or make the whole dough and freeze half of it. This one is very unique. You can make them very, very thin. You can even make them for your soup.

Pizza Flavor Cracker Recipe
Dry Ingredients
1 1/4 cup Tapioca flour
1 cup + 2 T Arrowroot Flour
2 1/4 cups Oat flour
1/2 cup Brown Rice flour
1 cup Nutritional yeast
2 T Psyllium Husk <u>powder</u> *
3 T Pizza Blend (See below)
2 tsp Salt

Wet Ingredients
1 3/4 cup cashew milk**(or any plant based milk)
1/3 cup + 2 T Aquaschata™
2 T Red Wine (*optional*)

Pizza Blend
2 T dried Oregano
2 T dried Basil
1 T + 1 tsp roasted Garlic powder
1/4 crushed Red Pepper Flakes (optional)

- Grind all of the Pizza Blend ingredients into a fine powder using a seed grinder.

Cooking Instructions:

1. In a small pot warm cashew milk and red wine (*optional*) over medium heat (just under a boil). Add Aquaschata™ once it's heated.
2. In a mixer bowl (using the dough hook) combine tapioca flour, arrowroot flour, oat flour, brown rice flour, psyllium husk powder, nutritional yeast, Pizza blend and salt. Mix at medium speed for 5 minutes adding in the cashew milk and Aquaschata™ liquid until it forms a nice dough ball that is sticky but firm. If it

needs more liquid, add 1 T of oat milk at a time.

3. Remove dough onto a floured surface (I use brown rice flour). Make sure your hands are floured too. Knead for 2 more minutes, putting your body weight into it. You want the dough supple, not dry.
4. Divide in half using a knife or pastry cutter.
5. Depending on your use, you can freeze half the dough.
6. Divide into pieces that will fit into the pasta machine or are easy to work with.
7. Next, either use the pasta machine to make the pieces thin or a rolling pin. This dough can be stretched to the last setting on the pasta machine and not tear. It is quite magical that way. Keeping settings to #5 or #7 seem to be sufficient. Since it's a cracker, you get to decide how thin or thick you'd like it.
8. Preheat the oven to 400 degrees F.
9. Lay the thin dough on a lined cookie sheet with parchment paper. Score with a knife or the pastry cutter, making indented marks, without cutting through the cracker dough, indicating where you will break them up. Depending on how thin the dough is, will determine how quickly they cook. Start with 8 - 10 minutes to see how quickly they golden brown. Remove and cool on a rack. Break with your hands or with a knife cutting where they were scored. Because there is a lot of dough, you can play around with sizes and thickness. That's where the fun is.

Notes:
* Psyllium husk powder can be found in the bulk herbs section at natural grocery stores. This recipe only works with the powder. Not the course fiber.

**Making your own Cashew milk is easy. Soak 1/2 cup raw cashews for a few hours in water. Blend with 1 ¾ cup water for 2 - 3 minutes. Add to saucepan and heat.

Rebekah's Herb Crackers
☆☆☆☆☆
Simply delicious and flavorful.

Dry Ingredients
1 1/4 cup tapioca flour
1 cup + 2 T Arrowroot Flour
2 1/4 cups oat flour
1/2 cup Brown Rice flour
2 T psyllium husk powder *
3 T Herb blend (See below)
2 tsp salt

Wet Ingredients
1 3/4 cup cashew milk**(or any plant based milk)
1/3 cup + 2 T Aquaschata™

Herb Blend
1/2 T dried Basil
1 T dried Thyme
1 T dried Marjoram
1 T dried Rosemary
9 Whole dried Bay Leaves
1 T Onion powder

- Grind all of the ingredients into a fine powder using a seed grinder. Store in an airtight container.

Cooking Instructions:
1. In a small pot, warm cashew milk over medium heat (just under a boil). Add Aquaschata™ once it's heated.
2. In a mixer bowl (using the dough hook) combine tapioca flour, arrowroot flour, oat flour, brown rice flour, psyllium husk powder, herb blend and salt. Mix at medium speed for 5 minutes, adding in the cashew milk and Aquaschata™ liquid until it forms a nice dough ball that is sticky but firm. If it needs more liquid, add 1 T of oat milk at a time.
3. Remove dough onto a floured surface (I use brown rice flour). Make sure your

hands are floured too. Knead for 2 more minutes, putting your body weight into it. You want the dough supple, not dry.
4. Divide in half using a knife or pastry cutter.
5. Depending on your use, you can freeze half the dough.
6. Divide into pieces that will fit into the pasta machine or are easy to work with.
7. Next, either use the pasta machine to make the pieces thin or a rolling pin. This dough can be stretched to the last setting on the pasta machine and not tear. It is quite magical that way. Keeping settings to #5 or #7 seem to be sufficient with whatever was being made. Since it's a cracker, you get to decide how thin or thick you'd like it.
8. Preheat the oven to 400 degrees F.
9. Lay the thin dough on a lined cookie sheet with parchment paper. Score with a knife or the pastry cutter, making indented marks without cutting through the cracker dough, indicating where you will break them up. Depending on how thin the dough is, will determine how quickly they cook. Start with 8 - 10 minutes to see how quickly they turn golden brown. Remove and cool on a rack. Break with your hands or with a knife cutting where they were scored. Because there is a lot of dough, you can play around with sizes and thickness. That's where the fun is.

Notes:
* Psyllium husk powder can be found in the bulk herbs section at natural grocery stores. This recipe only works with the powder. Not the course fiber.

**Making your own Cashew milk is easy. Soak 1/2 cup raw cashews for a few hours in water. Blend with 1 3/4 cup water for 2 - 3 minutes. Add to saucepan and heat.

Bread

English Muffins..................................185

Cinnamon Raisin Bread..................................187

Spiced Pumpkin Bread..................................189

Spicy Banana Bread..................................191

Farmhouse Bread..................................193

Multi Grain Sandwich Bread..................................196

Pumpernickel Bread..................................198

Sun-dried Tomato and Olive Bread..................................200

Challah Bread..................................202

Rosemary Breadsticks..................................206

More Bread Favorites

Continued ...

Herb Dinner Rolls..208

Onion and Dill Dinner Rolls..........................210

Biscuits with Green Onions............................212

Corn Bread...213

Indian Style Naan..214

Best Pizza Crust...215

Cauliflower Pizza Crust..................................216

Cinnamon Raisin Bagels.................................219

Onion Poppyseed Bagels................................222

Pumpernickel Bagels.......................................225

Belgium Soft Pretzel..227

English Muffins *makes 14*

☆☆☆☆☆

Who doesn't like fresh bread? Adding this delightful English muffin to your new allergy friendly foods is a wonderful addition to your breakfast or snack. Kids will love the versatility and the freshness of them. Better yet, have the kids make them with you, empowering them through kitchen life skills. The color on these English muffins looks as if they were bought from the store. They don't look "Whole Foods," "Healthy looking" or "cardboard tasting." They look, smell, and taste amazing.

Wet Ingredients
1/2 cup Oat milk (any plant based milk)
1 tsp Lemon Juice
1/2 tsp Date Nectar
1 3/4 tsp Yeast
3/4 cup warm water

2 T Angel Butter (2 T Coconut cream, 2 tsp ground Chia Seeds, 1/8 tsp Turmeric, 1 T Aquaschata™)

Dry Ingredients
2 1/2 cups Sorghum flour
1 cup Millet flour
2 T Tapioca flour
1/2 T Coconut flour
2 - 3 T Brown Rice flour (for the final kneading of dough if too sticky)
1 tsp Xanthan Gum
1/2 tsp Baking powder
1 tsp Salt

Cooking Instructions:

1. Heat the milk and water to the temp of 110 Degrees F. Add the yeast and syrup and set aside for 5 min.
2. In a seed grinder make the Angel Butter. Adding the Coconut Cream, (remember to refrigerate the coconut milk overnight and take only the cream, not the liquid) the chia seeds, Aquaschata™, ground chia seeds and turmeric.
3. In a stand mixing bowl, add all the dry ingredients.
4. Add the lemon juice and Angel Butter to the yeast milk and whisk to dissolve.

5. Using the stand mixer, on low, pour the liquid into the flour and mix. Turn it up to #5 and mix until all the flour blends and makes a dough ball.
6. On a Silpat, add 2 - 3 T Brown rice flour and knead into the dough so it's not sticky and make a ball. Place in a bowl in a warm spot and cover with a damp cloth. Or place it in an instant pot and cover with a damp cheesecloth (you will have to wet this 2 or 3 times through the rise). Turn instant pot to the dehydrator setting at 100 degrees F and let rise for 45 minutes to 1 hour. Until the dough doubles in size.
7. Once it's risen, place it on a floured Silpat mat and using a rolling pin, roll out to 1/2 inch thick. Using 3" size round cookie cutters, or mason jar lids or a glass, cut the shape of the muffins.
8. Place them on a cookie sheet lined with parchment paper. Re-roll the dough making it a 1/2 inch thick until you use up all the dough.
9. Cover with another damp cloth and let rest for another hour. If it's cold, place them in the oven. (Turn oven on to 200 degrees for 5 min) and then turn oven off and place dough to rest in oven with the door cracked open. If it's warm out, just set them on the counter.
10. Heat a non - stick griddle to 400 degree F. Place all the English muffins on the griddle and cook them for 4 - 5 minutes on one side until they get beautiful golden brown markings on them. Flip them over and cook another 2 - 3 min. Remove and they are done. You can slice them once they cool. Keep them unsliced and store in a bag for up to a week in the refrigerator and toast or warm to eat. They also freeze well.
11. Serve with nut butter and jams, my Herb Cream Cheese or as bread for sandwiches.

Cinnamon Raisin Bread *1 loaf*

☆☆☆☆☆

Dry Ingredients
1 cup Buckwheat flour
2 1/2 cups Sorghum flour
1/2 cup Brown Rice flour
1/2 cup Arrowroot powder
2 - 3 T Cinnamon
1/2 - 1 cup Raisins
1/2 - 1 tsp Salt

Wet Ingredients
2 1/2 cups warm water
1 T active dry Yeast
1/2 tsp Date Nectar
4 T Aquaschata™
4 T Applesauce
1/3 cup ground Chia seeds
1/3 cup Whole Psyllium Husks

Cooking Instructions:

1. Place the warm water in a bowl or 4 cup liquid glass measure. Add the yeast and 1/2 tsp of date nectar, whisk together. Cover and let rest for 5 - 10 minutes to activate the yeast. The mixture should get foamy or bubbly. If not, dump it and start again.
2. While the yeast is activating, mix together the dry ingredients in a large bowl.
3. After the yeast is activated, whisk in the Aquaschata™, applesauce, chia seeds and psyllium husks into the water-yeast mixture. Let stand for about 2 minutes to let the chia and psyllium release their gelatinous substances. Whisk again.
4. Pour the wet ingredients into the dry and fold in raisins and mix together with a rubber spatula until it is combined and stiff. Then knead the dough in the bowl to incorporate the flour. Add more flour if it's sticky. You want it to be moist without the sticky. If it's too dry, add more Aquaschata™ to it. 1 T at a time.
5. Next, form the dough into a ball.

Rise, you have several options, depending on how warm or cold it is.

1) If it's hot/warm, place on a cookie sheet lined with a piece of parchment paper and cover with a damp cloth (A damp, hefty, cheesecloth placed over the top is all you need to do) and set aside for an hour (until it's doubled).

2) If it's cold, a hot water bath works really well. Find a shallow container that you can place the bread loaf pan into (if making a loaf pan) place it in the container with a lid, and pour boiling water to fill the container part way (be sure not to get any of the dough wet). Allow this to rise for an hour.

3) Ninja Foodie 8 qt (or similar instant pot) - Place parchment paper or a Silpat mat on the bottom of the pot. Next, add the dough and cover it with a wet/damp cheesecloth and set the dehydrator setting to 100 degrees F for 30 min.

Baking:
1. **In the instant pot**, brush the Aquaschata™ on top with a pastry brush (it acts as an egg wash) and then sprinkle tops with poppyseeds or Everything Topping (Page 123) It also gives it a gorgeous color when it's baked. Bake at 375 degrees F for 1 hour.
2. **Oven**, remove cloth and brush with Aquaschata™. Sprinkle with poppyseeds or Everything Topping (Page 123) Bake on stoneware or loaf pan (if you chose that) at 375 degrees F for 1 hour.
3. Place on cooling rack when done and let cool completely. At least a few hours. If it's gummy inside, there wasn't enough flour. If it's too dry, there wasn't enough wet. You can freeze slices or whole loaf. Store the bread in a large nut bag (to breathe) and place inside a paper bag. It prevents extra moisture from collecting making it go sour. This works for 3 days before it begins drying out. At this point, if there is bread remaining, slice it and freeze it.

Spiced Pumpkin Bread   *makes 4 mini loaf pans*
☆ ☆ ☆ ☆ ☆

This Spiced Pumpkin bread goes great with tea, good company and a familiar holiday treat. Make them in mini loaf pans and gift them to your neighbors or friends in the fall. It makes a delightful gift.

Dry Ingredients
2 1/2 cups Buckwheat flour (or, 1 cup millet and 1 1/2 cups Sweet brown rice flour)
3/4 cup Tapioca flour (arrowroot powder works also)
3 T Pumpkin pie spice blend
3/4 cup Xylitol
1 tsp Vanilla powder
1/2 tsp Salt

Wet Ingredients
2 cups Pumpkin (canned) or cooked Butternut Squash
1/2 tsp Pumpkin Spice Stevia
1/2 cup Applesauce
1/4 cup Aquaschata™
1/2 cup Oat Milk
1/4 cup Chia Seeds

2 Egg Replacer
3 T Tapioca flour
2 tsp Baking powder
1/2 tsp Xanthan gum
1/4 tsp Cream of Tartar
1/4 cup +2 T warm filtered Water

Cooking Instructions:
1. Preheat oven to 350 degrees F.
2. In a mixing bowl, add all the dry ingredients and set aside.
3. In a blender, add the wet ingredients and blend for 1 minute.
4. In a seed grinder, make your egg replacer for 2 eggs. Take the egg replacer and whisk into the wet ingredients, by hand, in a bowl.

5. Take the bowl with the combined wet ingredients and egg replacer and fold it into the dry ingredients being careful to not over mix.
6. Line 4 mini loaf pans with parchment paper on the bottom. Pour into mini loaf pans for best results. Bake in a 350 degree F oven for 40 - 45 minutes or until a toothpick comes out clean. Remove from oven and let cool in loaf pan 10 - 15 minutes. Take a small stiff spatula or a butter knife to cut the edges and remove from pan. These are meant to be eaten right away but do well after freezing.

Spicy Banana Bread *1 loaf*
☆☆☆☆☆

This takes some time to prepare and bake but it's well worth it. Since it's more Wholesome, it's more filling. The bread can be cut into smaller pieces and go twice as far. Serve warm at brunches or along with soup and salad for lunch or eat just simply by itself.

1 Egg Replacer:
1 1/2 T Tapioca flour
1 tsp Baking powder
1/4 tsp Xanthan gum
1/8 tsp Cream of Tartar
3 T Warm water

Wet Ingredients
1/2 cup Pumfu (pumpkin seed tofu)
2 T Aquaschata™
2 T Applesauce unsweetened
1 cup mashed Banana
9 - 15 drops Liquid Stevia

Dry Ingredients
1 cup Sorghum flour
1/2 cup Brown Rice flour
1/2 cup Arrowroot flour
3/4 cup Xylitol
1/2 tsp Baking powder
1/2 tsp Baking soda
1 tsp Vanilla powder
1 tsp Cinnamon
1/4 tsp Nutmeg
1 tsp Allspice
1 T Poppyseeds
dash of Salt

Cooking Instructions:
1. Preheat oven to 350 degrees F. In a food processor, cream tofu, liquid stevia,

banana, and spices.

2. In a seed grinder or with a hand mixer, add egg replacer ingredients all together and blend or mix. It will froth immediately. Set aside.

3. In a food processor or blender, combine the remaining wet ingredients and blend until creamy smooth.

4. In a small bowl, add both the creamy smooth wet ingredients to the egg replacer froth and mix together with a spatula.

5. In a mixing bowl, combine flours, baking powder, and baking soda, xylitol, spices salt and vanilla. Add wet mix to dry mix. Using a mixer or by hand, work it until well blended. Fold in poppy seeds.

6. I like to use stoneware, as there is rarely any sticking. If you don't have one, line a 9"x5"x3" inch bread loaf pan with parchment paper. Sprinkle the top of loaf with poppy seeds as well. (If using a glass baking dish, place on cookie sheet to conduct the heat more evenly throughout). If you have a convection oven it will bake in approximately 30 - 35 minutes, however with regular oven it may take closer to an hour, but check after 35 minutes. Make sure cake tester or toothpick comes out perfectly clean from the center. Cool on a wire rack for 30 minutes before removing from pan.

Variation: Omit nutmeg and allspice for a regular banana bread.

Farmhouse Bread *1 loaf*
☆☆☆☆☆

This is a very rustic loaf of bread with a hard crust. You will feel like you are eating "real" homemade bread. This is one of the most well loved and satisfying loaves of bread made in my house.

Included are two sets of instructions for rising and baking. You can use an **Instant Pot** (done in an 8 qt to rise it and bake it.) Adjust to your particular quart capacity. You can also use a water bath which will be explained in the recipe.

Wet Ingredients
2 1/2 cups warm water (105 - 110 degrees F)
1 T Active Dry Yeast
1/2 tsp Date Nectar
4 T Aquaschata™
2 T Applesauce (unsweetened)
1/3 cup ground Chia Seeds
1/3 cup Whole Psyllium husks

Dry Ingredients
1/2 cup Teff flour
1/2 cup Arrowroot flour
1/2 cup Brown Rice flour
1 1/4 cup Sorghum flour
2 T Protein Powder (optional)
1/4 cup Millet (whole grain)
2 T Poppyseeds
2 T dried Rosemary
1 T dried Onion powder
2 T Sunflower seeds (optional)
1 1/2 tsp Salt

Cooking Instructions:
1. Place the warm water in a bowl or 4 cup liquid glass measure. Add the yeast and 1/2 tsp of date nectar, whisk together. Cover and let rest for 5 - 10 minutes to activate the yeast. The mixture should get foamy or bubbly. If not, dump it and start again.

2. While the yeast is activating, mix together the dry ingredients in a large bowl.
3. After the yeast is activated, whisk in the Aquaschata™, applesauce, chia seeds and psyllium husks into the water-yeast mixture. Let stand for about 2 minutes to let the chia and psyllium release their gelatinous substances. Whisk again.
4. Pour the wet ingredients into the dry and fold in the sunflower seeds and mix together with a rubber spatula until it is well combined and stiff. Then knead the dough in the bowl to incorporate the flour. Add more flour if it's sticky. You want it to be moist without the sticky. If it's too dry, add more Aquaschata™ to it. 1 T at a time.
5. Next, form the dough into a ball.

Rise, you have several options, depending on how warm or cold it is.

1) If it's hot/warm, place on a cookie sheet on top of a piece of parchment paper and cover with a damp cloth (A damp, hefty, cheesecloth placed over the top is all you need to do) and set aside for an hour (until it's doubled)

2) If it's cold, a hot water bath works really well. Find a shallow container that you can place the bread loaf pan into (if making a loaf pan) place it in the container with a lid, and pour boiling water to fill the container part way (be sure not to get any of the dough wet). Allow this to rise for an hour.

3) Ninja Foodie 8 qt (or similar instant pot) - Place parchment paper or a Silpat mat on the bottom of the pot. Next, add the dough and cover with a wet/damp cheesecloth. Set the dehydrator setting to 100 degrees F for 30 min.

Baking:
1. In the **Instant Pot**, brush the Aquaschata™ on top with a pastry brush (it acts as an egg wash), then sprinkle poppyseeds or Everything Topping (Page 123). It also gives it a gorgeous color when it's baked. Bake at 375 degrees F for 1 hour.
2. **Oven**, remove cloth and brush with Aquaschata™. Sprinkle with poppyseeds or Everything Topping (Page 123). Bake on stoneware or loaf pan (if you chose that) at 375 degrees F for 1 hour.
3. Place on cooling rack when done and let cool completely. At least a few hours. If it's gummy inside, there wasn't enough flour. If it's too dry, there wasn't enough wet. You can freeze slices or whole loaf. Store the bread in a large nut bag (to breathe). Place inside a paper bag. This prevents

extra moisture from collecting making it go sour. This works for 3 days before it begins drying out. At this point, if there is bread remaining, slice it and freeze it.

Farmhouse Bread Version 2. Use these as the Dry Ingredients, instead. Follow the same cooking instructions.

☆☆☆☆☆

1/2 cup Teff flour
1/2 cup Arrowroot powder
1/2 cup Millet flour
1 1/4 cup Sorghum flour
2 T White Bean flour
2 T Poppyseeds
2 T ground Rosemary
1 T Onion powder
1/4 cup Pumpkin seeds
1 1/2 tsp Salt

Multi Grain Sandwich Bread *1 loaf*
☆☆☆☆☆

Wet Ingredients
2 1/2 cups warm water (105 - 110 degrees F)
1 T Active Dry Yeast
1/2 tsp Date Nectar
4 T Aquaschata™
2 T Applesauce (unsweetened)
1/3 cup ground Chia Seeds
1/3 cup Whole Psyllium Husks

Dry Ingredients
1/2 cup Sorghum flour
1 cup Brown Rice flour
1 1/2 cup Teff flour
1/2 cup Arrowroot
3/4 cup Almond meal (or substitute w/ Millet flour)
1 T Onion powder
2 T Poppyseeds
1 1/2 Salt

Cooking Instructions:
1. Place the warm water in a bowl or 4 cup liquid glass measure. Add the yeast and 1/2 tsp of date nectar, whisk together. Cover and let rest for 5 - 10 minutes to activate the yeast. The mixture should get foamy or bubbly. If not, dump it and start again.
2. While the yeast is activating, mix together the dry ingredients in a large bowl.
3. After the yeast is activated, whisk in the Aquaschata™, applesauce, chia seeds and psyllium husks into the water-yeast mixture. Let stand for about 2 minutes to let the chia and psyllium release their gelatinous substances. Whisk again.
4. Pour the wet ingredients into the dry and mix together with a rubber spatula until it is combined and stiff. Then knead the dough in the bowl to incorporate the flour. Add more flour if it's sticky. You want it to be moist without the sticky. If it's too dry, add more Aquaschata™ to it. 1 T at a time.
5. Next, form the dough into a ball.

Rise, you have several options, depending on how warm or cold it is.

1) If it's hot/warm, place on a cookie sheet on top of a piece of parchment paper and cover with a damp cloth (A damp hefty cheesecloth placed over the top is all you need to do) and set aside for an hour (until it's doubled)

2) If it's cold, a hot water bath works really well. Find a shallow container that you can place the bread loaf pan into (if making a loaf pan) place it in the container with a lid and pour boiling water to fill the container part way (be sure not to get any of the dough wet). Allow this to rise for an hour.

3) Ninja Foodie 8 qt (or similar instant pot). Place parchment paper or a Silpat mat on the bottom of the pot. Next, add the dough and cover it with a wet/damp cheesecloth and set the dehydrator setting to 100 degrees F for 30 min.

Baking:

1. **In the Instant Pot**, brush the Aquaschata™ on top with a pastry brush (it acts as an egg wash) and then sprinkle tops with poppyseeds or Everything Topping (Page 123) It also gives it a gorgeous color when it's baked. Bake at 375 degrees F for 1 hour.
2. **Oven**, remove cloth and brush with Aquaschata™. Sprinkle with poppyseeds or Everything Topping (Page 123) Bake on stoneware or loaf pan (if you chose that) at 375 degrees F for 1 hour.
3. Place on cooling rack when done and let cool completely. At least a few hours. If it's gummy inside, there wasn't enough flour. If it's too dry, there wasn't enough wet. You can freeze slices or whole loaf. Store the bread in a large nut bag (to breathe) and place inside a paper bag. It prevents extra moisture from collecting making it go sour. This works for 3 days before it begins drying out. At this point, if there is bread remaining, slice it and freeze it.

Pumpernickel Bread *1 loaf*

☆☆☆☆☆

Rye bread and pumpernickel bagels have always been my favorite growing up. This recipe is as close to a wheat based rye bread as I have ever found. The color is dark and rich from the Chicory root. And the texture is smooth and really satisfying. Combine this with an herb cream cheese and you have a perfect snack or breakfast.

Dry Ingredients
1 cup Buckwheat flour
1 1/2 cup Sorghum flour
1/2 cup Brown Rice flour
1 cup Arrowroot powder
2 1/2 T Caraway seeds
1 T Cacao powder
1 tsp salt

Wet Ingredients
1 cup hot water with 2 1/2 T roasted Chicory root steeped for 5 minutes.
1 1/2 cups Hot water with 1 T Yeast
1/2 tsp Date Nectar
4 T Aquaschata™
2 T Applesauce
1/3 cup ground Chia seeds
1/3 cup whole Psyllium Husks
15 drops Liquid Chocolate Stevia

Cooking Instructions:
1. In 1 cup of hot water, steep the chicory root tea. Place the warm water in a bowl or 4 cup liquid glass measure. Add the yeast and 1/2 tsp of date nectar, whisk together. Cover and let rest for 5 - 10 minutes to activate the yeast. The mixture should get foamy or bubbly. If not, dump it and start again.
2. While the yeast is activating, mix together the dry ingredients in a large bowl.
3. After the yeast is activated, whisk in the Aquaschata™, Chicory root water, applesauce, chia seeds and psyllium husks and Chocolate Stevia into the water-yeast mixture. Let stand for about 2 minutes to let the chia and psyllium release

their gelatinous substances. Whisk again.
4. Pour the wet ingredients into the dry and mix together with a rubber spatula until it is combined and stiff. Then knead the dough in the bowl to incorporate the flour. Add more flour if it's sticky. You want it to be moist without the sticky. If it's too dry, add more Aquaschata™ to it. 1 T at a time.
5. Next, form the dough into a ball.

Rise, you have several options, depending on how warm or cold it is.

1) If it's hot/warm, place on a cookie sheet on top of a piece of parchment paper and cover with a damp cloth (A damp, hefty, cheesecloth placed over the top is all you need to do) and set aside for an hour (until it's doubled).

2) If it's cold, a hot water bath works really well. Find a shallow container that you can place the bread loaf pan into (if making a loaf pan) place it in the container with a lid, and pour boiling water to fill the container part way (be sure not to get any of the dough wet). Allow this to rise for an hour.

3) Ninja Foodie 8 qt (or similar instant pot) Place parchment paper or a Silpat mat on the bottom of the pot. Next, add the dough and cover it with a wet/damp cheesecloth and set the dehydrator setting to 100 degrees F for 30 min.

Baking:
1. **In the Instant Pot**, brush the Aquaschata™ on top with a pastry brush (it acts as an egg wash) and then sprinkle tops with poppyseeds or Everything Topping (Page 123) It also gives it a gorgeous color when it's baked. Bake at 375 degrees F for 1 hour.
2. **Oven**, remove cloth and brush with Aquaschata™. Sprinkle with poppyseeds. Bake on stoneware or loaf pan (if you chose that) at 375 degrees F for 1 hour.
3. Place on cooling rack when done and let cool completely. At least a few hours. If it's gummy inside, there wasn't enough flour. If it's too dry, there wasn't enough wet. You can freeze slices or whole loaf. Store the bread in a large nut bag (to breathe) and place inside a paper bag. It prevents extra moisture from collecting making it go sour. This works for 3 days before it begins drying out. At this point, if there is bread remaining, slice it and freeze it.

Sun-dried Tomato and Olive Bread *1 loaf*

☆☆☆☆☆

Wet Ingredients
2 1/2 cups warm water (105 - 110 degrees F)
1 T Active Dry Yeast
1/2 tsp Date Nectar
4 T Aquaschata™
2 T Applesauce (unsweetened)
1/3 cup ground Chia seeds
1/3 cup Whole Psyllium husks

Dry Ingredients
1/2 cup Teff flour
1/2 cup Arrowroot flour
1/2 cup Brown Rice flour
1 1/4 cup Sorghum flour
2 T Protein Powder (optional)
1/4 cup Millet (whole grain)
1 T dried Garlic powder
1/4 cup soften diced Sun-dried Tomatoes
1/4 cup Kalamata Olives (diced)
1/2 tsp Salt

Cooking Instructions:

1. Place the warm water in a bowl or 4 cup liquid glass measure. Add the yeast and 1/2 tsp of date nectar, whisk together. Cover and let rest for 5 - 10 minutes to activate the yeast. The mixture should get foamy or bubbly. If not, dump it and start again.
2. While the yeast is activating, mix together the dry ingredients in a large bowl.
3. After the yeast is activated, whisk in the Aquaschata™, applesauce, chia seeds and psyllium husks into the water-yeast mixture. Let stand for about 2 minutes to let the chia and psyllium release their gelatinous substances. Whisk again.
4. Pour the wet ingredients into the dry and fold in the Sun-dried tomatoes and olives. Mix together with a rubber spatula until it is combined and stiff. Then knead the dough in the bowl to incorporate the flour. Add more flour if it's sticky. You want it to be moist without the sticky. If it's too dry, add more Aquaschata™ to it. 1 T at a time.

5. Next, form the dough into a ball.

Rise, you have several options, depending on how warm or cold it is.

1) If it's hot/warm, place on a cookie sheet lined with a piece of parchment paper and cover with a damp cloth (A damp, hefty, cheesecloth placed over the top is all you need to do) and set aside for an hour (until it's doubled).

2) If it's cold, a hot water bath works really well. Find a shallow container that you can place the bread loaf pan into (if making a loaf pan) place it in the container with a lid, and pour boiling water to fill the container part way (be sure not to get any of the dough wet). Allow this to rise for an hour.

3) Ninja Foodie 8 qt (or similar instant pot) - Place parchment paper or a Silpat mat on the bottom of the pot. Next, add the dough and cover it with a wet/damp cheesecloth and set the dehydrator setting to 100 degrees F for 30 min.

Baking:
1. **In the Instant Pot**, brush the Aquaschata™ on top with a pastry brush (it acts as an egg wash) and then sprinkle with poppyseeds or Everything Topping (Page 123). It also gives it a gorgeous color when it's baked. Bake at 375 degrees F for 1 hour.
2. **Oven**, remove cloth and brush with Aquaschata™. Sprinkle with poppyseeds. Bake on stoneware or loaf pan (if you chose that) at 375 degrees F for 1 hour.
3. Place on cooling rack when done and let cool completely. At least a few hours. If it's gummy inside, there wasn't enough flour. If it's too dry, there wasn't enough wet. You can freeze slices or whole loaf. Store the bread in a large nut bag (to breathe) and place inside a paper bag. It prevents extra moisture from collecting making it go sour. This works for 3 days before it begins drying out. At this point, if there is bread remaining, slice it and freeze it.

Challah Bread *1 large loaf*
☆☆☆☆☆

This was one of my favorite breads growing up. My grandmother would bake this weekly for Shabbat. I began baking my Aunt Sarah's recipe in high school. It isn't something I have eaten in decades as most people do not make it gluten free and egg free. However, I believe I have succeeded in both flavor and texture with this recipe. And, although it is unconventional, it brings comfort and satisfies my memory of what a conventional loaf looks like on Shabbat. For that I am grateful.

Serve with Avocado, or herb cream cheese

Dry Ingredients
2 cups Tapioca flour
1 1/2 cups Brown Rice flour
1 1/2 cups Oat flour
2 T Psyllium powder
1 tsp Xanthan gum
1 1/2 tsp Salt

1 cup Oat milk heated
1 cup water (105 - 110 Degrees F)
1 T Dry Yeast
1/2 tsp Date Nectar

Wet Ingredients
2 Flax eggs (2 T ground Flax seeds and 4 T warm water 2 T Aquaschata™
1/3 tsp Liquid Stevia

Crust Wash
9 T plant based milk + 3 T Aquaschata™
8 drops of Liquid Stevia

Cooking Instructions:
1. Measure out the dry ingredients into a bowl.
2. Prepare and activate the yeast water with date nectar. Add warmed Oat milk.

3. While yeast is activating, make the flax eggs and set them aside for 5 - 10 min.
   Next, add the stevia to the flax egg. Once the yeast is activated, add the flax eggs into your yeast water/milk.
4. Have the dry ingredients mixed already in the stand mixer. With a dough hook, start your mixer on low speed. Add 1/4 of the liquid to the flour and mix well scraping the sides of any flour sticking. Increase to medium speed and continue adding the remaining liquid, 1/4 at a time until it forms a dough ball.
   Make sure to stop and scrape down the sides a few more times with a rubber spatula. When the dough has completely formed, remove and dust the mat with rice flour and knead by hand to make sure it's not sticky at all. It should be warm, malleable and ready for rising. Make a ball and set it aside to rise.

First Rise - Take the dough ball and choose one of several options, depending on how warm or cold it is.
1. If it's hot/warm, place on a cookie sheet on top of a piece of parchment paper and cover with a damp cloth (A damp hefty cheesecloth placed over the top is all you need to do) and set aside for an hour (until it's doubled).

2. If it's cold, a hot water bath works really well. Find a shallow container that you can place the dough pan into. Place it in the container and pour boiling water to fill the container part way (be sure not to get any of the dough wet). Cover container with a lid. Allow dough to rise for an hour.

3. Ninja Foodie 8 qt (or similar instant pot) Place parchment paper or a silicon mat on the bottom of the pot. Next, add the dough and cover it with a wet/damp cheesecloth and set the dehydrator setting to 100 degrees F for 30 min.

Second Rise -
1. Divide the dough into 3 pieces. You are about to make the first strand. On your work surface, gently make a long 6 or 7 inch log rolling it out to be 12 - 13 inches long. Rolling it back and forth on

your palm of your hands gently lengthening it. Start in the middle and work your way out rolling as you move your hands out. It's OK if your strands are thicker in the middle than on the ends. Actually, its preferable, as that's what gives Challah its beautiful shape as long as it's even on both ends. Do this 2 more times making each strand the same size. You can measure each piece out in weight or eyeball it and cut the ends off and add it to another strand.

2. Making a three-strand loaf, just braid the outside strands alternately - over, under, over, under.
3. Lay your strands on top of parchment paper. It will be much easier to transfer the Challah at that point.
4. Starting with the right-most strand, bring it over the strand directly to its left, then under the next one, and then over the last one. Repeat that process until you get to the bottom.
5. When you get to the bottom and you can't weave the strands anymore, pinch them together like you did the top. Again, you may need a dab of water to accomplish this.
6. Move the braided Challah to your lined baking tray. If you braided your Challah on top of parchment paper, just slide the whole paper onto your baking tray. Cover with a damp cheesecloth for a second rise for 30 min. Letting it rest and double in size again.
7. When it's ready for baking, brush with the Aquaschata™ stevia mixture all over the Challah, except the bottom. Make sure to get all the crevices and the sides.
8. **Baking:** Bake on stoneware or loaf pan (if you chose that) at 375 degrees F for 1 hour. I recommend removing the pan from the oven halfway through and brushing it again with Aquaschata™ wash to make it nice and brown. You'll find that some areas look like they never got the wash during this step. That's because the Challah expands in the oven when it's baking. Concentrate first on brushing the sections that don't have the wash, then brush the whole thing again. This is what makes those shiny brown knots on top of the finished Challah.
9. Place on cooling rack when done and let cool completely. At least a few hours. If it's gummy inside, there wasn't enough flour. If it's too dry, there wasn't enough wet. You can freeze slices or whole

loaf. Store the bread in a large nut bag (to breathe) and inside a paper bag. It prevents extra moisture from collecting making it go sour. This works for 3 days before it begins drying out. At this point, if there is bread remaining, slice it and freeze it.

10. Bake it until it has a nice crust. It will have a lot of cracks and textures in it.
11. Let the Challah fully cool before attempting to slice it. You can either easily pull it apart or slice it using a serrated knife. Enjoy!
12. Store bread in a nut milk bag or wrapped in cheesecloth and in a paper bag for up to 3 days. After that, slice and freeze to keep the bread fresh. You can freeze your baked Challah for up to 3 months. I recommend wrapping it tightly with plastic wrap AND freezer paper or something else freezer safe.

Rosemary Breadsticks *makes 1 1/2 dozen*

☆☆☆☆☆

These are perfect for dipping in a tomato sauce, pesto, herb cream cheese or eating just by themselves. Children love helping in the kitchen, and this recipe is perfect for that. My children started helping me with shaping dough as early as 4 years old. They love to eat what they have made, so give them as much artist expression on this as possible. It's extremely rewarding.

Dry Ingredients
1 1/4 - 1 1/2 cup Sorghum flour
1/2 cup Almond flour or Teff flour
1/2 cup Millet flour
3/4 cup Arrowroot powder
1 T Onion powder
2 T ground Rosemary
2 T Poppyseeds
1/2 tsp Salt

Wet Ingredients
2 cups warm water
1 T Active Dry Yeast
1/2 tsp Date Nectar
4 T Aquaschata™
2 T Applesauce
1/3 cup ground Chia Seeds
1/4 cup whole Psyllium Husks

Cooking Instructions:
1. Place the warm water in a bowl or 4 cup liquid glass measure. Add the yeast and 1/2 tsp of date nectar, whisk together. Cover and let rest for 5 - 10 minutes to activate the yeast. The mixture should get foamy or bubbly. If not, dump it and start again.
2. While the yeast is activating, mix well the dry ingredients in a large bowl.
3. After the yeast is activated, whisk in the Aquaschata™, applesauce, chia seeds and psyllium husks into the water-yeast mixture. Let stand for about 2 minutes to let the chia and psyllium release their gelatinous substances. Whisk again.
4. Pour the wet ingredients into the dry and mix well with a rubber spatula until it

is combined and stiff. Then knead the dough in the bowl to incorporate the flour. Add more flour if it's sticky. You want it to be moist without the sticky. If it's too dry, add more Aquaschata™ to it. 1 T at a time.

5. Next, form the dough into a ball and divide the dough into 8 pieces and then again into 8 more pieces.
6. On a Silpat mat, dust with flour if the dough appears sticky. Take each piece and roll them out with the palms of your hands until they are approximately 10 inches long. Place them on a cookie sheet on parchment paper or Silpat mat unless you have a stoneware cookie sheet. For this, stoneware works best. Fill the sheet with all the breadsticks.

Rise and Baking:
7. Cover with a damp cloth or damp cheesecloth and place in a warm place. One option is to let oven warm to 200 Degrees F, turn off and leave door ajar. Let them rise and double in shape. This takes about 45 min. Bake at 375 degrees F for 45 minutes or until golden brown.
8. Place on cooling rack when done and let cool completely. At least a few hours. If there are any leftover breadsticks, place in a large nut bag (to breathe) and inside a paper bag. It prevents extra moisture from collecting making it go sour. This works for 2 days before it begins drying out. At this point, if there are bread sticks remaining, store in a zip lock bag, and freeze.

Notes: A hot water bath will cut the rise time in half. Take a Pyrex dish that holds the bread sticks and that fits inside a shallow container that has a cover. Then pour a couple of inches of hot water into the container, keeping it from getting into the Pyrex dish.

Herb Dinner Rolls *makes 14 - 16 Rolls*
☆☆☆☆☆

Fresh rolls with soup are delicious. Spread an herb cream cheese or sun-dried tomato pesto.

Dry Ingredients
1 cup Buckwheat flour
2 1/2 cups Sorghum flour
1/2 cup Brown Rice flour
1/2 cup Arrowroot powder
2 - 3 T Rosemary
1 T Onion powder
1/2 - 1 tsp Salt

Wet Ingredients
2 1/2 cups warm water
1 T active Dry Yeast
1/2 tsp Date Nectar
4 T Aquaschata™
4 T Applesauce
1/3 cup ground Chia seeds
1/3 cup Whole Psyllium Husks

Cooking Instructions:

1. Place the warm water in a bowl or 4 cup liquid glass measure. Add the yeast and 1/2 tsp of date nectar, whisk together. Cover and let rest for 5 - 10 minutes to activate the yeast. The mixture should get foamy or bubbly. If not, dump it and start again.
2. While the yeast is activating, mix together the dry ingredients in a large bowl.
3. After the yeast is activated, whisk in the Aquaschata™, applesauce, chia seeds and psyllium husks into the water-yeast mixture. Let stand for about 2 minutes to let the chia and psyllium release their gelatinous substances. Whisk again.
4. Pour the wet ingredients into the dry and fold in raisins and mix together with a rubber spatula until it is combined and stiff. Knead the dough in the bowl to incorporate the flour. Add more flour if it's sticky. You want it to be moist without the sticky. If it's too dry, add more Aquaschata™. 1 T at a time.

5. Next, form the dough into a ball.

First Rise: you now have several options, depending on how warm or cold it is.

1) If it's hot/warm, place the dough on a cookie sheet on parchment paper and cover with a damp cloth (A damp, hefty, cheesecloth placed over the top is all you need to do) and set aside for an hour (until it's doubled).

2) If it's cold, a hot water bath works really well. Find a shallow container, with a lid, that you can place a bread loaf pan into. Place it in the container and pour boiling water to fill the container part way (be sure not to get any of the dough wet). Cover container with lid. Allow this to rise for an hour.

3) Ninja Foodie 8 qt (or similar instant pot) - Place parchment paper or a silicon mat on the bottom of the pot. Next, add the dough and cover it with a wet/damp cheesecloth and set the dehydrator setting to 100 degrees F for 30 min.

Second Rise and Baking:
1. Divide the dough into 8 pieces and then again into 8 more pieces. On a cookie sheet with parchment paper or Silpat mat, roll each piece in a round roll and set aside to rise again. Cover with a damp cloth and place back in the oven that was set at 200 Degrees F, turned off and the door left open. Or if it's warm enough, just set them aside for another 30 min.
2. When you are happy with the rise, remove cheesecloth, brush with Aquaschata™ to give it a nice golden color and bake at 375 degrees F for 35 - 45 min. Depending on their size.
3. Place on cooling rack when done and let cool completely. At least a few hours. You can freeze any leftovers. Store the rolls in a large nut bag (to breathe) and inside a paper bag. It prevents extra moisture from collecting, making it go sour. This works for 3 days before it begins drying out. Freeze leftovers.

** Use an herb cream cheese or sun-dried tomato pesto spread for a tasty snack. **

Onion and Dill Dinner Roll *makes 8*

☆☆☆☆☆

These yeast free herb Popover like rolls are heaven. You can eat them plain or cut them open and make them your sandwich bread, bun or even a hot dog roll. They are fun to watch when they puff up and even more fun to eat! Kids love them.

2 Egg Replacer
3 T Tapioca flour
2 tsp Baking powder
1/2 tsp Xanthan gum
1/4 tsp Cream of tartar
1/4 cup + 2 T warm water

Choux Pastry
Dry Ingredients
1/2 cup Brown Rice flour
1/2 cup Arrowroot flour
4 T + 1 tsp Psyllium powder
2 tsp Xanthan gum
1 T Onion powder
1 tsp Dill weed
1/2 tsp Salt

Wet Ingredients
1 cup + 2 T Oat milk (any plant based milk)
1/2 cup of Angel Butter (Page 107)

Cooking Instructions:
1. Preheat oven to 425 degrees F. Either use a Silpat mat or line with parchment paper.
2. In a seed grinder, add the 2 egg replacer ingredients and blend until it's frothy.
3. In a small bowl, add the dry ingredients.
4. In a small pan, melt the Angel Butter with the milk on very low heat. Do not heat mixture up. You want this to only melt the cream, do not bring to a boil or raise the temperature past the melting part. Remove from heat.
5. Add the dry ingredients into the milk and mix with a wooden spoon. It will have a mushy texture while having an elastic firm texture at the same time.

6. Next, add the 2 egg replacer into the pot and mix thoroughly.
7. Place the mixture into a piping bag without a tip, make sure the opening is bigger for the hot dog rolls. What you pipe is the width of it. It will be firm but squeezable.
8. Pipe the mixture into 2 - 3 inch rounds or 5 - 6 inch long. The middle will sink in the longer they are. Since they will be cut open afterwards, this doesn't matter.
9. Lightly wet your finger to smooth out any points left from piping.
10. Bake for 20 - 25 min. They will puff up and brown nicely. If after 20 - 25 minutes, they appear, crusty and golden brown, lower the heat to 350 Degrees F for 5 - 8 more minutes. Then, open the oven door part way, turn off the heat, and allow them to cool down another 20 minutes to prevent them from deflating. They are ready to eat after 15 - 20 minutes of cooling down.

Biscuits with Green Onions *12 Biscuits*

☆☆☆☆☆

Serve this with your favorite gravy or an herb cream cheese. It's a delicious comfort food that resembles corn bread without the corn.

Ingredients
1 cup Teff flour
1 cup Almond flour (Or white bean flour)
1/2 cup Brown Rice flour
2 tsp Baking Powder
1/2 tsp Sea Salt
10 drops of Liquid Stevia
3 T Angel Butter (Page 107)
2 T Coconut Cream
1 1/4 cups Green Onions
1 cup Almond Milk (plant based milk)

Egg wash
Brush with Aquaschata™

Cooking Instruction:
1. Preheat oven to 400 degrees F.
2. In a food processor add flour, baking powder, baking soda, salt.
3. Blend Liquid Stevia with Coconut cream.
4. Add blended Coconut Cream and Angel Butter to dry mix. Pulse 6 - 8 times until the Angel Butter is cut into the flour.
5. Place mixture in mixing bowl and fold in green onions. Add milk and mix until a ball of dough is formed. Add more rice four if necessary, so it's not sticky. It will be moist without the stickiness.
6. Make 12 Biscuit size dough balls on a baking dish and brush with Aquaschata™ on their tops. Bake for 5 minutes at 400 degrees and then lower to 300 degrees for 20 - 30 minutes. The top will have a lot of cracks giving it a beautiful pattern. Eat warm with an herb cream cheese or make a gravy to pour over it.

Corn Bread

☆☆☆☆☆

Cooking in a cast iron skillet is a traditional way to make this. Enjoy with soup or salad.

Ingredients
2 cups Cornmeal
1/2 cup Sorghum flour
1/3 cup Almond flour (Use arrowroot powder for a nut free version)
1/3 cup Millet flour
4 tsp Baking powder
5 drops Liquid Stevia
1 1/2 cups Oat milk
1/4 cup Angel Butter (Page 107)
1 tsp Salt

2 Egg replacer
3 T Tapioca flour
2 tsp Baking powder
1/2 tsp Xanthan gum
1/4 tsp Cream of tartar

Cooking Instructions:
Preheat oven to 375 degrees F.
- Best baked in a cast iron skillet. If not, use a cake pan or stoneware. Bake at 375 degrees F for 20 - 30 minutes until done. Use parchment paper to prevent sticking.

Indian Style Naan
☆☆☆☆☆

1 tsp Yeast
1/2 tsp Date Nectar
1/2 cup Oat Milk
4 T Aquaschata™
1/2 cup Arrowroot powder
1/2 cup + 1 1/2 T Sorghum flour
1 tsp Baking powder
1 tsp Salt
2 T Psyllium powder
2 tsp whole Chia Seeds
3/4 tsp Xanthan gum

Cooking Instructions:
1. Preheat oven to 500 degrees F.
2. Heat up oat milk in a pot. Do not bring it to a boil, just hot.
3. Place Yeast in a small bowl. Add Hot milk, Aquaschata™, 1/2 tsp Date Nectar. Cover to activate yeast.
4. Add flours, salt, chia seeds and psyllium powder and mix together.
5. Add wet yeast mix to dry ingredients.
6. Knead the dough and let sit in warm spot for 30 min.
7. Divide into 6 pieces. Keep covered. Roll one into a ball and using a rolling pin, shape into 3 x 5 inch size. Place on Silpat mat.
8. Bake for 17 min. Some may puff and some may not. Do not overcook as they will get dry.

Best Pizza Crust - *makes 4 small or 2 large*
☆☆☆☆☆

Dry ingredients
1 cup White Bean flour
1 cup Brown Rice flour
1/4 Buckwheat flour
1/2 cup Arrowroot powder
1/2 T Garlic powder
1 tsp Salt

Wet ingredients
1 cup warm water
2 1/4 tsp Dry Yeast
2 T Chia seeds
Mix 1/3 cup Aquaschata™ with 1 T tahini and 1 cup water. Use 1/4 cup of this mix per batch. Refrigerate or freeze for next time.

Rice flour for rolling if sticky

Cooking Instructions:
1. Preheat oven to 450 degrees F.
2. Mix the wet ingredients first. Then in a separate bowl mix the dry ingredients.
3. In the dry bowl, add the wet ingredients and mix into a dough. Let it rest for 5 minutes in plastic wrap.
4. Divide dough with what size pizzas you'd like.
5. Prebake for 5 minutes and freeze. Or use immediately with toppings.

Note: Tripling the batter is well worth your time for freezing.

Cauliflower Pizza Crust *makes 2 large pizzas or 4 personal size*

☆ ☆ ☆ ☆ ☆

This is a Grain free crust.

Ingredients

6 cups white Cauliflower (Medium size head)
1 1/2 T Ground Chia Seeds* (making a chia egg)
4 T Aquaschata™ (heated)
1 - 2 tsp Garlic powder
1 tsp dried Oregano
1 1/2 T Psyllium Husk **powder (Not Whole)**
1 T Tapioca flour
3 T Nutritional Yeast (optional)
1/2 tsp Salt

Notes:
If substituting the chia seeds with flax seeds, you will need to add an additional 1 T of arrowroot powder and 2 1/2 T psyllium husk powder.

Cooking Instructions:

1. To prepare the cauliflower, using a food processor, rice 1 head of cauliflower (equivalent to 6 cups). Pulse until you get the texture of rice. Depending on the size of the cauliflower head, you may have to do this in more than one batch.
2. Place in a bowl and rinse with water removing any large pieces.
3. Using a large skillet or wok, add the cauliflower and cover with water. Remove any large pieces. Bring to a boil and cook on medium high heat for 5 min. It will get foamy and frothy. Next, using a large sieve or a drum strainer, strain water, pressing out all the water with the large plastic scraper. At this point, you can use a nut bag to squeeze out the remaining water. It is hot, so be careful to not burn yourself. If you don't have a nut milk bag, a thin, clean kitchen towel will work also, but it Is harder to get all the pieces out. A wooden spoon will also push all the water out but the large scraper is best. Once you feel all the water has been removed, place the cauliflower in a large tray or container and set it in the freezer for 10 minutes.
4. Mix the hot Aquaschata™ with the ground chia seeds in a small bowl to thicken.

5. Once the cauliflower has completely cooled, add the remaining ingredients. Using your hands, mix it all together to form a "dough." It will be mushy. It should form a ball. Taste and adjust flavor as needed, adding more vegan parmesan or nutritional yeast for cheesy flavor, salt for saltiness, or herbs/garlic for intense flavor.
6. Preheat the oven to 375 degrees F. Line a baking sheet or pizza stone/pan with parchment paper. Sprinkle with a little cornmeal or gluten-free flour to help prevent the pizza from sticking when slicing.
7. Depending on the size, on a piece of parchment paper, divide into the size you'd like to shape. Then use your hands to carefully spread the dough into a circle or square (depending on shape of pan) and keep the crust slightly less than a 1/2-inch thick with a slightly thicker outer perimeter.
8. Bake crust for 30 - 40 minutes depending on how thick it is. Then remove from oven and carefully flip the crust. Do so by first loosening the crust from the bottom layer of parchment with a spatula and then laying another sheet of parchment paper on top of the crust. Then grab both sheets of parchment and gently flip. Arrange the crust back on the baking pan. Not crisp and not cracker like. You've over baked it if it's cracker like.
9. Return to the oven and bake for an additional 10 - 12 minutes or until the edges appear golden brown and the center feels mostly firm to the touch.
10. Remove from oven and top with desired toppings (cooked or fresh). I recommend going light on the sauce as it can make the crust soggy if too much is applied. Bake for another 10 or so minutes or until toppings are tender. Watch the edges of the crust, which can get brown before the toppings. They are thin and pliable.
11. Enjoy hot with any additional garnishes, such as fresh basil, red pepper flake, or vegan parmesan cheese.
12. Best when fresh. This pizza is best eaten with a fork – I find that it doesn't quite support itself when eaten with hands.

Note: You could bake your crust ahead of time and then freeze for later use if desired.

Cinnamon Raisin Bagels *makes 10 Large Bagels or 16 small Bagels*

☆☆☆☆☆

Bagels are another childhood favorite of mine. Top this with hazelnut butter or my herb cream cheese. These definitely won't stick around.

Dry Ingredients
1 cup Buckwheat flour
2 1/2 cups Sorghum flour
1/2 cup Brown Rice flour
1/2 cup Arrowroot powder
2 - 3 T Cinnamon
1/2 - 1 cup Raisins
1/2 - 1 tsp Salt

Wet Ingredients
2 1/2 cups warm water
1 T active Dry Yeast
1/2 tsp Date Nectar
4 T Aquaschata™
4 T Applesauce
1/3 cup ground Chia Seeds
1/3 cup Whole Psyllium Husks

Cooking Instructions:
1. Place the warm water in a bowl or 4 cup liquid glass measure. Add the yeast and 1/2 tsp of date nectar, whisk together. Cover and let rest for 5 - 10 minutes to activate the yeast. The mixture should get foamy or bubbly. If not, dump it and start again.
2. While the yeast is activating, mix together the dry ingredients in a large bowl.
3. After the yeast is activated, whisk in the Aquaschata™, applesauce, chia seeds and psyllium husks into the water-yeast mixture. Let stand for about 2 minutes to let the chia and psyllium release their gelatinous substances. Whisk again.
4. Pour the wet ingredients into the dry and fold in raisins and mix together with a rubber spatula until it is combined and stiff. Knead the dough in the bowl to incorporate the flour. Add more flour if it's sticky. You want it to be moist without the sticky. If it's too dry, add more Aquaschata™ to it. 1 T at a time.

5. Place the warm water in a bowl or 4 cup liquid glass measure. Add the yeast and 1/2 tsp of date nectar, whisk together. Cover and let rest for 5 - 10 minutes to activate the yeast. The mixture should get foamy or bubbly. If not, dump it and start again.
6. While the yeast is activating, mix together the dry ingredients in a large bowl.
7. After the yeast is activated, whisk in the Aquaschata™, applesauce, chia seeds and psyllium husks into the water-yeast mixture. Let stand for about 2 minutes to let the chia and psyllium release their gelatinous substances. Whisk again.
8. Pour the wet ingredients into the dry and fold in raisins and mix together with a rubber spatula until it is combined and stiff. Knead the dough in the bowl to incorporate the flour. Add more flour if it's sticky. You want it to be moist without the sticky. If it's too dry, add more Aquaschata™ to it. 1 T at a time.
9. Next, form the dough into a ball.

First Rise, you have several options depending on how warm or cold it is.

1) If it's hot/warm, place on a cookie sheet on top of a piece of parchment paper and cover with a damp cloth (A damp, hefty, cheesecloth placed over the top is all you need to do) and set aside for an hour (until it's doubled)

2) If it's cold, a hot water bath works really well. Find a shallow container that you can place a bread loaf pan into. Place it in the container and pour boiling water to fill the container part way (be sure not to get any of the dough wet). Place lid on container and allow this to rise for an hour.

3) Ninja Foodie 8 qt (or similar instant pot) Place parchment paper or a silicon mat on the bottom of the pot. Next, add the dough and cover it with a wet/damp cheesecloth and set the dehydrator setting to 100 degrees F for 30 min.

2nd Rise, Boiling and Baking:
1. Divide dough into 10. This makes 10 large bagels. If you want them smaller, then divide into 16 pieces. On a Silpat mat, dust with rice flour if sticking. Roll out one at a time into a cigar like shape about 8 inches long and an inch thick. Make a circle and wetting one end, stick it to the other end shaping it the way a bagel looks. Set aside. Repeat this step with all the cut pieces. If you have a dehydrator, place them on the racks on parchment paper, cover with damp cheesecloth; or put back in Instant pot for another 30 minutes to

get another rise. If it's warm in the house, set on counter and cover with a damp cheesecloth and let rise for another 30 min.
2. Preparing the water bath. In a large pot, fill with water and bring to a boil. Once the bagels have risen again, take 3 - 5 at a time and place in boiling water for 30 seconds per side. When that is done, place back on cookie sheet with parchment paper or a Silpat mat. As they come out of the water bath, sprinkle with poppy seeds generously.

3. Preheat the oven to 375 degrees F. Bake for 1 hour.

4. Place on cooling rack when done and let cool completely. At least a few hours. Slice in half if freezing. Store the bread in a large nut bag (to breathe) and inside a paper bag. It prevents extra moisture from collecting making it go sour. This works for 3 days before it begins drying out. At this point, if there is bread remaining, slice and freeze it.

Onion Poppyseed Bagels *makes 10 Large Bagels or 16 Small Bagels*

☆☆☆☆☆

Serve with an Herb Cream Cheese (Page 110)

Dry Ingredients
1 cup Buckwheat flour
2 1/2 cups Sorghum flour
1/2 cup Brown Rice flour
1/2 cup Arrowroot powder
2 T Onion powder
2 T Poppyseeds
1/2 - 1 tsp Salt

Wet Ingredients
2 1/2 cups warm water
1 T Active Dry Yeast
1/2 tsp Date Nectar
4 T Aquaschata™
4 T Applesauce
1/3 cup ground Chia Seeds
1/3 cup Whole Psyllium Husks

Cooking Instructions:
1. Place the warm water in a bowl or 4 cup liquid glass measure. Add the yeast and 1/2 tsp of date nectar, whisk together. Cover and let rest for 5 - 10 minutes to activate the yeast. The mixture should get foamy or bubbly. If not, dump out and start again.
2. While the yeast is activating, mix together the dry ingredients in a large bowl.
3. After the yeast is activated, whisk in the Aquaschata™, applesauce, chia seeds and psyllium husks into the water-yeast mixture. Let stand for about 2 minutes to let the chia and psyllium release their gelatinous substances. Whisk again.
4. Pour the wet ingredients into the dry and mix together with a rubber spatula until it is combined and stiff. Then knead the dough in the bowl to incorporate the flour. Add more flour if it's sticky. You want it to be moist without the sticky. If it's too dry, add more Aquaschata™ to it. 1 T at a time.
5. Next, form the dough into a ball.

First Rise, you have options depending on how warm or cold it is.

1) If it's hot/warm, place on a cookie sheet on top of a piece of parchment paper and cover with a damp cloth (A damp hefty cheesecloth placed over the top is all you need to do) and set aside for an hour (until it's doubled.)

2) If it's cold, a hot water bath works really well. Find a shallow container that you can place the bread loaf pan into (if making a loaf pan) place it in the container with a lid, and pour boiling water to fill the container part way (be sure not to get any of the dough wet). Allow this to rise for an hour.

3) Ninja Foodie 8 qt (or similar instant pot) - Place parchment paper or a silicon mat on the bottom of the pot. Next, add the dough and cover it with a wet/damp cheesecloth and set the dehydrator setting to 100 degrees F for 30 min.

2nd Rise, Boiling and Baking:

1. Divide dough into 10. This makes 10 large bagels. If you want them smaller, then divide it into 16 pieces. On a Silpat mat dust with rice flour if sticking. Roll out one at a time into a cigar like shape about 8 inches long and an inch thick. Make a circle and wetting one end, stick it to the other end shaping it the way a bagel looks. Set aside. Repeat this step with all the cut pieces. If you have a dehydrator, place them on the racks on parchment paper, cover with damp cheesecloth and put back in Instant pot or dehydrator for another 30 minutes to get another rise. If it's warm in the house, set aside on counter and cover with a damp cheesecloth and let rise for another 30 min.
2. Preparing the water bath. In a large pot fill with water and bring to a boil. Once the bagels have risen again, Take 3 - 5 at a time and place in boiling water for 30 seconds per side. When that is done place back on a cookie sheet with parchment paper or a Silpat mat. As they come out of the water bath, sprinkle with toppings generously. Everything topping (Page 123) or poppyseeds or sesame seeds.
3. Preheat the oven to 375 degrees F. Bake for 1 hour.

4.. Place on cooling rack when done and let cool completely. At least a few hours. Slice in half if freezing. Store the bread in a large nut bag (to breathe) and inside a paper bag. It prevents extra moisture from collecting and making it go sour. This works for 3 days before it begins drying out. If there are bagels remaining, slice them and freeze.

Pumpernickel Bagels *makes 10 Large Bagels or 16 Small Bagels*

☆☆☆☆☆

Serve with an Herb Cream Cheese

Dry Ingredients
1 cup Buckwheat flour
1 1/2 cup Sorghum flour
1/2 cup Brown Rice flour
1 cup Arrowroot powder
2 1/2 T Caraway seeds
1 T Cacao powder
1 tsp Salt

Wet Ingredients
1 cup hot water with 2 1/2 T roasted Chicory root steeped for 5 minutes.
1 1/2 cups Hot water with
1 T Active Dry Yeast
1/2 tsp Date Nectar
4 T Aquaschata™
2 T Applesauce
1/3 cup ground Chia seeds
1/3 cup whole Psyllium Husks
15 drops Liquid Chocolate Stevia

1. Place the warm water in a bowl or 4 cup liquid glass measure. Add the yeast and 1/2 tsp of date nectar, whisk together. Cover and let rest for 5 - 10 minutes to activate the yeast. The mixture should get foamy or bubbly. If not, dump it and start again.
2. While the yeast is activating, mix together the dry ingredients in a large bowl.
3. After the yeast is activated, whisk in the Aquaschata™, applesauce, chia seeds and psyllium husks into the water-yeast mixture. Let stand for about 2 minutes to let the chia and psyllium release their gelatinous substances. Whisk again.
4. Pour the wet ingredients into the dry and fold in raisins and mix together with a rubber spatula until it is combined and stiff. Then knead the dough in the bowl to incorporate the flour. Add more flour if it's sticky. You want it to be moist without the sticky. If it's too dry, add more Aquaschata™ to it. 1 T at a time.
5. Next, form the dough into a ball.

First Rise: You have several options depending on how warm or cold it is.

1- If it's hot/warm, place on a cookie sheet on top of a piece of parchment paper and cover with a damp cloth (A damp hefty cheesecloth placed over the top is all you need to do) and set aside for an hour (until it's doubled)
2- If it's cold, a hot water bath works really well. Find a shallow container that you can place the bread loaf pan into (if making a loaf pan) place it in the container with a lid, and pour boiling water to fill the container part way (be sure not to get any of the dough wet). Allow this to rise for an hour.
3- Ninja Foodie 8 qt (or similar instant pot) - Place parchment paper or a silicon mat on the bottom of the pot. Next, add the dough and cover it with a wet/damp cheesecloth and set the dehydrator setting to 100 degrees F for 30 minutes.

Second Rise, Boiling and Baking

1. Divide dough into 10. This makes 10 large bagels. If you want them smaller, then divide it into 16 pieces. On a Silpat mat dust with rice flour if sticking. Roll out one at a time into a cigar like shape about 8 inches long and an inch thick. Make a circle and wetting one end, stick it to the other end shaping it the way a bagel looks. Set aside. Repeat this step with all the cut pieces. If you have a dehydrator, place them on the racks on parchment paper, cover with damp cheesecloth and put back in Instant pot or dehydrator for another 30 minutes to get another rise. If it's warm in the house, set aside on counter and cover with a damp cheesecloth and let rise for another 30 min.
2. Preparing the water bath. In a large pot fill with water and bring to a boil. Once the bagels have risen again, Take 3 - 5 at a time and place in boiling water for 30 seconds per side. When that is done place back on cookie sheet with parchment paper or a Silpat mat. As they come out of the water bath, sprinkle with toppings generously. Everything topping or (Page 123) poppyseeds or sesame seeds.

Cooking Instructions Preheat the oven to 375 degrees F.

1. Bake for 1 hour.
2. Place on cooling rack when done and let cool completely. At least a few hours. Slice in half if freezing. Store the bread in a large nut bag (to breathe) and inside a paper bag. It prevents extra moisture from collecting making it go sour. This works for 3 days before it begins drying out. If there is bread remaining, slice it and freeze it.

Belgium Soft Pretzel *makes 8 Large Pretzels***
☆☆☆☆☆

Dry Ingredients
1 1/4 cup Tapioca flour
1 cup + 2 T Arrowroot flour
2 1/4 cups Oat flour
1/2 cup Brown Rice flour
2 T Psyllium Husk powder *
2 tsp Salt

Wet Ingredients
1 T Active Dry Yeast
1/2 tsp Date Nectar to activate yeast
1 3/4 cup Cashew Milk**(or any plant based milk)
1/3 cup + 2 T Aquaschata™

Topping
1 T coarse sea Salt
Everything Toppings (Page 123)
Cooking water
10 cups water
1/3 cup baking soda

Cooking Instructions:
1. In a small pot, warm cashew milk over medium heat (just under a boil). Transfer into a glass container for yeast activation. Add yeast and maple syrup, stir and let sit for about 15 minutes while yeast activates.
2. In a mixer bowl (using the dough hook) combine tapioca flour, arrowroot flour, oat flour, brown rice flour, psyllium husk powder, and salt. Mix over medium speed for 5 minutes, adding in the cashew milk yeast mixture. Add the Aquaschata™ until it forms a nice dough ball that is sticky but firm.
3. Remove dough onto a floured surface (I use brown rice flour). Make sure your hands are floured too. Knead for 2 more minutes, putting your body weight into it. You want the dough supple, not dry.
4. Shape dough into a ball and transfer into an instant pot. Put on dehydrator at

100 degrees F for 30 - 45 min. Cover with a moist cheese cloth. If you don't have an instant pot, you can use the toaster oven or regular oven at its lowest setting. You might need to moisten the cheesecloth several times in case it dries out. Rise it for 45 - 60 min. You can also put it in a warm sunny spot in your house and rise it for 60 min. Dough should rise twice its size.
5. 10 minutes before making the dough get your water and baking soda bath prepared in a large pot.
6. Transfer dough onto your rolling surface and divide into 8 sections. (keep all but the one you are about to work, covered in plastic wrap to prevent them from drying out. It's VERY temperamental.
7. Roll out one piece of dough into a 15 - 18 inch rope and shape it into a U. Take both ends and cross over each other twice. Fold them down and dip your finger into some water and where it meets in 3 spots of the pretzel, wet it and stick the dough to each other gently pressing. Carefully transfer pretzel with a large spatula into the boiling baking soda bath for 30 seconds. Gently lift out of the water and transfer onto the lined baking sheet or Silpat. Repeat the process with the remaining pieces of dough. In general, 3 pretzels fit into the bath at once.
8. Let pretzels sit on the baking sheet for 10 minutes while the oven is preheating to 450 degrees F.
9. Sprinkle with course salt and bake in the oven for 15 - 17 minutes until pretzels are golden brown.
10. Serve while still warm. Leftovers go in the freezer. Defrost in oven before serving again. As they dry out the next day, spritz with water and warm in toaster oven and it will bring it back to the first day. Or freeze uneaten ones on the first day.

Notes:
* Psyllium husk powder can be found in the bulk herbs section at natural grocery stores. This recipe only works with the powder. Not the course fiber. I use the other for my bread recipes.

**Making your own Cashew milk is easy. Soak 1/2 cup Raw Cashews for a few hours in water. Blend with 1 ¾ cup water for 2 - 3 minutes. Add to saucepan and heat.

***Cut recipe in half if you prefer to eat them fresh only.

Tortillas & Wraps

Grain Free Tortillas..230

Coconut Flour Tortillas..231

Homemade Corn Tortillas - Soft and Hard..........................232

Cauliflower Wrap…………………………………….....233

Collard Green Wraps..235

Grain Free Tortillas *makes 8*
☆☆☆☆☆

Ingredients
3/4 cup + 1 T Arrowroot flour
1/4 cup Chickpea flour (Use cassava flour as a substitute)
4 T Psyllium Husks, whole
1/4 tsp Salt
3/4 cup water
2 T Aquaschata™

Cooking Instructions:
1. In a small bowl mix together the flours, psyllium husks and salt.
2. Mix the Aquaschata™ and water together and add it into the flour, vigorously mixing until a dough forms. It won't take much.
3. Divide into 8 balls and place in a zip lock bag to keep moist.
4. Between two pieces of parchment paper, place a round ball and flatten with your hand. With a rolling pin, roll until it's very thin.
5. Place on a 300 degree F griddle and heat one side for a couple of minutes and then flip and heat the other side.
6. Set on a plate and repeat the process.
7. Store in a zip lock bag in the freezer to maintain freshness. They make a perfect tortilla wrap.

Coconut Flour Tortillas *Makes 4 large or 6 small*
☆☆☆☆☆

Ingredients
1/2 cup Coconut flour
2 T Whole Psyllium husks
Optional: teaspoon fine sea salt (more or less to taste)
1 cup water

Cooking Instructions:

1. In a small mixing bowl, whisk the coconut flour, psyllium husks and (optional) salt, breaking up any lumps in the coconut flour.
2. Add the water to the bowl, stirring until combined. Let stand 5 minutes to thicken and then shape dough into a ball (it will feel moist & springy).
3. Cut the dough into 4 equal pieces. Shape each piece of dough into a ball.
4. Place one dough ball between two large pieces of wax paper or parchment paper (plastic wrap will also work). Using a rolling pin, roll dough into a 7-inch (17.5 cm) circle. Carefully peel off top layer of paper.
5. On a non stick griddle or skillet, heat over medium high heat until hot. Place tortilla, dough side down, into skillet and carefully peel off second piece of paper.
6. Cook the tortilla for 2 to 3 minutes until it begins to puff and the bottom is browned in spots (when you lift tortilla with a spatula). Flip the tortilla and cook the other side for 2 to 3 minutes longer until puffed and golden brown in spots.
7. Transfer tortilla to a metal cooling rack and repeat with remaining pieces of dough.
8. The tortillas are delicious warm or room temperature.

Notes: *Store the cooled tortillas in an airtight container at cool room temperature for 2 days, the refrigerator for 2 weeks or the freezer for up to 6 months. Double the recipe for extra.*

Tip for Removing Tortillas from Paper: *if the paper is really sticking to the tortilla, place the tortilla (in its paper) in the freezer for 3 to 4 minutes (not much longer). The tortilla will come off with ease.*

Homemade Corn Tortillas - Soft and Hard *makes about 17 soft shells.*
☆☆☆☆☆

These are so easy to make, with only 2 ingredients. Once you've tasted a fresh homemade corn chip, you won't be filling deprived as the baked version are equally satisfying if not better than the ones cooked in oil. A rolling pin and parchment paper, a griddle and or a cookie sheet. You are set! Make a double batch and freeze them and you are double set!

Ingredients
1 1/2 cups organic, dry Hominy flour or Masa Harina
1/2 cup hot water
1/2 tsp Salt (optional)

Cooking Instructions:
1. In a bowl, mix the hot water with the flour until a non sticky dough is formed.
2. On a Silpat mat, knead the dough for 5 to 7 minutes. The dough will feel like play dough. Airy and light. At some point you will have a sense of it connecting and it feels different. It no longer feels like air. Place it in a zip lock baggy and set aside for 5 -10 min.
3. Prepare two pieces of parchment paper 12 x 12, approximately, and set aside.
4. With a knife, divide the dough into 8 pieces. Then divide those into 8 more pieces. Make a small ball, about golf ball size, and place in the middle of the two parchment papers. With a rolling pin, roll out to approximately 1/4 inch thickness. Using a 4 inch round cookie cutter, cut the shape of the tortilla and set aside on a plate. Repeat this until you have used up all the dough. I like to make half the batch and cook them, then make the other half.
5. Heat a non stick griddle to 300 degrees F. Place on the surface and cook for 25 seconds on one side and flip and cook for 15 seconds on the second side. Wrap them in foil. They will dry and crack if they are not kept wrapped. Once they are all cooked either eat them, freeze them or bake them to be hard shells or chips.
6. If you are making hard shells, drape them on the wrack upside down and bake (making sure they don't touch any heat element. If you are making chips, cut each one into 4 triangles and place on a cookie sheet. Sprinkle salt, or chili lime powder on them and bake at 400 degrees F for 5 - 10 min. Watch them carefully.
7. If you baked all of them and aren't eating all of them, let them cool off and store in an airtight container. Serve warm with your homemade Pico de Gallo salsa.

Cauliflower Wrap
☆☆☆☆☆

This is a very versatile crepe like wrap. You can make any size from small to large. You can use them like a wrap, a soft taco or eat it like a crepe with a filling such as cream cheese and blueberry compote. They have no flavor of cauliflower whatsoever, so don't be fooled by the name. They actually remind me of hash browns. They are elastic and don't crumble. You can change up the flavors in them. Make a big batch and freeze them. This is an ideal grain free, nut free, bean free allergy friendly food. Perfect for kids, both at home and at school as well as adults on very restricted diets. This recipe delivers a strong satisfaction level to "fit in" and feel "normal."

Ingredients
6 cups white or yellow Cauliflower (Medium size head)
1 1/2 T Ground Chia Seeds (making a chia egg)
4 T Aquaschata™ (heated)
2 tsp Garlic powder or 3 Cloves fresh
2 heaping T fresh crushed Basil (in seed grinder) or 1/2 T dried basil
1 1/2 T dried Oregano
1 1/2 T Psyllium Husk **powder**
1 T Arrowroot powder
3 T Nutritional Yeast (optional)
1/2 tsp Salt
Water for cooking

*Notes: *If substituting the chia seeds with flax seeds, you will need to add an additional 1 T of arrowroot powder. And 2 1/2 T psyllium husk powder.*

*If you are making this as a breakfast crepe, remove the garlic, basil, oregano and nutritional yeast. Replace with 1 1/2 T Cinnamon and 1/4 tsp of nutmeg or 1/2 tsp Ground Cardamom, 1 1/4 tsp Vanilla Powder, 1/2 drops Liquid Stevia. Add 2 T Arrowroot powder and 1 T Protein powder or 1 T of Cacao powder. This extra T allows the moisture to dry just enough to form a ball. Follow cooking instructions below. Serve with non dairy whipping cream or vanilla ice cream (page 402).

*Filling ideas are listed below in step 7.
*To make crackers, remove the Psyllium powder and replace with Protein powder and follow the recipes for making crackers. Yes, crackers are made from a batter.

Cooking Instructions:

1. To prepare the cauliflower, using a food processor, rice 1 head of cauliflower (equivalent to 6 cups). Pulse until you get the texture of rice. Depending on the size of the cauliflower head, you may have to do this in more than one batch.
2. Place in a bowl and rinse with water removing any large pieces.
3. Using a large skillet or wok, add the riced cauliflower and cover with water. Remove any large pieces. Bring to a boil and cook on medium high heat for 5 min. It will get foamy and frothy. Next, using a large sieve or a drum strainer, strain water out and press out all the water with a large plastic scraper. At this point, you can use a nut bag to squeeze out the remaining water. It is hot, so be careful to not burn yourself. If you don't have a nut milk bag, a clean kitchen towel will work also, but it is harder to get all the pieces out. A wooden spoon will also push all the water out but the large scraper is best. Once you feel all the water has been removed, place the cauliflower in a large tray or container and set it in the freezer for 10 minutes to cool.
4. Mix the hot Aquaschata™ with the ground chia seeds in a small bowl to thicken.
5. Once the cauliflower has completely cooled, add the remaining ingredients. Using your hands, mix together to form a "dough." It will be mushy. It should be able to hold it's form as a ball.
6. Preheat the oven to 375 degrees F.
7. Depending on the size, on a piece of parchment paper, divide into the size you'd like to shape. Using your hands to make the flat shaped crepe, press into a round shape either 5 inches, 6 inches or 8 inches. Use 1/3 or 1/2 cup measurement cups to keep the shapes consistent.
6. Bake them in the oven for 30 minutes or until they are somewhat firm. Not crisp and not cracker like. You've over baked it if it's cracker like. They will be thin and pliable.

***For Savory, serve with my lemon basil pesto, sun-dried tomato pesto or hummus.
   Or, my creamy chive cream cheese and diced tomatoes or thin cucumbers and lettuce.
   Or, gingered mashed potatoes, wild rice, cranberries, pecans and Mushrooms.
***For Sweet, serve with my blueberry compote and cream cheese or whipping cream.
   Or Vanilla ice cream (Page 402) for a dessert crepe. Apricots or apples diced and
   sautéed in a pan work deliciously. Grate fresh ginger and sauté in water
   with some extra Liquid Stevia.

Collard Green Wraps
☆☆☆☆☆

Collard Greens, where I live, are often huge in the summertime. Substituting this dark green leaf for tortillas is a perfect solution when one can't eat grains and wishes to have some kind of "normal." This is a good recipe to satisfy that comfort need for a wrap. To be able to pick up your food with your hands and eat it. These work great will any kind of filling, including portabella mushrooms. I use this as a wrap in my Portabella Wellington.

Ingredients
large skillet
1 bunch Collard Greens
water

Cooking Instructions:
1. Rinse any dirt off of the collard greens before cooking them.
2. Cut and remove 2 - 3 inches of the thick stem.
3. Fill a large skillet with approximately 1/4 inch or 1/3 inch water and turn to medium high heat.
4. Place the large leaf inside the skillet. It should mostly fit. As the leaf steams, it will soften and fit better.
5. Steam for 3 - 4 minutes or until soft and pliable but not tearing. Set aside. Steam the remaining.
6. To fill, simply use it like any wrap. Folding the top over and bringing the sides in and rolling the top down in a wrap fashion.

Filling ideas: Cooked lentils, Portabella Wellington (Page 253), Carrot Beet Salad (Page 146), Tofuna (Page 149), Pumfu scramble, Rice and beans, Quinoa or Jasmine rice.

Entrées
Breakfast Style

Basic Crepe Recipe..237

Crepes with Nectarine and Raspberry Coulis....................239

Mini Waffle Bowls...240

Fluffy Pancakes with Marionberry Compote.....................241

Potato Latkes..243

Jalapeno Sweet Potato Pancake..244

Basic Crepe Recipe *makes 14 - 6" crepes*
☆☆☆☆☆

This is a delicious and very simple recipe. What I love about it is you can be as creative as you'd like with it. Add Basil for a savory crepe. Add Pumpkin Spice for a delicious holiday treat filled with a dessert filling. Other variations are listed below.

Ingredients
1 cup Millet flour
1/2 cup Arrowroot flour
3/4 cup White Bean flour (Baby Lima Bean)
1 T Coconut cream
1 T Aquaschata™
1/4 tsp Vanilla powder
1 T Cinnamon
15 drops Liquid Stevia
2 cups Oat milk (or any plant based milk)
1/2 tsp Salt

Cooking Instructions:
1. Place all the ingredients into the blender and blend on med. to high for a minute or two. Make sure everything is well blended.
2. Use a non stick pan, heat on medium to high heat. Crepes are VERY picky for temperature! Extremely picky. You may end up losing the first 2 or 3 crepes until you get it right. One trick, if you don't want to use oil, is to get the first crepe in a well seasoned perfect temperature pan. Take a little oil from a nut butter and drip in the pan. Using a paper towel, wipe the oil on the entire pan. An 8 inch pan works best. That way you have better control. After you've wiped the nut butter oil to season the pan, pour in 3 T of batter or so making a 6 inch crepe. Move the batter around by lifting the pan by its handle, so it's thinly distributed. **This is key.** The thinner it is, the quicker it will cook. Sometimes throwing out the first 2 or 3 crepes happens to get the correct temperature. Don't give up. Trust. It works!
3. Once you have the perfect heat in the non stick skillet, cook on one side for 2 minutes and then flip as soon as it appears to be drying out. Flip and cook 30 seconds on the other side. Remove onto plate. Stack them as you go.
4. Store in refrigerator up to 4 days. Because they have beans in them, they tend to spoil quicker. Freezing them is best if you can't eat all of them right away.. Use

freezer paper or parchment paper between crepes so they don't stick together.

Notes: These are not considered sweet crepes. They are a perfect balance. The stevia in these cuts any bean flavor out. Ironically, the cinnamon can't be detected much either. It is a true reflection of a "normal" tasting crepe. Add a pinch of black salt for the sulfur of eggs to come through and create a flavor similar to a real egg crepe ... it's amazing. Any adjustments made will alter the flavor for savory or sweet, as you choose. If not, let the filling do all the sweet and savory for you.

Crepes with Nectarine and Raspberry Coulis *serves 5*
☆☆☆☆☆

Melt in your mouth crepes. Fill with peaches, blueberry compote or any other fruit that calls to you.

Ingredients
1 Recipe Basic Crepes (Page 237)
1 Recipe Raspberry Coulis (Page 399)
1 Recipe Coconut Whipping Cream, *optional (Page 377)*

3 cups White Nectarines, chopped (roughly 5 nectarines)
1 T Cinnamon
15 drops Liquid Stevia
2 T Lemon juice
1/4 cup Filtered Water

Cooking Instructions:
1. Prepare the nectarines. In a bowl, add the remaining ingredients, except the water.
2. In a large skillet, cook over medium high heat sweating down the nectarines. Approximately 5 - 8 minutes. Halfway through, as the pan begins to get dry, add the 1/4 cup water and watch it caramelize the nectarines.
3. Take a 1/3 cup measurement and scoop the filling and place in the crepe. Roll it up and tuck the seam side down. Drizzle the Raspberry coulis on top and a dollop of Coconut Whipping Cream or vanilla ice cream if it's a dessert crepe.

Suggested Variations for fillings: *Fill with Hazelnut Cream Cheese or Hazelnut Cauliflower Ricotta Filling. Fill with Basil and Collard Greens Pesto Ricotta. Or the Raspberry filling from the Cannoli. These can be eaten savory or sweet. Use them as a sandwich wrap and use the Cilantro Garlic Aioli as a spread.*

Mini Waffle Bowls *makes 13 (Will need Mini Waffle Bowl Maker)*
☆☆☆☆☆

This is definitely a different way of enjoying your waffles. What is a waffle bowl? A waffle bowl is made with a mini waffle iron shaped like a small bowl. There are some that are double and some single. It goes quicker with the double. It doesn't need oil as it has a non-stick surface. They can be a bit slow to make, however, once you have them made, they store in the freezer and you can pull one out anytime. Just pop it in the toaster oven and bake it again, like a frozen waffle. It's perfect with ice cream, sorbet, yogurt, fresh fruit, or whipped cream. They can be used in so many ways.

Wet Ingredients
1/2 cup mashed bananas (the blacker they are the sweeter they will be)
1 T Aquaschata™
1 tsp ground Flax seeds
1 1/4 cup Oat Milk (any plant-based milk works)

Dry Ingredients
1 cup Sweet Rice flour
1/2 cup Millet flour
3/4 tsp Baking powder
3 T ground, roasted Walnuts
3 tsp Cinnamon
1/2 tsp Vanilla powder (optional)
1/2 tsp Salt

Cooking Instruction:
1. In a small bowl, add all the wet ingredients.
2. Mix the dry ingredients in another bowl.
3. Add the wet ingredients into the dry bowl and mix until a batter is formed.
4. Turn on your mini waffle bowl waffle maker.
5. Add 2 T of batter and allow for 2 cycles to go through before they are done. Remove and shape if necessary. Use a firm spatula to peel it out if necessary. Allow it to cool and then place in a container in the freezer.
6. For serving, use toaster oven until it is to your desired cook. Add yogurt, fruit, ice cream, compote, coulis, sorbet. Whatever puts a smile on your face! Very Kid friendly!

Fluffy Pancakes with Marionberry Compote *makes 16 pancakes*

☆☆☆☆☆

These are super light and fluffy. One of the best pancake recipes that the whole family enjoys. These are a winner. Serve with Coconut Whipping cream and they are hands done the kids favorite! Serve with Vanilla ice cream (Page 402) and it makes a great dessert.

Dry Ingredients
1 cup Sorghum flour
1/2 cup Arrowroot powder
1/2 cup Brown Rice flour
2 T ground Chia Seeds
2 T Baking powder
1 - 2 T Cinnamon
1 T Cold Inulin
1 tsp Vanilla powder
1/2 tsp Salt

Wet Ingredients
1 1/2 cups Oat milk
1/2 cup Applesauce
2 T Aquaschata™

Marionberry Compote
2 cups Marionberries (frozen)
2 T Lemon Juice
2 tsp Arrowroot powder
9 - 15 drops of clear Liquid Stevia

Cooking Instructions:
1. In a Mixing bowl add all the dry ingredients.
2. In a smaller bowl add all the wet ingredients.
3. Add the wet ingredients to the dry Mixing bowl. Mix thoroughly.
4. On a hot griddle (350 degrees F) or non stick pan, scoop 1/4 cup of the batter and pour onto cooking surface. Cook until top surface looks a bit dry before you cook the other side. If you flip them too soon, they will be messy. If you wait till the bottom are golden brown they will flip easily.

5. In a small saucepan add 2 cups of frozen Marionberries and lemon juice and stevia. Bring to a boil and simmer on medium heat for a few minutes. Berries are cooked when they are soft. Add 1 T cold water in a small cup with the arrowroot powder and mix into a liquid. Stir it into the pot of cooked berries and it with thicken immediately. If it doesn't add another tsp of arrowroot powder and water mixture.

Note: *You can make blueberry or strawberry sauce the same way. Just change out the fruit.*

Potato Latkes *makes 8 – 10 Patties*
☆☆☆☆☆

These are so delicious. Another comfort food to add to the healthy alternatives. Serve with some homemade applesauce and enjoy.

Ingredients
1/4 cup Oat milk
2 Potatoes cubed (if you desire, leave skin on, for more nutrients)
3 T Nutritional yeast
1/4 cup + 3 T Brown Rice flour (any flour will do)
1 small Onion, diced
1 tsp Salt
1 T Bragg® Liquid Aminos
1/2 tsp Xanthan gum
1/4 tsp Cream of tartar
1/4 cup +2 T warm water

2 Egg replacer
3 T tapioca flour
2 tsp Baking powder
1/2 tsp Xanthan gum
1/4 tsp Cream of tartar
1/4 cup +2 T warm water

Serve with Applesauce

Cooking Instructions:
1. In food processor, blend all ingredients for 10 seconds.
2. On a non stick griddle, over med. High temperature, spoon about ¼ of potato batter and fry 5 – 10 min. on each side, until golden brown. Remove and set aside.
3. Keep in warm oven (300 degrees) until all are done.

Jalapeño Sweet Potato Pancake *makes 8 – 6" pancakes*
Served with Cilantro Cream Cheese or Green Salsa
☆☆☆☆☆

This grain free pancake is a complete meal all by itself. It's not often that we have savory pancakes, so, offering this recipe expands your dinner options!

Dry Ingredients
1 cup Cassava flour
1/2 cup Teff flour
1/4 cup Arrowroot powder
1 T Baking powder
1/2 tsp Turmeric powder
1 tsp Salt* (omit if salting vegetables first to draw out moisture)

1 ½ cup Filtered water (Add 2 – 4 T to adjust)
2 T Aquaschata™

Vegetables
8 Green onions, cut into 1 inch pieces
2/3 cup Leek, sliced thinly 1 inch pieces
1 cup Zucchini matchsticks
2 Jalapeños, diced
1 Onion, diced
2/3 cup Sweet potato, shredded
1/2 cup Mushrooms, diced

Serve it with Cilantro Cream Cheese (Page 112)
or *Green Salsa (Page 125)*

Cooking Instructions:
1. Prepare all the vegetables.
2. In a large mixing bowl, add all the dry ingredients. Mix well.
3. Slowly pour in the water while mixing. Mix until you've reached a thick batter consistency. If the batter is too thick, adjust with extra water.
4. Mix the vegetables into the batter making sure to coat evenly.
5. Preheat your non stick griddle or pan to 350 degrees F or Medium high heat.

Your pancake will be the size of your pan. Or, if using a griddle, its best to keep them 3 – 4 inches in diameter. Once hot enough, use a ½ cup measuring cup to pour the batter. This also keeps them consistent in size. Using the back of the spoon to spread evenly making them as thin as possible without exposing the griddle or pan. If there are any holes, feel free to scoop more batter into the pan to cover them.

6. Cook for 4 – 5 minutes or until the batter starts to dry up. You can also cover the pan to help cook down the veggies. If using a griddle, cover with a 9 x 13 baking pan.
7. If you covered your pancake, remove the cover and allow the excess steam to evaporate. Press down on the center of the pancake. Once the top of the pancake and sides start to dry up, carefully scrape the sides and check underneath to see if it's lightly golden brown. If so, flip the pancake with a spatula. Cook the other side until golden brown and crisp. If you want extra crispiness, cook over low heat for another 3 – 4 minutes on each side or until it is a deep golden brown. By doing this, you will evaporate any excess moisture and they will be even more crispy and less doughy pancakes.
8. Slice pancake into small squares of bite sized pieces to enjoy with green salsa or Cilantro Cream cheese.

Note: For grain free, use ½ cup of Almond flour to replace teff flour.
A great way to remove excess water is to salt your vegetables first and squeeze out excess liquid before mixing it in the batter. This way the extra moisture is drawn out. If you do that, skip the salt in the batter.

Entrées
Dinner Style

Side Dish

Corn on the Cob with "Butter Sauce"..249

Barbeque Quinoa..250

Jasmine Rice with Lemongrass & Green Onions...............................251

Millet Stuffing with Cashew Gravy...252

Main Dish

Portabella Wellington with Cashew Gravy..253

Pecan Patties...255

Taco Salad...256

Black Bean Yam Quesadillas...257

Entrees
Dinner Style
Continued ...

Main Dish

Mexican Style Millet Polenta	258
Classic Vegan Chili	259
Sunlight Burger	260
Gardenesque Burger	261
Classic Vegan Burger Served with Tahini Sauce	262
Falafels	264
Falafel Waffle Bowl	265
Coconut Lemongrass Thai Dish	266
Vegan BBQ Sauce with Jack Fruit	268

Corn on the Cob with "Butter Sauce" serves 3 - 6
☆☆☆☆☆

What in the world do I put on corn??? This will surprise the whole family to know something can be as delicious as butter on corn ... or at least come close.

Ingredients
1/2 tsp pressed Garlic, or 1/2 tsp Garlic powder
1/4 tsp ground Cumin
1/4 tsp Paprika
dash of Cayenne
dash of Chili powder
2 T Aquaschata™
6 ears Corn, fresh or frozen

Cooking Instructions:
- Combine spice, garlic and Aquaschata™
- Grill or Steam the corn on the cob until tender and done.
- Remove and brush with sauce.

Barbecue Quinoa *serves 6*

☆☆☆☆☆

A wonderful summer picnic dish or buffet table dish. It's light and has a rich flavor.

Ingredients
2 cups uncooked Quinoa
2 T Veggie Paste
4 cups water
1/2 Red Onion, diced
2 Scallions, chopped
1 cup Corn (fresh or frozen)
1 medium Zucchini, grated
1 stalk Celery, diced
1/4 Yellow pepper, diced
1/4 Green pepper, diced
10 Cherry Tomatoes (*Avoid for low Histamine diet*)
3/4 cup Pea Pods
8 - 10 Asparagus stalks, halved
3 - 4 cloves Garlic
2 - 3 tsp Onion powder
1/4 - 1/3 cup chopped Parsley
2 tsp Salt
Pepper to taste
9 drops liquid Stevia
1 can Butter Beans
1 1/2 - 2 cup Barbecue sauce (Page 124 - 125)
Lettuce
Avocado garnish

Cooking Instructions:
1. In a medium size skillet bring to a boil 4 cups of water. Add veggie paste. Add quinoa. Simmer for 15 - 20 minutes until water is gone. Fluff with a fork.
2. Prepare Barbecue Sauce
3. Prepare all the vegetables while quinoa is cooking. In a large skillet, water sauté red onions until soft. Add peppers, asparagus and pea pods and lightly cook them. Do not overcook. Add the cooked quinoa. Add everything else. Heat through. Serve on lettuce greens and garnish with an avocado.

Jasmine Rice with Lemongrass & Green Onions
☆☆☆☆☆

Jasmine rice is a specialty grain that is used often in Thai foods. It has a fragrance that swirls through the kitchen while cooking. It isn't brown so it is not as high in nutrients, but it is another transition to trying new foods. It goes well as a side dish to fish or perhaps, barbecued shish kabobs for a nice outdoor dinner on a hot summer night. Lemongrass can be bought in the bulk herb section of any natural food stores.

Ingredients
1 cup uncooked Jasmine Rice
1 3/4 cup water
2/3 cup yellow Onion, chopped
1/4 tsp Turmeric
1 - 2 T Lemongrass
1 tsp Lemon zest
2 T Lemon juice

Cooking Instructions:
1. In a medium saucepan bring to a boil 1 3/4 water.
2. In the meantime, in a skillet, use water to sauté the onions on medium high heat. After they've softened 3 - 5 minutes, add the turmeric and sauté another 5 minutes.
3. When the water has boiled, add the rice, onions and lemongrass. Cover and simmer until rice is done and all liquid is absorbed, about 18 minutes. Remove from heat and keep covered for another 10 minutes. Fluff with a fork and add lemon zest, lemon juice and green onions.

Millet Stuffing with Cashew Gravy *makes a lot*

☆☆☆☆☆

This has been my Thanksgiving stuffing for over 30 years. Obviously, a family favorite.

Ingredients
4 cups cooked Millet
1 cup Pecans, finely chopped
1 medium Onion, diced
2 stalks Celery, diced
1 1/2 cups Shitake Mushrooms
1/4 cup Parsley, chopped
1 tsp Herbamare® Seasoning
1 T Onion powder
1 T Poultry Seasoning
Salt and Pepper to taste

Cashew Gravy
2 cups water (adjust as needed)
1/2 cup Raw Cashews (soaked for 2 hours in water)
2 T Arrowroot powder
1/2 tsp Salt
1/4 tsp Black Pepper
1 - 2 Green Onions or 1/2 tsp onion powder
2 - 3 T Bragg® Liquid Aminos (optional)
1 T Parsley, minced

Cooking Instructions:
1. Prepare the millet ahead of time. Cooking millet in general is 2 1/2 cups water to 1 cup of millet. Dry toasting the millet will give it a nutty flavor. Cooking millet until fluffy will make this dish more enjoyable.
2. Water sauté in a skillet, the onions, celery and shitake mushrooms.
3. In a large bowl, combine the millet, sautéed veggies and remaining ingredients.
4. In a blender, add the water, cashews, green onions, parsley and Salt or Bragg® Liquid Aminos. Blend for a minute and pour into a saucepan, heating it up. In a small cup, mix the arrowroot flour with 1 or 2 T of cold water and pour it into the gravy. Cook on medium high until the gravy thickens.

  Notes: *Serve with Portabella Wellington (Page 253) or a sweet potato soup.*

Portabella Wellington with Cashew Gravy *serves 4*
☆☆☆☆☆

This is an adapted recipe that originally won 2nd place in Vegetarian Times magazine (Oct. 95). The original dish was made with puff pastry. I also have adapted it using Phyllo dough. This version is the best way to keep it oil free and gluten free. The Portabella mushroom has a meaty consistency and has a full bodied flavor. If you wanted to marinate it before putting it together, I'm sure it would work well. This recipe is extremely quick to put together and has an elegant appearance, so a dinner party would be a good time to serve this, or even Thanksgiving dinner.

Ingredients
8 medium Collard green leaves
4 small-medium size Portabella mushrooms

Filling
10 - 14 Cremini Mushrooms
2 cloves Garlic
1 Green Scallion
1/4 cup raw Pecans

Cooking Instructions:
1. Preheat oven to 400 degrees F.
2. Rinse any dirt off of the collard greens before cooking them.
3. Cut and remove 2 - 3 inches of the thick stem.
4. Fill a large skillet with approximately 1/4 inch or 1/3 inch water and turn to medium high heat.
5. Place the large leaf inside the skillet. It should mostly fit. As the leaf steams, it will soften and fit better.
6. Steam for 3 - 4 minutes or until soft and pliable but not tearing. Set aside. Steam the remaining.
7. In food processor combine button mushrooms, garlic, scallion and pecans. Mix until a fine crumb appears and then drizzle oil in to make a paste.
8. Remove stems from portabella and brush clean. (Do not rinse!) With stem side up, in the center of the mushroom, spread the filling 1/4 inch thick. Do this with each mushroom. Cut them in half with a sharp knife. Place half of the mushroom on a collard green leaf and wrap it by

rolling it, tucking the sides underneath.
9. Place mushrooms with creased side down onto a parchment covered cookie sheet or baking dish. Cover with foil. Bake at 400 degrees for approximately 40 minutes to cook the mushroom all the way through. They vary in size, so bake accordingly.

Creamy Cashew Gravy
2 cups water (adjust as needed)
1/2 cup raw Cashews (soaked for 2 hours in water)
2 T Arrowroot powder
1/2 tsp Salt
1/4 tsp Black Pepper
1 - 2 Green Onions or 1/2 tsp onion powder
2 - 3 T Bragg® Liquid Aminos (optional)
1 T Parsley, minced

- In a blender place all the ingredients. Add to a saucepan and heat until thickens.

Variation - Use the Phyllo Like Dough for wrapping the mushroom (Page 365)

Pecan Patties *serves 6 - 8*
☆☆☆☆☆

1 cup Pecans (grounded up)
1 cup cold water (I added some veggie stock to it)
1 T Bragg® Liquid Aminos
1 1/2 clove Garlic
1/4 cup Onion, chopped
2 T Nutritional Yeast
1 cup quick rolling Oats
1 cup crumbled firm Pumfu (Pumpkin seed tofu)
2 Carrots, shredded
1 - 2 Celery Stalks, diced finely
1/2 tsp Cumin
Red Hot Pepper flakes
Salt and Pepper to taste
Brown Rice flour for dusting patties at end

Cooking Instructions:
1. Preheat Oven to 300 degrees F
2. In a food processor add pecans and grind up. Remove.
3. In processor, add tofu, garlic and onion and combine all ingredients to a crumble. In a med. sized bowl, add the tofu mixture, pecans and all the remaining ingredients. If too moist add more oats and if too dry add more water. Mix well by hand. Using a 1/3 cup measurement or 1/2 cup measurement make patties and coat in flour to keep from sticking. In a non stick skillet or griddle, cook patties on both sides 'til brown.
4. Place in 300 degree F oven for 15 - 20 minutes.
5. Serve as a sandwich with favorite condiments and lettuce, tomatoes if desired.
Freeze any leftover, cooked patties.

Taco Salad *serves 4 - 6*

☆☆☆☆☆

This is a fun family recipe because everyone gets to build their own. It is a very satisfying dish and requires little time in the kitchen. If you're making a transition to eating less meat this would be a wonderful dish to provide those necessary comforts that go in changing your ways. Always make more than you need. It's very addicting and you'll probably want more.

1 1/2up. Black Beans or pinto beans, organic
3/4 cup water
1 large Red Onion, chopped
1 Green Pepper, chopped
1 Red Pepper, chopped
1 Recipe Pico de Gallo (Page 124)
1/4 cup frozen Corn or 1 ear of Fresh Corn (*optional*)
1/2 tsp Taco Seasoning (Page 124)
1 - 2 T Water for sautéing
1 - 2 Tomatoes, chopped
1 Avocado (opt.)
lettuce (shredded)

Homemade corn tortilla recipe (Page 232)

Cooking Instructions:

1. Prepare the Vegan sour cream and refrigerate until served.
   Vegan Sour Cream
   3/4 cup Water
   1 cup Raw Cashews
   1 1/2 tsp Lemon Juice

- Blend water, lemon and cashews until smooth and creamy. Add more nuts if necessary. Then blend in vinegar.

2. In a skillet, sauté onions in water for a few minutes. Add the peppers, corn, Taco Seasoning, and Pico de Gallo. Cook until done. Serve with lettuce, tomatoes and avocado.

Black Bean Yam Quesadillas *serves 6*

☆☆☆☆☆

These quick quesadillas are excellent served with Smoky Apple Salsa (below), but any prepared salsa would be tasty.

Ingredients
1 - 2 T water for sautéing
1/2 Red Onion, finely chopped
1/2 tsp ground Cumin
1 medium Yam, grated (about 3 cups)
15 oz. can Black Beans, drained (any bean works - Adzuki, Pinto, - etc.)
2 cups packed Spinach leaves, chopped
1/4 cup water
1 Recipe Tortillas, 6 - 8 large (Page 229)
Salt
Salsa, for garnish

Cooking Instructions:
1. Heat 1 - 2 T water in a large skillet over medium high heat. Add onion and sauté for 5 minutes until onion begins to soften and brown. Stir in cumin and sauté an additional minute. Add yam, black beans, spinach leaves and water; stir to combine. Cover and cook for 5 - 7 minutes, stirring once, until yam is tender but not mushy. Season with salt.
2. Heat another skillet or nonstick griddle over medium high heat. Place one tortilla in skillet and spoon 1/2 cup of the yam-black bean mixture onto half the tortilla. Fold and cook for 3 minutes, until the bottom is golden, flip the quesadilla and cook for 2 additional minutes. Repeat with remaining tortillas. Serve quesadillas with salsa.

Note: Black beans can be an allergen factor. If you are not able to eat Black beans, you are welcome to try any kind of bean that works for your body type.

Mexican Style Millet Polenta *serves 6 - 8*
☆☆☆☆☆

This is a nice change from the original use of corn. It is easy to digest because millet is considered alkaline and is beneficial for those with corn allergies. Served with corn chips and steamed kale it makes a filling dinner.

Ingredients
2 cups Millet
5 cups water
1 cup Onion
1/2 cup frozen Corn
1/2 cup Salsa (Your choice, red, green or?)
1/2 Green Pepper, chopped
1/2 Red Hot Pepper, diced
2 T Cilantro, minced
1 cup Black Beans
2 T Garlic, minced
1 T Taco seasoning (Page 121)

Cooking Instructions:
1. In a blender, blend millet until it is flour texture.
2. In a large skillet, sauté onions and garlic for 1 - 2 minutes, then add peppers, corn and cilantro for about 8 minutes. Next, add water and salsa and bring to a boil.
3. Mix in millet, black beans and taco seasoning and simmer 10 - 15 minutes, until water is absorbed. Be careful not to burn bottom of pan.
4. Add polenta to a 2 quart loaf pan. Bake for 15 minutes, uncovered at 350 degrees F.
5. Cool for 5 minutes.

Note: *Add a vegan cheese of your choosing and bake until cheese is melted or soft.*

Classic Vegan Chili serves 8
☆☆☆☆☆

This vegan chili is so thick and flavorful, you won't miss the meat! It's a crowd pleasing hit with vegan, vegetarian, and meat eaters alike.

Ingredients
3 medium Yellow Onions
6 cloves Garlic, crushed
2 T Aquaschata™
3 - 15 ounce cans Beans or 4 1/2 cups cooked, dried beans (black, pinto, or kidney)
2 - 32 ounce cans diced Tomatoes
2 - 4 ounce cans Roasted Green Chilies
1 cup Quinoa
1 cup frozen Corn
1/3 cup Chili Powder (standard, not spicy)
3 T dried Oregano
2 tsp Garlic powder
2 tsp Salt
1/4 tsp Black Pepper
9 drops Liquid Stevia
1/8 teaspoon Chipotle Powder

Hot sauce, vegan sour cream, nut cheese, cilantro, or chives for garnish (for vegan, garnish with vegan nacho cheese)

Cooking Instructions:
1. Chop the onions. Mince the garlic. In a large pot, sauté the onions until softened over medium heat, about 5 minutes. Add the garlic and cook another minute.
2. Add the remaining ingredients beans (drained), tomatoes with their juices, green chilies, corn, chili powder, garlic powder, oregano, chipotle powder, Stevia, salt and pepper. Mix to combine. If necessary, add a bit of water to make sure everything is covered. It might be up to 1 cup.
3. Bring to a boil, then simmer for 20 - 30 minutes. Taste and add additional seasonings as desired. Serve with cilantro or chives, vegan sour cream (Page 108) and homemade corn chips (Page 232). And remember … it's always better the second day.

Sunlight Burger

☆☆☆☆☆

This is a grain free Raw Foods Burger option "cooked" in a dehydrator.

Ingredients
1 cup Almonds, soaked 12 - 48 hours
1 cup Sunflower seeds, soaked 6 - 8 hours & rinsed
8 stalks Celery, finely chopped
1/2 cup Red Onion, finely chopped
1/2 cup fresh Parsley, chopped
1 Lemon, juiced
2 T Tahini
1 Garlic, minced to taste
Cilantro, chopped to taste
Salt, to taste

Cooking Instructions:

1. Process all items in a blender or food processor. Make into burgers and dehydrate at 105 degrees for 12 - 24 hours until dry. I had to flip my burgers to get them to dry.

   **The burgers seemed very lemony to me. You might start with a smaller amount of juice and adjust to taste.

Gardenesque Burger

☆☆☆☆☆

Simple and easy. Freeze for a quick meal on busy days.

Ingredients
1 cup Uncooked Brown Rice
2 cups water
Salt

2 cups Raw sunflower Seeds, (toasted optional)
1 tsp Garlic powder
1/2 tsp Thyme
1/2 tsp Oregano
1/2 tsp Cumin
1/2 tsp Herbamare®
1 small Carrot, coarsely chopped
2 T minced Parsley

Cooking Instructions:
1. Cook Rice.
2. Food process sunflower seeds and herbs 'til ground up.
3. Add carrots and parsley and grind coarsely.
4. Add cooked rice and pulse more. (Don't over process)
5. Make patties and cook on non stick griddle.
6. Bake in oven for 20 minutes at 400 degrees F.

Classic Vegan Burger Served with a Tahini Sauce *serves 8*
☆☆☆☆☆

Delicious and supports a busy lifestyle. Make a stack of them and freeze to make these available anytime you need a quick meal. Enjoy in a Cauliflower wrap.

Ingredients
1 med. Sweet Potato
1 cup Millet uncooked
1 1/2 tsp salt
1 med. Carrot, peeled and cut into 1/2 inch rounds
1 Celery stalk, cut into 1 inch pieces
1 small Onion, peeled & quartered
3 med. Garlic cloves
1 cup shelled fresh or Frozen peas
1 cup cooked Garbanzo beans
1 1/2 T Lemon juice
1/4 cup Sunflower seeds, toasted (optional)
1/4 cup Chives, diced
1/4 cup Parsley
1/4 cup Arrowroot flour (OR Brown Rice flour, Oat flour or White Bean flour)
Salt and Pepper to taste

Seasonings:
1 tsp Coriander
1 tsp ground Fennel
1 tsp ground Cumin
1/4 tsp Cayenne pepper flakes

Tahini Sauce
1/4 to 1/2 cup Tahini
3 T Lemon Juice
1/2 tsp Garlic powder or 1 clove garlic
salt and pepper to taste

Cooking Instructions:
1. Bake sweet potato till done, peel and mash. Set aside.
2. Cook millet, add mashed sweet potato to pot of millet.

3. In a food processor, add carrot and celery and chop finely.
4. In a medium skillet, sauté in water, onions and garlic until soft. Add onion and garlic to carrot mix. Use Pulse setting to combine.
5. Cook peas and drain, rinse with cold water and process with Garbanzo beans in food processor until they are a medium fine texture.
6. Add flour, seasonings, lemon juice, chives, parsley, salt and pepper.
7. On a non stick griddle, measure 1/4 cup of batter and make burgers. Cook on griddle for 4 or 5 minutes per side to brown the surface and bake in 350 degree F oven for 20 min.
8. While those are baking, make the Tahini Sauce. Add all ingredients into a seed grinder and blend. Refrigerate until ready to serve.

Notes* serve with Cauliflower Wrap adding lettuce and sprouts.
   When freezing, place wax paper or parchment between patties.

Falafels

☆☆☆☆☆

Ingredients
2 cups Garbanzo Bean flour
4 med Garlic cloves, minced
2 tsp (or 3) Cumin, ground
1 tsp Turmeric
1 tsp Salt
1/2 cup red Onion, minced
1/2 cup water
2 T Lemon Juice
1/4 cup minced Parsley, packed
dash Cayenne Pepper
1 tsp Smoked Paprika or Smoked Salt (optional)

Tahini Sauce
1/4 to 1/2 cup Tahini
3 T Lemon Juice
1/2 tsp Garlic powder or 1 clove garlic
salt and pepper to taste

Cooking Instructions:
1. Mix all the ingredients together. Adjust water if needed. Form large patties or spoon sized ones. On a non stick skillet or griddle, cook for a few minutes on each side.
2. Place in preheated oven at 400 degrees. Using a baking pan, bake for 15 minutes or so (careful not to dry them out). Serve with a Tahini Sauce, cucumbers, tomato, lettuce and shredded carrots, on Naan (Page 214). Or in the following Waffle Bowl.

Falafel Waffle Bowl *makes 13 Mini Waffle Bowls (See photo Page 133)*
☆☆☆☆☆
(Requires Mini Waffle Bowl Maker)
This is a fun creative way of eating a falafel. Make a salad on top with a Tahini or Caesar salad dressing. Or, pipe Beet Hummus on top, giving it a colorful and festive meal. It's a big success at any potluck or gathering.

Ingredients
1/2 cup cooked Chickpeas
1 clove Garlic
1/2 Onion
1/4 cup Parsley
1 cup baby Spinach or Kale
1/4 cup Aquaschata™
1 cup Chickpea flour
1 tsp Cumin
1/2 tsp Salt

Serve with salad or beet hummus.
1 recipe Caesar dressing (Page 152) or Sesame Cream (Page 156)

Cooking Instructions:
1. In a food processor, add garlic, onions, parsley, and Chickpeas. Blend until minced and combined. Add all the remaining ingredients except chickpea flour.
2. Pour into a bowl and mix by hand while adding the Chickpea flour. Add Salt and pepper to taste.
3. Plug in the Mini Waffle Bowl Maker and wait till it heats up. Add about 3 T to the waffle iron and push down to evenly spread batter. It cooks in one round. Use a firm rubber spatula to take them out. If they don't come out easily, they aren't done yet.
4. Eat them right away or store in the freezer.

Coconut Lemongrass Thai dish

☆☆☆☆☆

This is a win, win dish for the whole family. This grain free recipe is a base that allows for the rest of the family to add to it. So, if there are meat eaters in the house, shrimp or chicken can be added to their dishes, allowing you to enjoy this plant based version. There's always a lot of compromises being made in split meals. So, when you can get one that works for everyone, it's a win, win.

Ingredients
1 - 2 stalks Lemongrass, depends on size
1 1/2 cups Broccoli, in florets
1 1/2 cups Cremini Mushrooms, chopped
1 cup Oyster Mushrooms, separated into individual stems
1 1/2 cups Black Kale, chopped
1 1/2 cups Shallots, diced (Onion works too)
1 1/2 cups Carrots, chopped
3 - 4 inches Thai Ginger root (Galangal), sliced
Handful of Thai Basil leaves
1 cup Fresh Basil leaves
1 cup Heirloom Tomatoes, chopped
3 cloves Garlic, chopped and powder
2 Limes, juiced
1/2 tsp Veggie Paste
1 cup Pumfu, cubed
1 quart Coconut milk (Oat Milk is a good substitute)
Water to Sauté
Salt to taste

Cooking Instructions:
1. Prepare all vegetables. With the back of the knife, on the bottom white part, smash the lemongrass, crushing it allowing the fragrance to come out. Chop off about 4 - 5 inches of the bottom.
2. In a large skillet or wok, Sauté the onions and the garlic in water to start. Add the Veggie paste. After the onions sweat for a few minutes, add the carrots, cremini mushrooms and the broccoli. Next, add a quart of Coconut milk. *Oat milk works as well in this dish too.* Next, add the coconut milk to infuse the lemongrass, lime, ginger.

3. Add whole stems of Basil to the dish. Stir every now and then. Add the black kale next. If you need more coconut milk, add it. Start with 3 T lime juice, add garlic powder, and salt.
4. Taste and see what else it needs. Add 1/2 tsp turmeric for color if you'd like. After 10 min, add the oyster mushrooms, tofu and tomatoes. Cover and cook for another 5 min. You want the lemongrass flavors to come through. Add more Veggie paste if the flavors aren't quite there yet.
5. Serve it alone or on a bed of Jasmine rice or grain free pasta. When serving, remember to remove the lemongrass and ginger.

Vegan BBQ Sauce with Jack Fruit

☆☆☆☆☆

Jack fruit offers a "pulled pork" meat effect. With a BBQ sauce, it works brilliantly. Although it doesn't offer protein, it does offer a lot of fiber.

BBQ sauce:
makes 1/2 cup, double it if you need more.
4 T Tomato paste
2 1/2 T Chicory tea (1 1/2 T Chicory crystals steeped in 1/2 cup hot water)
1 T Aquaschata™
1/4 tsp Liquid Stevia
1/2 tsp Onion powder
1/4 + 1/8 tsp roasted Garlic powder (it's less clumping)
1/2 tsp Lemon juice
1/8 tsp Smoked Paprika
1/8 tsp Chili powder (optional)
1/4 tsp salt
1 can Jack fruit

Cooking Instructions

1. Add 1/2 cup of Boiling water into a cup with 1 1/2 T Chicory crystals. Let it steep for 1 min. Strain and set the liquid aside. The longer it steeps, the more bitter it gets. Darken the sauce by changing the amount and steep time of the crystals. The chicory crystals darken the sauce. That is its only purpose.
2. In a small bowl, add Chicory tea to the tomato paste, along with the Aquaschata™, lemon juice, Stevia, garlic powder, onion powder, smoked paprika and salt.
3. Mix all together until you get the desired taste. If you would like it spicier, add chili powder or other hot peppers.
4. To prepare the Jack fruit. Drain a can of Jack fruit and rinse under cold water. Using your fingers, break apart the pieces so they are "shredded." There are some pieces that are hard. Do not use those pieces. Everything you use should be soft enough to break down. The seeds can be mashed if they are soft.
5. Mix 1/2 cup of BBQ sauce into the Jack fruit. Add extra salt.
6. In a small saucepan, heat the mixture for 4 - 5 min.
7. Serve with tortillas (Page 232), bread (Page 183) or rice.
   Optional: *Add different color peppers in the saucepan for added color and crunch.*

Notes

Pasta
Lasagna, Ravioli, Fillings, Red & White Sauces

Pasta Dough..272

Lasagna with Basil & Collard Pesto & Macadamia Cauliflower Ricotta Cheese...273

Cannelloni with Bechamel Sauce................................275

Lemon Basil Pesto Ravioli..278

Sun-dried Tomato Basil & Mushroom Ravioli..........................279

Pumpkin Ravioli with Herbed Brazil Nut Cream Sauce........280

Pasta Dough

☆☆☆☆☆

This is basic pasta dough for Fettuccine, Lasagna sheets, Manicotti, Ravioli or any other pasta you're making. You don't need anything fancy to make this. A simple rolling pin works. However, a pasta machine will make the sheets much thinner. This recipe is exact. Do not try to use less flour or more liquid.

3 T Flax meal
1/2 cup + 2 T Aquaschata™ + 1 T water (heated)
2/3 cup Brown Rice flour
2/3 cup Sorghum flour
1/3 cup Arrowroot powder
1 tsp Xanthan gum
1/2 tsp Salt

Cooking Instructions:

1. Heat Aquaschata™ and water.
2. In a small bowl add the flax meal and Aquaschata™ to make the flax egg.
3. In another bowl mix the remaining ingredients.
4. On a table, mound the flour into a small dome and use a spoon to make a well in the center.
5. Pour the flax egg in and with a fork, pulling from the inside flour dome, mix in the flax egg until it's all combined. With your hands, start forming a dough until its all come together. Knead it for a few minutes. Let rest for 5 minutes in a zip lock bag.
6. Depending on what you are making, you will begin dividing up the dough into appropriate sizes for making different pastas or ravioli.

Note: For a grain free version - I've tried making this with white bean flour. It's not stable for spaghetti or fettuccine because I found it breaks easily. However, it is suitable for lasagna sheets or manicotti.

Lasagna with Basil & Collard Pesto & Macadamia, Cauliflower Ricotta Cheese

☆☆☆☆☆

Serves 4 - 6 Prep time 1 hour, Bake time 45 min.

Lasagna is one of those foods that takes a lot of time prepping the sauce and making the pasta dough. There are some shortcuts that have been included here, making the prep time less. If you are busy, then you can make this in stages. The ricotta cheese is only fresh the first day. If you make this ahead of time, then freeze it until you use it.

Ingredients
1 Recipe Pasta Dough (Page 272) or 1 package gluten free Lasagna Noodles

1 28 ounce can Organic Whole Plum Tomatoes
1 14.5 oz. can of Organic fire roasted diced Tomatoes
1 cup Sun dried Tomatoes, cut into desired pieces *(optional)*
1 large Onion, sliced
2 - 3 cups Mushrooms, sliced
Green, Red or Yellow Peppers, diced *(optional)*
2 T dried Oregano
1/4 diced Parsley *(optional)*
Freshly ground Pepper to taste
1 - 2 tsp Salt
1/4 tsp Red Pepper Flakes (optional)

2 cups Zucchini rounds
Spinach or Kale leaves, chopped

Basil & Collard Green Pesto
(half goes into Ricotta recipe and half goes into Tomato sauce)
2 cups Fresh Basil leaves
2 large leaves raw Collard Greens (remove stems)
5 cloves Garlic
1/2 cup Artichoke Hearts (1/2 can)

1 Recipe Macadamia Cauliflower Ricotta Cheese (Page 109)

Cooking Instructions:

1. If you are making the pasta dough, prepare the dough and cut them into appropriate lasagna noodle shapes. 3 x 10 inches.
2. Cook approximately 12 lasagna noodles for a 9 x 13 baking pan. Be careful not to break them when you are removing them out of the water with tongs. If you are making the pasta yourself, you can always make more since there's plenty of leftover dough. Rinse under cold water and place on a cookie sheet flat until you are ready to work with them.
3. Prepare the cauliflower to make the ricotta cheese (Page 109)
4. Prepare the Pesto in a food processor.
5. In a large skillet, over medium - high heat, sauté the onions in water for a few minutes, until they are translucent. Add the mushrooms and peppers and sauté another few minutes.
6. While those are sautéing, in a blender, add all the cans of tomatoes and seasonings. One half of this mixture will be added into the pesto in the blender. The other half will be mixed into the pesto, for flavoring the Ricotta cheese.
7. After blending the sauce, pour into the sauté of vegetables. Cover and let simmer for 30 min. Add water if necessary. Taste and season. Does it need more salt? More garlic powder? There's a lot of garlic in the pesto, so it doesn't necessarily need it yet. Take that into consideration. Does it need more nutritional yeast?
8. Building your lasagna. Using a ladle, spoon 2 or 3 scoops on the bottom of your pan. Just barely enough to cover it. Add a layer of noodles, 3 in one direction touching and one going horizontal covering the whole pan. Next, ladle another batch of sauce over the noodles. Place a layer of zucchini rounds from one end to the other, touching each other. Next, add the macadamia nut and cauliflower ricotta cheese, spreading it over the zucchini slices. Add another few ladles of sauce and place the next layer of lasagna noodles, just like the first layer. Add the kale or spinach in a nice thick layer cover. Next, add another layer of ricotta cheese and more sauce. Finally, the last layer of lasagna noodles. Add more sauce on top and garnish with some decorative noodles strips or diced basil leaves. Something to give it a finishing touch.
9. Cover dish with Aluminum foil and bake at 350 degrees F for 30 minutes. Remove foil and bake another 10 min. Remove from oven and let it rest for 5 minutes. Serve with a salad and bread.

Cannelloni with Béchamel Sauce

★☆☆☆☆

This recipe delivers the depth and flavor of its classic version. This makes double the amount for the effort involved. So you can freeze one for another time. This is a perfect holiday dish or birthday celebration as a lot of steps are involved. It is worth it though!

Ingredients
1 Recipe Pasta Dough (Page 272)

1 28 ounce can Organic Whole Plum Tomatoes
1 14.5 oz. can of Organic fire roasted diced Tomatoes
1/2 cup Sun dried Tomatoes, cut into desired pieces
1 large Onion, sliced
1 package frozen Spinach or equivalent fresh Spinach
1/2 can Black Olives, chopped
2 T dried Oregano
3 tsp Garlic powder
Freshly ground Pepper to taste
1 - 2 tsp Salt

Filling
1 Recipe Macadamia Cauliflower Ricotta Cheese (Page 109)

Macadamia Basil Pesto (makes 1 cup)
1/2 cup Macadamia Nuts (optional, leave out and double the cauliflower)
2 cups Fresh Basil leaves (packed)
2 T Nutritional yeast
1/2 tsp fresh grated Nutmeg
3 T Shallots (diced)
1 T Aquaschata™
1/4 tsp salt
White pepper

White Sauce

Brazil Nut Cream Sauce Makes 1 - 1 1/2 cups

1 T Onion powder
2 stalks Celery, chopped
2 cups Mushrooms, sliced
3 T Coconut cream
1/3 cup Brazil Nuts *(Optional Macadamia or Pili Nuts)*
1 1/2 cups Filtered Water
1/2 T Arrowroot powder
3 fresh Garlic cloves
2 T Nutritional yeast
Salt and Black Pepper to taste

Cooking Instructions:

1. Prepare the Pasta Dough. Make the noodles 6 x 6 squares or 8 x 6 inch rectangle.
2. Make approximately 12 Cannelloni noodles for 2 - 9 x 13 casserole dishes or a baking pan. Be careful not to break them when you are removing them out of the water with tongs. You can always make more since there's plenty of leftover dough. Rinse under cold water and place on a cookie sheet, flat until you are ready to work with them.
3. Prepare the cauliflower to make the ricotta cheese (Page 109) Prepare the Pesto in a food processor.
4. In a large skillet, over medium-high heat, sauté the onions in water for a few minutes, until they are translucent.
5. While those are sautéing, in a blender, add all the cans of tomatoes and seasonings.
6. After blending the sauce, pour that into the sautéed onions. Cover and let simmer for 20 - 30 minutes. Add water if necessary. Taste and season. Does it need more salt? More garlic? Add the olives and the spinach. Does it need more nutritional yeast?
7. Prep the Brazil nut cream sauce and set aside.
8. Building your Cannelloni. In a casserole dish or baking dish, add 6 Cannellonis. Each individual pasta square goes in the dish, one at a time and is filled with the filling. It is folded over itself like a log, so the

filling goes lengthwise. Start with 1/3 cup and fold over and see what that looks like. Does it need more stuffing? Less? It all depends on the size of the cannelloni. Once each of them is filled, start on the next casserole dish for freezing. Then cover both dishes with Sauce generously. Making sure there's plenty in-between.

9. Cover dish with Aluminum foil and Bake at 350 degree F, for 30 minutes. Remove foil and bake another 10 min. Remove from oven and let it rest for 5 minutes. Heat the Brazil nut cream sauce up and pour over each Cannelloni. Serve with a salad and fresh rolls or bread sticks. They are great for soaking up the sauce.

Cooking Instructions for Brazil nut Cream Sauce (Béchamel Sauce):
1. In a med-large skillet sauté onions in water 2 - 3 minutes. Add mushrooms and sauté another 3 - 4 minutes.
2. In a seed grinder, grind Brazil nuts to a fine powder. In a blender Add water and blend 1 - 2 minutes.
3. Add milk to saucepan and bring to a boil and mix continuously. Heat until thickens and remove from heat. Pour over cooked Cannelloni.

Cooking Instructions for Macadamia Basil Pesto:
1. In a seed grinder, grind the Macadamia nuts to a fine ground.
2. Add all the remaining ingredients in the seed grinder and blend until smooth and creamy.

   Note: Macadamia nuts will have grit in the pesto (especially in ravioli it will be noticeable) if you don't cream it completely. Test for big chunks or pieces.

Lemon Basil Pesto Ravioli *makes 1 cup*

☆☆☆☆☆

Ingredients
1 Recipe Fresh Pasta dough (Page 272)

Filling
1/2 cup Macadamia Nuts
1 cup Fresh Basil leaves (packed)
3 T Lemon Juice
2 T Nutritional Yeast
1/2 tsp fresh grated Nutmeg
3 T Shallots (diced)
1 T Aquaschata™
1/4 tsp Salt
White pepper

Cooking Instructions:

1. Prepare one recipe of fresh pasta dough and set aside to make the filling.
2. In a food processor, add all ingredients and process until it has a super smooth texture. You don't want the macadamia nut to be gritty. If you need to add it to a seed grinder to blend it even further, please do so. It needs to be smooth or the grit of the macadamia nut takes away from being the perfect ravioli.
3. Prepare the dough in the pasta machine (or hand roll) to make thin sheets.
4. There are many different ways to make ravioli. A round circle folded in half makes a half moon and is the quickest. Use only 1/2 tsp of filling per ravioli.
5. Wet the edges of the dough by dipping a pastry brush in water. Using your fingers to pinch the edges will easily seal the ends.
6. You can take a round and place it on top of another round cut out to have twice as much dough and filling. It's a personal choice how you like your ravioli. There are many shapes. Many different kinds of cutters with straight edges and frilly edges. In general, the rule of thumb is 1/2 tsp of filling. If you were making Tortellini, then use 1/4 tsp.
7. Boil a pot of water (with salt) and boil pasta 3 - 4 min. It cooks quickly, but not as fast as regular pasta dough. If there are no holes in the dough, it will not fall apart.
8. Serve it with Brazil nut cream sauce (Page 280), or Oat milk Cream Sauce.

Sun-dried Tomato Basil & Mushroom Ravioli
☆☆☆☆☆

The Sun-dried tomato filling is very versatile. It can also be used in a spaghetti sauce. It has a "meat-like" appearance. It's been a big family favorite.

Ingredients
1 Recipe dough for Fresh Pasta (Page 272)

Filling
1/4 cup Sun-dried Tomatoes
1/4 cup boiling water
1/2 cup Pecans (roasted, optional)
2 cups Cremini Mushrooms (chopped)
1 - 2 T Garlic, minced
1/3 cup Fresh Basil leaves (packed)
1/4 tsp Salt
Pepper to taste

Cooking Instructions:
1. Prepare one recipe of fresh pasta dough, set aside to make the filling.
2. Soak Sun-dried tomatoes in hot water for 10 - 15 min.
3. Sauté garlic and mushrooms in water.
4. Add all ingredients (including the liquid from the sun-dried tomatoes) into a blender or food processor and blend until it has a smooth texture.

Prepare the dough
Work dough in the pasta machine (or hand roll) to make thin sheets.
1. There are many different ways to make ravioli. A round circle folded in half makes a half moon and is the quickest. Use only 1/2 tsp of filling per ravioli.
2. Wet the edges of the dough by dipping a pastry brush in water. Using your fingers to pinch the edges will easily seal the ends.
3. You can take a round and place it on top of another round cut out and have twice as much dough and filling. It's a personal choice how you like your ravioli. There are many shapes. Many different kinds of cutters with straight edges and frilly edges. In general, the rule of thumb is 1/2 tsp of filling. If you are making Tortellini, that uses 1/4 tsp.
4. Boil a pot of water (with salt) and boil pasta 3 - 4 min. It cooks quickly.
5. Serve with Brazil Nut Cream Sauce (Page 280) or an Oat milk cream sauce.

Pumpkin Ravioli with Herbed Brazil Nut Cream Sauce

☆☆☆☆☆

makes 1 - 1 1/2 cups

This cream sauce has such a full body flavor and is such a totally satisfying experience, you will want to eat all of it. So, make plenty if you want leftovers.

Pumpkin Ravioli Ingredients
1 Recipe Pasta Dough (Page 272)

3 cups cooked Pumpkin or Butternut squash
1 cup Onion, diced
3 cloves Garlic, minced
1/2 tsp dried Sage (or poultry seasonings)
1/2 tsp fresh grated Nutmeg
2 T Nutritional Yeast
1 T Lemon Juice
9 drops of Pumpkin Spice Liquid Stevia (or plain)
4 ounces Pumfu (or 1/2 cup Roasted Cashews ground up)
1/2 tsp Salt
Pepper

Sauce Ingredients
1 red Onion, chopped
2 stalks Celery, chopped
2 cups Mushrooms, sliced
2 T Coconut cream
1/2 cup Brazil Nuts *(Optional Macadamia or Pili nuts)*
2 cups water
1 T Parsley
1 T Currants
1/2 Arrowroot Powder
1/4 tsp Cinnamon
1 - 2 tsp Garlic Powder
1/2 tsp Poultry Seasonings
1/2 tsp Rosemary
1 - 2 T Nutritional Yeast
1 T Bragg® Liquid Aminos (optional)
Salt and White Pepper to taste

Cooking Instructions:

1. Prepare the Ravioli filling. Using cooked or canned pumpkin (or Butternut Squash) add to food processor with remaining filling ingredients. Blend until completely smooth and creamy. Set aside.
2. Prepare the Pasta dough and follow instructions for making ravioli. Make the ravioli and add 1/2 tsp of filling per ravioli. You can pipe it from a piping bag or use a 1/2 tsp measurement. Boil the water, cook the ravioli and prepare and serve with the Herbed Brazil Nut cream sauce.
3. In a med-large skillet sauté onions in water 2 - 3 minutes. Add mushrooms and sauté another 3 - 4 minutes.
4. In a seed grinder, grind Brazil nuts to a fine powder. In a blender, add water and blend 2 minutes or so. Add parsley and blend again.
5. Add milk to skillet and bring to a boil. Add flour and mix continuously. Add currants, seasonings, Bragg® Liquid Aminos to taste and nutritional yeast. Heat until thickens and remove from heat. Pour over pasta of choice.

Desserts
Muffins, Donuts, Pastries, Cookies, Eclairs & Profiteroles

Basic Muffin Mix..286

Spiced Squash Nut Muffins with Apricot & Ginger........288

Millet & Sweet Rice Muffins with Apricot Puree

    & Raspberries………………………………………289

Basic Donut Recipe..291

Chocolate Donuts..293

Cinnamon Hole..295

Cinnamon Rolls with Yeast & Rise Time............................297

Profiteroles & Mini Eclairs..300

Oatmeal Walnut Currant Cookies..303

Hemp Teff Cookies..305

Chocolate Hemp Cookies...307

Basic Cookie Recipe………………………………………309

  Cream Filled Cookies...311

  Cashew Butter Cream Frosting……………………………313

  Cacao Hazelnut Pinwheel Cookie……………………….314

  Raspberry Cannoli...317

  Gingersnap Cookies or Gingerbread Houses...................321

Baking Tips; Tricks that develop with a lot of practice.

- Baking with whole foods can be tricky. The light, spongy texture does not always happen when the timer says they're done. Since there is no oil, or sugar, there are a few noticeable differences. I offer recipes that deliver the "missing" component. And it's not noticeable. Since baking without sugar lacks caramelization and has a different color. This book offers way to counter that… results are, no sugar will not be noticeable.

- The weather does play a role in how bread/baked goods turn out. Depending on how much moisture is in the air, it can delay something from cooking at a "normal time." The Northwest tends to be generally moist outside (that is an understatement); so you may want to use a little more flour than called for in the recipe. It's difficult to give instructions for this because it comes right down to the feel of the batter. Which comes with experience. If the batter seems soupy, then add a bit more dry ingredients. If it seems overly dry, then add just a tiny bit of water at a time.

- Inserting a toothpick in the center and throughout the cake lets you know if the batter has been cooked. If the toothpick comes out clean, then you're doing okay. If not, pop it back in the oven for another 5 minutes or so.

- Cookies are another tricky item, if you overcook them, they'll be dry, so at first, begin with a habit of undercooking them. Remember they will continue to cook on the cookie sheet 1 - 2 minutes longer after they are removed from the oven. Now, the size of the cookie will determine how long they stay in the oven. The bigger they are, the longer they take. You want them to be lightly browned on the bottom and golden on top.

- Scooping cookies - Use an ice cream scoop for consistent shape and size. They vary in size from a 2 T scooper to 1/2 cup scooper.

- Storing - If you like moist and chewy cookies, store them in a Tupperware container with a piece of bread. The cookies draw the moisture out of the bread keeping the freshness of the cookies at their peak. If you like them crunchier, then this doesn't matter.

- Coconut Cream - to get the cream easily, after its been refrigerated, open the can upside down and pour out the liquid. The remaining is all cream.

- Parchment paper can be used many times after it's been in the oven.

- Psyllium Husk powder makes an excellent "gluten" substitute in recipes that are gluten free and need some kind of "elasticity" in the end product.

- Xylitol works exceptionally with citrus lemons and limes removing the weirdness of it. That also goes away in baking.

- Monk fruit and xylitol works well in a 1/32 tsp to 1 T ratio. This balances out the weirdness of their flavors as well.

- Zesting citrus fruits like lemons, oranges and limes are easier to do before you cut them or juice them. It's easy to forget this step. Carrot peelers work well at removing the skin of citrus fruits. Then, using a knife, dice it. You can also put the peels in a dehydrator and once dehydrated, put them into a seed grinder making your own citrus powder.

- Essential oils - Using essential oils not only adds a bonus flavor, they have properties that are healing as well.

- Brushing Aquaschata™ on the bread, or anything that you'd like to have a golden brown color, works beautifully.

- Brush Aquaschata™ or coconut milk on cake pans, and add flour on bottom and sides of cake pans to prevent sticking. Or, use parchment paper on the bottom and sides of cake pans.

- Zip lock bags work well for a "quick fix" for a piping bag. With and without the piping tip.

Basic Muffin Mix *makes 24 mini muffins*
☆☆☆☆☆

I get asked a lot if there is a muffin recipe that works. I like this one because it allows for the variations to be used. Below is a list of many different variations. Get creative ... come up with your own variations, as well.

Dry Ingredients
2/3 cup Brown Rice flour
1/4 cup Buckwheat flour
1/2 cup Oat flour
1/2 cup Sorghum flour
1 tsp Baking powder
1 tsp Xanthan Gum
3/4 tsp Salt

Egg Replacer for 3 Eggs
4 1/2 T Tapioca flour
3 tsp Baking powder
3/4 tsp Xanthan gum
1/2 tsp Cream of tartar
1/2 cup + 1 T warm water

Wet Ingredients
1 cup + 2 T Oat Milk or Nut milk
1/4 cup Angel Butter (Page 107)
3 T Aquaschata™
1/2 tsp Liquid Stevia

Cooking Instructions: Preheat oven to 350 degrees F
1. In a large mixing bowl stir together the dry ingredients.
2. Make the 3 egg replacer and mix in with Aquaschata™.
3. Make a well in the center of the dry ingredients.
4. Pour wet mixture into well, blend thoroughly.
5. Using non stick mini muffin pans, Silpat mini muffin molds or line with paper baking cups; fill 3/4 full.
6. Bake in a 350 Degree F oven for 25 - 30 minutes or until golden brown. Set cooking rack just below center for best results. Remove from pans. Let cool.

Variations:

Blueberry Muffins: Prepare the basic mix above, and add combine 3/4 cup frozen blueberries, thawed, and 2 T Xylitol. Add 1 teaspoon finely shredded lemon peel. Carefully fold into batter.

Cranberry Muffins: Prepare the basic mix above, and add coarsely chop 1 cup fresh or frozen cranberries and combine with 1/4 cup Xylitol. Fold into batter.

Apple-Cinnamon Raisin Muffins: Prepare the basic mix above and add stir 1 T ground cinnamon into the flour mixture. Fold 1 cup chopped, peeled apple and 1/2 cup Raisins or Currents into batter.

Jelly Muffins: Any coulis makes an excellent "jelly" filling. Or, make the Macadamia nut cauliflower ricotta filling. (Eat fresh or freeze) That makes an excellent frosting or filling. Prepare the basic mix above, pipe the coulis with a #12 tip, into the muffin.

Banana-Chocolate Muffins: Prepare the basic mix above, except, decrease milk to 1/2 cup. Stir in 1 cup mashed banana and 3 T Cacao powder into.

Pumpkin Muffins: Prepare the mixture above, adding 2 T Date Nectar and 1/4 cup Xylitol. Add 1/2 cup canned pumpkin to egg replacement mixture. Combine 1 T ground cinnamon and 1/2 teaspoon ground nutmeg into flour mixture. Stir 1/2 cup raisins into batter.

Lemon Poppyseed: add 1/2 cup lemon juice, 1/4 cup + 2 T Oat milk and 1/2 tsp lemon stevia and 2 T poppyseeds.

Spiced Squash Nut Muffins with Apricot and Ginger

☆☆☆☆☆

makes 18 muffins

This is my sons first birthday "cake." It is allergen friendly, and loaded with vitamin A.

Dry Ingredients
1 cup Teff flour
1 cup Brown Rice flour
1/2 cup Arrowroot powder
1/2 cup Millet flour
1 T Baking powder
1 tsp Salt
1 tsp Vanilla powder
1 tsp Cinnamon
2 tsp ground Cloves
2 tsp ground Cardamom

Wet Ingredients
2 cups cooked Squash - mashed or pureed Hubbard or butternut
5 Dried Apricots (soak 30 minutes in 1/2 cup hot water)
1 T grated Ginger or 1 tsp ginger powder (mix into apricots)
1/2 - 3/4 cup unsweetened Applesauce
1/2 cup Oat Milk (or rice milk)

2 cups Pecans or Walnuts, chopped (optional)

Cooking Instructions:
1. Preheat oven to 375 degrees F. Use non stick muffin tins or line with paper muffin cups.
2. Process softened apricots with soaking water and ginger in seed grinder.
3. Mix together flours, baking powder, salt and spices in a large bowl. Set aside.
4. Put squash, applesauce, oat milk, vanilla and apricot puree. Mix together in blender or by hand.. Add wet ingredients to dry and fold gently, using a minimum of strokes.
5. Gently fold pecans into batter. Fill muffin cups to top with batter. Bake 25 - 35 minutes, until a toothpick comes out clean.

Millet and Sweet Rice Muffins with Apricot Puree and Raspberries
☆☆☆☆☆
makes 12 muffins

This muffin recipe is light and airy giving the texture of muffins as they normally are. Millet and Sweet Rice make a good pairing of flours. The puree and raspberries make up for the dryness these two flours tend to be, making for a good muffin.

Dry Ingredients
1 cup Millet flour
1/4 cup Sweet Brown Rice flour
1/4 cup White Bean flour
3/4 cup Xylitol
2 T Poppyseeds
1 tsp Baking powder
1/2 tsp Baking soda
1/2 tsp Cinnamon
1/2 tsp Salt
1 1/4 cup Raspberries (fresh or frozen)

Wet Ingredients
1 Chia Egg (1 1/2 T chia ground chia seeds to 4 T hot water)
2 T Aquaschata™
1/2 tsp Liquid Stevia
1/2 cup filtered water (varies)
1/2 cup Apricot puree, 3 med size apricots (soak in 1/2 cup hot water for 30 min, discarding the water when done).
Add soaked apricots to 1/4 cup warm water, puree in seed grinder. Add enough water to make 1/2 cup puree.

Cooking Instructions: Preheat oven to 350 degrees F
1. Combine all the dry ingredients and set aside.
2. Combine the chia egg, Aquaschata™, water, apricot puree and Stevia. Mix well.
3. Add the wet ingredients, except 1/2 cup water, to the dry and mix (do not over mix). Fold in the raspberries. After its all been mixed together and it's showing how thick it is, then add in 1/4 cup of water and stir until it's a batter for muffins. It will take anywhere from 1/4 to 1/2 cup water for a perfect batter.

4. Pour into muffin tins or Silicone baking mold and bake in a preheated 350 degree F oven for 20 - 30 minutes or until a toothpick comes out clean.

Variations: Blueberry lemon muffins, Blackberry muffins. There are many, many, variations.

Basic Donut Recipe *makes 18 donuts*

☆☆☆☆☆

I can't believe I can eat Donuts again ... When was the last time you had a donut? Exactly! It was that long ago. This recipe is baked not fried. This is also the recipe used for cake pops. It's fun and easy with a 15 minutes prep time and 15 minutes bake time. They freeze great. There are lots of topping ideas. They have been loved by all ages. Especially at a birthday party. Kids can't believe these are healthy.

Dry Ingredients
1 cup Teff flour
1 cup Sorghum flour
1 cup Arrowroot powder
1 T Baking powder
2 tsp Cinnamon
1 tsp Vanilla powder
1/2 tsp Salt

Wet Ingredients
3 T Applesauce
1 cup + 2 T Oat milk
1/2 cup Mashed Bananas (the blacker the better)
1/4 cup Aquaschata™
1/2 tsp Liquid Stevia

Topping ideas
Chocolate Ganache
Cashew Cream - lots of flavors (Chai, Raspberry, Blueberry, Chocolate, Lemon etc.)
Raspberry or Marionberry Coulis
Freeze Dried fruit powders like Raspberry, Passion fruit
Cacao powder
Caramel

Cooking Instructions:
1. Preheat oven to 350 degrees F.
2. Place all the dry ingredients in a large bowl.
3. Mash bananas in a separate bowl and add applesauce, Aquaschata™, Oat milk and Stevia. Whisk to blend.

4. Pour the wet ingredients into the dry ingredients bowl. The batter consistency must be able to come out of a piping bag. If it's too runny, it will make a mess. If it's too stiff it will be hard to pipe the batter. Adding more teff flour to stiffen it and more Oat milk to thin it, as needed.
5. Using a large piping bag and large tip # 808, 809, 824, anything that allows you to easily pipe. If you don't have a piping bag or tip, place batter in a zip lock bag and push it all to one corner. Cut one corner off by 1/2 inch or so and pipe that way.
6. This works best with non-stick donut pans. Usually, 6 on each, unless it's a whole sheet, then they have 18. I find that to be heavy. So the smaller ones work for me. Starting at the top of the circle, pipe your way around twice, ending in the same spot you started. Fill it up while making sure it doesn't spill into the middle.
7. Bake in a 350 degree F oven for 15 min. Or until a toothpick comes out clean. If they overcook, they will be dry. Pop them out of the pan with a rubber spatula right away and place on a cooking rack. Cool completely before topping them. While they are baking, make toppings (Page376 - 389) or prep toppings a day in advance to make it easier for you.

Notes: These are ideal for cake pops as well.

Chocolate Donut Recipe
☆ ☆ ☆ ☆ ☆

Dry Ingredients
1 cup Teff flour
1 cup Sorghum flour
1 cup Arrowroot powder
3 T Cacao powder
1 T Baking powder
2 tsp Cinnamon
1 tsp Vanilla powder
1/2 tsp Salt

Wet Ingredients
3 T Applesauce
1 1/4 cup + 1 T Oat milk (add 1 T at a time if it needs to be thinned)
1/2 cup Mashed bananas (the blacker the better)
1/4 cup Aquaschata™
1/2 tsp Stevia

Toppings
Caramel
Marionberry Coulis
Chocolate
Cashew Cream

Cooking Instructions:
1. Preheat oven to 350 degrees F.
2. Place all the dry ingredients in a large bowl.
3. Mash bananas in a separate bowl and add applesauce, Aquaschata™, Oat milk and Stevia. Whisk to blend.
4. Pour the wet ingredients into the dry ingredients bowl. The batter consistency must be able to come out of a piping bag. If it's too runny, it will make a mess. If it's too stiff it will be hard to pipe the batter. Adding more teff flour to stiffen it and more Oat milk to thin it, as needed.
5. Using a large piping bag and large tip # 808, 809, 824, anything that allows you to easily pipe. If you don't have a piping bag or tip, place in a zip lock bag and

push it all to one corner. Cut one corner off by 1/2 inch or so and pipe that way.

6. This works best with non stick donut pans. Usually, 6 on each unless it's a whole sheet, then they have 18. I find that to be heavy. So, the smaller pans work better for me. Starting at the top of the circle, pipe your way around twice, ending in the same spot you started. Fill it up while making sure it doesn't spill into the middle.
7. Bake in a 350 degree F oven for 15 min. Or until a toothpick comes out clean. If they overcook, they will be dry. Pop them out of the pan with a rubber spatula right away and place on a cooking rack. Cool completely before topping them. While they are baking, make toppings (Page 376 - 389) or prep toppings a day in advance to make it easier for you.

Notes: They are best the first day. After the second day they can dry too much and not be as good. However, if you spritz water on them (if not topped) and place in toaster oven and reheat, they will soften again. A little trick that works with bread, pretzels and donuts.

Cinnamon Holes - *yeast free*
☆☆☆☆☆

Just like a donut hole, the magic of a cinnamon roll is in the center. These Cinnamon holes are packed full of satisfaction. Bite-sized and worth having a recipe on its own.

Dry Ingredients
1 1/4 cup Sorghum flour
1/2 cup Buckwheat flour
3/4 cup Arrowroot powder
1 cup Brown Rice flour
1 T Baking powder
1/2 T Vanilla powder
1 tsp salt

Wet Ingredients
1 cup Applesauce
1/2 cup Aquaschata™
1/3 cup Baked (and cooled) Butternut Squash
1/2 tsp Liquid Stevia

Filling 1
1 cup Date paste (15 Medjool dates soaked in 1 cup hot water)
1 - 2 T Cinnamon

Filling 2 (if you can't have dates, this also works)
1/3 cup Sweet potato or butternut squash pureed
2 T Cinnamon
Yacon Syrup or 1/2 tsp Liquid Stevia

Frosting or Glaze
1 Recipe Cashew Butter Cream Frosting (Page 380)
Or 1 Recipe Cashew Cream (Page 379)

Cooking Instructions: Preheat oven to 375 degrees F

1. In a large mixing bowl, add the dry ingredients. In another bowl add the wet ingredients
2. Pour the wet into the dry and mix, forming a dough.
3. Make the filling. Filling 1, blend the water and the dates in a blender until

creamy and spreadable. Add 1 - 2 T of cinnamon to 1 cup of date paste. Filling 2, puree a sweet potato or butternut squash. Add cinnamon and stevia, or Yacon Syrup. It is another kind of zero calorie sugar that is molasses in texture.

4. Roll out dough, between parchment paper, into a large rectangle. Peel off the top layer and spread the filling nice and thick leaving 1/4 inch around the edges.
5. On the long side, begin rolling, making a nice long log. Place in the refrigerator and chill for 1 hour in order to cut easily.
6. With a sharp knife, cut them into 1 inch rolls and place on a lined cookie sheet. Bake in a preheated oven set at 375 degrees F for 40 - 45 minutes or until golden brown. Cool before eating.
7. Frost with the Cashew Butter Cream Frosting (Page 380) or drizzle with the Cashew Cream (Page 379).

Cinnamon Rolls with Yeast and Rise Time *makes 14*

☆ ☆ ☆ ☆ ☆

These are ooey, gooey good. Definitely worth trying once. Don't let the amount of work intimidate you. They freeze really well. If you can't have yeast, try the Cinnamon Holes recipe. If you can't have dates, there's another filling option just for you.

Activate 1 T active dry yeast in 2 1/2 cups hot water and 1/2 tsp Date Syrup

Dry Ingredients
1/2 cup Buckwheat flour
1/2 cup Arrowroot powder
1/2 cup Brown Rice flour
1 1/4 cup Sorghum flour
1 T Vanilla powder
1 tsp salt

Wet ingredients
4 T Aquaschata™
2 T Applesauce
1/3 cup whole Psyllium Husk
1/3 cup ground Chia Seeds
1 tsp Liquid Stevia

Filling 1
1 cup Date Paste (15 Medjool dates soaked in 1 cup hot water)
1 - 2 T Cinnamon (or to taste)

Filling 2 (if you can't have dates, this also works)
1/3 cup Sweet potato or butternut squash pureed
2 T Cinnamon (or to taste)
Yacon Syrup or 1/2 tsp Liquid Stevia

Frosting or Glaze
1 Recipe Cashew Butter Cream Frosting (Page 380)
Or 1 Recipe Cashew Cream (Page 379)

Cooking Instructions:

1. Place the warm water in a bowl or 4 cup liquid glass measure. Add the yeast and 1/2 tsp of date nectar, whisk together. Cover and let rest for 5 - 10 minutes to activate the yeast. The mixture should get foamy or bubbly. If not, dump it and start again.
2. While the yeast is activating, mix together the dry ingredients in a large bowl.
3. After the yeast is activated, whisk in the Aquaschata™, applesauce, chia seeds and psyllium husks into the water-yeast mixture. Let stand for about 2 minutes to let the chia and psyllium release their gelatinous substances. Whisk again.
4. Pour the wet ingredients into the dry and mix together with a rubber spatula until it is combined and stiff. Then knead the dough in the bowl to incorporate the flour.
   Add more flour if it's sticky. You want it to be moist without the sticky.
   If it's too dry, add more Aquaschata™ to it. 1 T at a time.
5. Next, form the dough into a ball.

First Rise: You have several options depending on how warm or cold it is.
1) If it's hot/warm, place on a cookie sheet on top of a piece of parchment paper and cover with a damp cloth (A damp hefty cheesecloth placed over the top is all you need to do) and set aside for an hour (until it's doubled).

2) If it's cold, a hot water bath works really well. Find a shallow container that you can place the cinnamon roll pan into. Place it in the container and cover with a lid. Pour boiling water to fill the container part way (be sure not to get any of the dough wet). Allow this to rise for an hour.

3) Ninja Foodie 8 qt (or similar instant pot) - Place parchment paper or a silicon mat on the bottom of the pot. Next, add the dough and cover it with a wet/damp cheesecloth and set the dehydrator setting to 100 degrees F for 30 min.

Make the filling. Filling 1, blend the water and the dates in a blender until creamy and spreadable. Add 1 - 2 T of cinnamon to 1 cup of date paste. Filling 2, puree a sweet potato or butternut squash. Add cinnamon and stevia, or Yacon Syrup. It is another kind of zero calorie sugar that is molasses in texture.

Second Rise: Roll out the dough on a Silpat mat in a large rectangle. It might be as large as the Silpat mat! Next, spread the filling nice and thick leaving 1/4 inch around the edges. Depending on what size this is, it might be done twice. Roll the log making a nice, long log.

1. With a sharp knife, cut them into 2 inch rolls and place in a 12 inch cake pan, a 9 x 12 baking pan or two 8 inch cake pans and cover with a damp cloth and set in a warm place. Rest them for an hour or until double in size. Bake in a Preheated oven set at 375 degrees F, for 45 minutes to 1 hour. They will get golden brown. Carefully separate them with a butter knife or a small stiff spatula. Cool on a cooling rack and frost.
2. Frost with the Cashew Butter Cream Frosting (Page 380) or drizzle with the Cashew Cream (Page 379)

Profiteroles and Mini Éclairs

☆☆☆☆☆

Have you ever noticed when you are on a diet, there's a tendency to dream about eating those guilty pleasures? Well dream no more! Inspired by baker and food blogger, Audrey Snowe, you can now delight yourself with this treat without the guilt. Enjoy them with my lemon pastry cream topped with whipping cream. Or fill them with whipping cream and dip them in chocolate. How about making a Raspberry Coulis? Pump it in and dip in chocolate. Top with whipping cream. Or fill them with Vanilla ice cream and dip in chocolate! There are so many ways to indulge with these unconventional treats. This is a very straight forward recipe with several steps to take, but it is worth it. Wow your friends, wow your family. What can be better?

Ingredients
Angel Butter (This makes 1/4 cup)
2 tsp ground Chia Seeds
2 T Coconut Cream (the top only not the liquid, so refrigerate first)
1 T Aquaschata™
1/8 tsp Turmeric powder

1 Egg Replacer
1 1/2 T Tapioca flour
1 tsp Baking powder
1/4 tsp Xanthan gum
1/8 tsp Cream of tartar

Choux Pastry
Dry Ingredients
1/4 cup Brown Rice flour
1/4 cup Arrowroot flour
1 1/2 T + 2 tsp Psyllium **powder**
1 tsp Xanthan gum
1 tsp Vanilla powder
1/8 tsp Salt

Wet Ingredients
1/2 cup + 1 T Oat milk (any plant-based milk works)
1/4 cup of Angel Butter (see above recipe)

15 drops Liquid Stevia

Sweet filling ideas - Lemon Pastry Cream, Coconut whipping cream, Cashew Butter Cream, Raspberry coulis, vanilla ice cream.

Topping ideas - chocolate ganache, raspberry coulis, coconut whipping cream, caramel

Savory Filling ideas - Lemon Basil Pesto, Sun-dried Tomato Pesto, Artichoke Pesto

Cooking Instructions:
1. Preheat oven to 425 degrees F. On a cookie sheet, either use a Silpat mat or line with parchment paper.
2. Prepare the Angel Butter. Make sure the coconut cream has been refrigerated. Have an extra can for the filling or topping as well. In a medium sized pot, whisk all the Angel Butter ingredients until blended. Set aside.
3. In a seed grinder, add the egg replacer ingredients and blend until it's frothy.
4. In a small bowl, add the dry ingredients.
5. Place the Angel Butter pan on a burner and add the Oat milk. On very low heat, melt the coconut cream in the Angel Butter mixture. Do not over heat. You want this to only melt the cream. Do not bring to a boil or raise the temperature past the melting point. Remove from heat.
6. Add the dry ingredients into the milk and mix with a wooden spoon. It will have a mushy texture while having an elastic texture at the same time.
7. Next, add the egg replacer into the pot and mix thoroughly.
8. Place the mixture into a piping bag without a tip. It will be firm but squeezable.
9. Pipe the mixture into 2 - 3 inch rounds or 3 - 4 inch long. Not too long as it will sink in the middle.
10. Lightly wet your finger to smooth out any points left from piping.
11. Bake for 20 - 25 min. at 425 degrees F. They will puff up and brown nicely. If after 20 - 25 minutes they seem like they are crusty and golden brown, lower the heat to 350 degrees F for 5 - 8 more minutes. Then, open the oven door part way and allow them to cool down another 20 minutes to prevent them from deflating. They will be ready to fill once cooled.

Prepare the Filling

While they are baking, you can make the toppings and fillings. If you are making Coconut Whipping Cream, first, place the mixing bowl and whisk into the refrigerator to chill. Make sure the coconut cream was refrigerated as well. See my recipes on how to make these toppings and fillings in the dessert section. Make sure the whipping cream, coulis and lemon pastry cream are all cooled in the refrigerator once made. The chocolate ganache needs to be liquidy and glossy to dip. If you let it cool too much, it will be thicker and sloppy (although it will still taste great).

Assembling:
1. You can either poke a hole in the small rounds and using a piping bag with a round piping tip, fill with your cream or coulis. Then dip the top. Making sure the bottom is able to stand up nicely.
2. You can also cut them in half. The long ones do best this way. However you fill them, they do puff up and can receive a lot of filling. So, play with which one is best. If it's longer, you will need to poke a hole on both sides to get the filling all the way through the center and not just one side to the middle.
3. You can dip the top in your choice of topping . They can be messy to make. Assemble them with kids and see how creative they can be. They freeze well.

Oatmeal Walnut Currant Cookies *makes 2 Dozen*

☆☆☆☆☆

This recipe has been adapted from the original oil, maple syrup recipe. However, it has always had flaxseed as the egg. This recipe is at least 30 years old and has been the most loved and most eaten cookie ever made. They are absolutely delicious and worth making. You can make a bigger cookie and double the recipe. This recipe does not disappoint!

Ingredients
1/2 cup hot water (not boiling)
1/4 cup Flax seeds
1/2 cup Applesauce (unsweetened)
1 tsp Vanilla powder
1/2 tsp liquid Stevia
1 cup Rolled Oats
3/4 cup chopped Walnuts
1/2 cup Currants, sulfur free
1 cup Brown Rice flour
1 tsp Cinnamon
1 tsp Baking powder
1/8 - 1/2 tsp Cardamom powder
1/2 tsp salt

Cooking Instructions:
1. Preheat oven to 350 degrees F.
2. Heat up 1/2 cup of filtered water. Do not boil it. In a small dish add flax seeds and cover with water. Let sit until ready to use.
3. In a bowl, add applesauce, stevia and vanilla and mix together.
4. In another bowl, combine oats, walnuts, currants and brown rice flour.
5. To the dry mix, add cinnamon, baking powder, cardamom and salt.
6. Pour applesauce mixture into the dry and fold until well blended. The flax seeds by now should look like egg white texture (gelatinous). Pour the flax seeds into the batter and with a mixer or hand blender combine and blend until it begins to get lighter in color and mixes altogether. If you need to add more water it's okay. (It will have an appearance of goop.)
7. Spoon or scoop with an ice cream scooper the batter on a Silpat or parchment lined cookie sheet.
8. Bake for 20 minutes or until golden brown on top and brown on

bottom. Let cool completely. Flavor is enhanced overnight if there are any left. These make very good, large cookies. Small too, but if you want a big cookie this will be a success.

Notes: These cookies need to sit for 24 hours in order for the fullness of the flavors to come together. They do not taste the same if you eat them right away. In order to have the perfect balance in flavors, waiting 24 hours will create the perfect cookie. It is well worth the wait. They are absolutely amazing.

Hemp Teff Cookies *makes 25 cookies*
☆☆☆☆☆

These are a great snack for hiking or biking. They are packed full of nutrition and are quite enjoyable. I love the texture. They have a firm, chewy texture, but are light at the same time. They are the perfect cookie for using as an ice cream cookiewich.

Dry Ingredients
1/2 cup Teff flour
3/4 cup Sorghum flour
1/2 cup Arrowroot powder
1/2 cup Hazelnut flour
1/2 cup Xylitol
1/2 tsp Salt
3/4 tsp Xanthan gum
1 tsp Vanilla powder
3/4 cup ground Hemp seeds

Wet Ingredients
1/4 cup Angel Butter (1 recipe) - 2 tsp ground chia seeds, 1 T Aquaschata™,
    2 T Coconut cream, 1/8 tsp Turmeric)
1/4 cup Aquaschata™
1/2 tsp English Toffee Liquid Stevia (optional), use regular Liquid Stevia

Egg Replacer for 1 egg
1 1/2 T Tapioca flour
1 tsp Baking powder
1/4 tsp Xanthan gum
1/8 tsp Cream of tartar
3 T warm water

Cooking Instructions:
1. Preheat oven to 350 degrees F.
2. Make your Angel Butter in a seed grinder and set aside.
3. Make the Egg Replacer egg. Add all the ingredients to either a bowl and use a hand mixer or a seed grinder and froth it. Whisk this into your 1/4 cup of Aquaschata™.
4. Combine all the dry ingredients into a stand mixer. Blend and add the egg

replacer mix with Aquaschata™ and mix for a minute. Next, add the Angel Butter and continue on medium to high speed until a dough is formed. Using a rubber spatula, stop and scrape sides occasionally.

5. Cover the dough in Saran Wrap and place in the refrigerator for 15 min. The dough will be very sticky if you don't.
6. Place a Silpat mat or parchment paper on 2 cookie sheets. With a 2 T ice cream scooper, scoop 2 T of dough and place it on the cookie sheet about 1 inch or so apart. Press down with the palm of your hand. Wet your fingers if sticky. Hot water helps to not stick. If you want this to be perfect rounds, use a small cookie cutter and remove excess dough. Push to about 1/4 to 1/3 inch apart. They don't spread, so you get to choose the size of the cookie. With thicker cookies, they can be cut in half for an ice cream cookiewich.
7. Bake in oven for 15 - 20 minutes.

Chocolate Hemp Cookies *makes 25 cookies*
☆☆☆☆☆

This is similar to the other hemp cookies, but they have cacao powder and chocolate stevia. They taste completely different when the cacao powder is added. They are more flavorful. If you cannot have cacao powder, then use the other recipe and add chocolate stevia to the batter for a chocolate flavor. It's subtle, but it's there. Add stevia to taste.

Dry Ingredients
1/2 cup Teff flour
3/4 cup Sorghum flour
1/2 cup Arrowroot powder
1/2 cup Hazelnut flour
1/2 cup Xylitol
1/2 tsp Salt
1 tsp Vanilla powder
3 T Cacao powder
3/4 tsp Xanthan gum
3/4 cup ground Hemp seeds
1 1/4 tsp Cinnamon

Wet Ingredients
1/4 cup Angel Butter (Page 107)
1/4 cup Aquaschata™
1/2 tsp Chocolate stevia

1 *Egg Replacer*
1 1/2 T Tapioca flour
1 tsp Baking powder
1/4 tsp Xanthan gum
1/8 tsp Cream of Tartar
3 T warm water

Cooking Instructions:
1. Preheat oven to 350 degrees F.
2. Make your Angel Butter in a seed grinder and set aside.

3. Make your Egg Replacer egg. Add all the ingredients to either a bowl and use a hand mixer or use a seed grinder and froth it. Whisk into your 1/4 cup of Aquaschata™

4. Combine all the dry ingredients into a stand mixer. Blend and add the egg replacer. Add Aquaschata™ and mix for a minute. Next, add the Angel Butter and continue on medium to high speed until a dough is formed. Using a rubber spatula, stop and scrape the sides occasionally.

5. Cover the dough in plastic wrap and place in the refrigerator for 15 min. This dough is not as sticky as the other Hemp Teff cookie.

6. Place a Silpat mat or parchment paper on 2 cookie sheets. With a 2 T ice cream scooper or Tablespoon, scoop 2 T of dough and place it on the cookie sheet about 1 inch or so apart. Press down with the palm of your hand. Wet your fingers if sticky. Hot water helps to not stick. If you want this to be perfect rounds, use a small cookie cutter and remove excess dough. Push to about 1/4 to 1/3 inch. They don't spread, so you get to choose the size of the cookie. With thicker cookies, they can be cut in half for an ice cream cookiewich. Ice Cream, Page 402.

7. Bake in oven for 15 - 20 minutes.

Basic Cookie Recipe
☆☆☆☆☆

This basic cookie recipe is a non-sugar, Sugar Cookie. They are great for the holidays because they are the perfect cookie to decorate. They are easy to make and are a base pastry for many other recipes in this book.

Dry Ingredients
1 1/2 cup Almond flour (or 3/4 cup oat flour and 3/4 cup brown rice flour blend)
1/2 cup Arrowroot flour
3 T White Bean flour (baby lima bean)
1 tsp Baking powder
1 tsp Vanilla powder
1/2 tsp salt
   ***Note** - if you don't have white bean flour, use arrowroot instead.*

Wet Ingredients
1/4 cup nut butter or Angel Butter (page 107)
1/4 cup Applesauce, unsweetened
2 T Aquaschata™
1/4 - 1/3 tsp Liquid Stevia

Cooking Instructions:
1. Preheat oven to 350 degrees F

2. Into a large mixing bowl, add in the nut butter (or Angel Butter), applesauce, Aquaschata™, stevia and vanilla, and whisk to combine. Then add in the dry ingredients. Use a silicon spatula and mix well until a dough forms. If it's a little too dry, add some plant based milk, 1 T at a time.

3. Cover work surface with parchment paper, dust surface with some arrowroot powder and then transfer the dough on top. Dust the top of the dough with more tapioca starch and roll it out using a rolling pin, around 1/4 of an inch in thickness.

4. Use a cookie cutter and cut into desired shapes/sizes. Gather scraps, re-roll out the dough and cut more cookies out. Repeat until you run out of dough.

5. Using a spatula, carefully transfer the cookies onto a parchment lined baking tray. Bake for 13 - 15 minutes, or until the edges are ever so slightly golden brown. Remove from the oven and let them cool for 2 minutes on the baking tray. Then, carefully transfer them onto a wire rack to cool completely. Enjoy as is or, after they cool sufficiently, get creative and frost/decorate them to your liking!

6. Store leftovers in an airtight container at room temperature for 2 - 3 days.

   Variations: Try almond flour and almond butter, or sun butter.

Cream Filled Cookies *makes about 24 cookies*

☆☆☆☆☆

Kids love these! Adults love these. I love these. Grain free options as well. Need I say more? This recipe makes a chocolate cookie, however, omit the cacao powder if you aren't eating chocolate.

Dry Ingredients
1 1/2 cup Almond flour (or 3/4 cup oat flour and 3/4 cup brown rice flour blend)
1/2 cup Arrowroot flour
3 1/2 T Cacao powder
3 T White Bean flour (baby lima bean)
1 tsp Baking powder
1 tsp Vanilla powder
1 tsp Xanthan gum
1/2 tsp salt
   *Note - if you don't have white bean flour, use the arrowroot instead.

Wet Ingredients
1/4 cup nut butter or Angel Butter (Page 107)
1/4 cup Applesauce, unsweetened
2 T Aquaschata™
1/4 - 1/3 tsp Liquid Stevia

1 Double Recipe Cashew Butter Cream Frosting (Page 313)

Cooking Instructions

1. Preheat oven to 350 degrees F.

2. Into a large mixing bowl, add in the nut butter (or Angel Butter), apple sauce, Aquaschata™, stevia and vanilla, and whisk to combine. Then add in the dry ingredients. Use a silicon spatula and mix well until a dough forms. If it's a little too dry, add some plant based milk, 1 T at a time.

3. Cover work surface with parchment paper, dust surface with some arrowroot powder and then transfer the dough on top. Dust the top of the dough with

more tapioca starch and roll it out using a rolling pin, around 1/4 of an inch in thickness.

4. Use a 2 inch cookie cutter or spice jar or lid, something that is 2 inches in diameter, and cut. Gather scraps, re-roll out the dough and cut out more cookies. Repeat until you run out of dough.

5. Using a spatula, carefully transfer the cookies onto a parchment lined baking tray. Bake for 13 - 15 minutes, or until the edges are ever so slightly golden brown. Remove from the oven and let them cool for 2 minutes on the baking tray. Then, carefully transfer them onto a wire rack to cool completely.

6. While they are baking, make the frosting. Take two cookies, once cooled, and add 1 - 2 T of frosting in between two cookies.

7. Store unfrosted cookies in an airtight container at room temperature for 2 - 3 days. If they are already frosted, freeze leftovers as they will soften the cookie.

Variations: Try almond flour and almond butter, or sun butter.

Cashew Butter Cream Frosting *(single recipe, so double this)*
☆☆☆☆☆

Ingredients
3/4 cup Raw Cashews* (soaked or ground up)
1/4 tsp Stevia
3 T Coconut cream
1/4 cup water

The fun is in the flavors. Add any Freeze dried fruit powder for color, or use a flavored stevia. Or, add 1/4 cup fresh mint leaves or fresh berries. Add Chocolate stevia, or melted cacao paste.

- Blend in seed grinder or blender on high speed.

  Use Macadamia or Pili nuts as a substitute for cashew. Or use the Macadamia Nut Cauliflower Ricotta recipe (Page 109). It is just as exciting as this one is.

Cacao Hazelnut Pinwheel Cookies *makes 22 Cookies*

☆☆☆☆☆

Enjoy this delightful grain free cookie with your favorite tea. This cookie is extremely light and airy and yet has body at the same time, with a distinct hazelnut flavor. It's crunchy on the outside and soft on the inside. It's a perfect sweet treat to satisfy your taste buds.

Dry Ingredients
- 1 1/2 cup Hazelnut flour
- 1/2 cup Arrowroot flour
- 3 T White Bean flour (baby lima bean)
- 1 tsp Baking powder
- 1/2 tsp salt

   ***Note** - if you don't have white bean flour, use the arrowroot instead.*

Wet Ingredients
- 1/4 cup Hazelnut butter
- 1/4 cup Applesauce, unsweetened
- 2 T Aquaschata™

   Filling
   Hazelnut Cream Cheese
   - 1 1/2 T Cacao powder
   - 3 1/2 T Coconut Cream (refrigerate beforehand, take only the cream)
   - 4 ounces Pumfu (pumpkin seed Tofu)
   - 1/8 tsp Liquid Stevia
   - 1/8 tsp Chocolate Stevia
   - 1 tsp Vanilla powder
   - 1 T Oat milk (Any Plant based milk)
   - 3 T water

Cooking Instructions

1. Preheat oven to 350 degrees F.

2. Place all the filling ingredients into a seed grinder. Make sure to crumble the tofu first. Mix until creamy smooth.

3. In another mixing bowl, add the Hazelnut flour, arrowroot powder, baking powder and salt. Mix well. Add the filling into the dry mix and with a

spatula, mix until a dough ball is formed. If it's too sticky, add some extra white bean flour or arrowroot flour.

4. Cover the work surface with parchment paper and then transfer the dough ball on top. Place another piece of parchment paper of equal size to the bottom piece. With the dough sandwiched between parchment paper, take a rolling pin and begin rolling out the dough, turning the paper every few rolls. Roll into a rectangle 1/4 of an inch thick. You can cut odd ends that aren't rolling equally and put back into the dough in order to reuse. Keep turning the parchment paper to keep the consistency of thickness.

5. Once you have achieved a large rectangle, roughly 16" x 11", remove the top parchment paper and spread the creamy filling on top with a frosting spatula. You will use just about all of the filling minus 1/8 of a cup. Make sure to leave 1/4 inch around all of the edges.

6. With the short side, gently and very carefully, begin rolling the end of the parchment paper, folding the dough onto itself, creating a roll. Peel gently and roll a little at a time. Working your way towards the other end. When you have a complete log rolled, keep it wrapped in the parchment paper and place on a cutting board and place in the freezer for 1 hour to firm up. This is enough time to allow the dough to chill and be cut without it flattening.

7. With a clean, sharp knife, cut 1/4 inch slices and place on a cookie sheet with parchment paper. Space them so they are not touching. There will be about 22 pinwheel cookies. This is a very easy dough to work with.

8. Bake for 25 - 30 minutes, or until the edges begin crusting up and browning. You can tell by the end pieces, which are smaller and bake faster, what they feel like when done. Remove from the oven and let them cool for 2 minutes on the baking tray. Then carefully transfer them onto a wire rack to cool completely. Enjoy with a cup of tea.

9. Store leftovers in an air tight container at room temperature for 2 days or freeze right away.

Notes: *Variations: *Add cinnamon or anise to the filling.*

*Make a fig paste or poppy seed butter.

*You can use almond flour, almond butter, walnut crumb and walnut butter or Sunflower butter.

*You can also make cookies out of the dough without the filling. Roll out the dough 1/4 inch thick and chill dough in the fridge for 15 min. Using a cookie cutter, cut shapes out of the dough and carefully transfer to a cookie sheet with parchment paper. Bake at 350 degrees F for 13 - 15 min. Remove and cool.

Decorate with different frosting ideas starting on page 376 .

Raspberry Cannoli
☆☆☆☆☆

Cannoli are Italian pastries consisting of tube-shaped shells of fried pastry dough, filled with a sweet, creamy filling, usually containing ricotta – a staple of Sicilian cuisine. They range in size from 3 ½ to 8 inches. In mainland Italy, they are commonly known as Cannoli Siciliana. This baked version and dairy free ricotta

will simply wow any guests you have.
There are many steps to putting this together, yet each one is simple. You can prep many of the steps ahead of time. You can freeze the shell and the filling separately. The riced cauliflower tastes the best on the first day. The day after, it begins to have a faint taste of cauliflower. So freezing is the best solution if you know there will be some leftovers.

This recipe calls for a 3 inch round cookie cutter and makes 17. I found this to be the perfect balance of size and satisfaction. Feel free to use whatever cookie size that works for you. You will need to adjust the cannoli molds accordingly if you change the size. The filling makes 2 cups. In order to match up the amount of shells and filling, adjust the recipes accordingly. Having leftover filling to freeze allows you to use it on other things. You can frost cupcakes and cookies as well. It's very versatile that way. You may also like to have more than one flavor. So doubling the batch allows multiple flavors and freeze any extra.

If you are making your own 3 inch cannoli molds preparation includes:
*If you don't have cannoli molds to wrap, you can easily make them out of aluminum foil. Simply take your aluminum foil and tear it off at 10 or 11 inches long. Fold it in half on the longer side (the side not torn). Household foil is 12 inches in width. Fold that 12 inches in half to 6 inches.

*Now fold the side that is 10 or 11 inches in half. You want to end with a square of 5 or 6 inches. It doesn't have to be exact.

*Taking the longer side and roll it around a tube that is 1/2 inch to 1 inch in diameter. I use the handle of an ice cream scooper as it's the perfect round size for me. Wrap it around several times forming a tube. Pinch one end (that's sticking off the tube or slide it to allow for one end to be pinched just enough to close). Slide off the other end and fold the open end that has the loose foil onto itself so it doesn't unravel. It's ok to have an open hole here, it doesn't need to be pinched off. If you have wrapped it a few times, it is sturdy enough to hold the shape in place.

*You will be wrapping your 3 inch cookie dough around it so they overlap or touch lightly and place on a cookie sheet with a Silpat mat or parchment paper. You will be baking it this way. I find with the 3 inch size, I still need to take a mini rolling pin and just stretch it a little bit more for the ends to touch. After you make 2 or 3, you will catch on easily.

*Removing them is super easy as the shell is baked. I just take both ends of the foil and twist it making it as thin as possible and pulling it out.

Prepare the Cauliflower Rice (Page 106)

Pastry:
Dry Ingredients
1 1/2 cup Almond flour (or 3/4 cup oat flour and 3/4 cup brown rice flour blend)
1/2 cup Arrowroot flour
3 T White Bean flour (baby lima bean)
1 tsp Baking powder
1 tsp Vanilla powder
1 tsp Xanthan gum
1/2 tsp salt
***Note** - if you don't have white bean flour, use the arrowroot instead.*

Wet Ingredients
1/4 cup nut butter or Angel Butter (Page 107)
1/4 cup Applesauce, unsweetened
2 T Aquaschata™
1/4 - 1/3 tsp Liquid Stevia

Sweet Macadamia Cauliflower Ricotta Cheese recipe - makes 2 cups
1 1/2 cup cauliflower, riced (roughly 1/2 a head)
1/2 cup Macadamia nuts, ground into a meal
1/2 tsp Liquid Stevia (Flavored Stevia works well)
1 tsp Vanilla powder
1 1/2 cup fresh Raspberries
1 T Cold Inulin
3 T Coconut Cream

Or Freeze dried Raspberry powder
Or Raspberry Coulis (Page 399)

17 Cannoli tubes or make your own

Cooking Instructions:
1. Prep the Cauliflower and add all the dry ingredients into a food processor. Blend until smooth and cream. Refrigerate.
2. Prepare the pastry dough. Preheat oven to 350 degrees F.
3. In a large mixing bowl, add the nut butter (or Angel Butter), applesauce,

Aquaschata™, stevia and vanilla and whisk to combine. Then add in the dry ingredients. Use a silicon spatula and mix well until a dough forms. If it's a little too dry, add some plant based milk, 1 T at a time.

4. Cover work surface with parchment paper, dust surface with some arrowroot powder and then transfer the dough on top. Dust the top of the dough with more tapioca starch and roll it out using a rolling pin, around 1/4 of an inch in thickness.
5. Use a cookie cutter and cut into 3 inch rounds. Gather scraps, re-roll out the dough and cut more cookies out. Repeat until you run out of dough.
6. Prepare the Cannoli molds as above and follow the baking instructions. Carefully place the pastry on their molds, then, onto a parchment lined baking tray. Bake for 13 - 15 minutes, or until the edges are ever so slightly golden brown. Remove from the oven and let them cool for 2 minutes on the baking tray. Carefully remove the molds and transfer onto a wire rack to cool.

Notes: Because the shell will get soggy sitting with the filling over time, pipe them close to serving time. If you plan on freezing , do so quickly after they have been filled.

Variations:
Add fresh fruit coulis like mango, blueberry or blackberry, or add 4 - 6 T of any freeze dried fruit when not in season, melted chocolate, ginger, orange zest, lemon zes t…
Use cacao powder to replace the nutritional yeast.

* Autumn Cannoli - Add the zest of 1 orange, 1/2 tsp of ground ginger, 1/2 tsp cinnamon, 1/8 tsp nutmeg and 1/16 tsp of cloves. And reduce the vanilla by half. Fold in 1 cup of raisins, dried apples or golden raisins.

*Lemon Cannoli - Add the zest of a lemon and a tsp of lemon stevia or 4 T lemon juice. Don't add the vanilla.

*Chocolate Mint Cannoli - Add 1/4 cup cacao powder to replace the nutritional yeast. Replace the vanilla powder with 1/4 cup crushed mint leaves.

*Key Lime Cannoli - 3 T lime juice, 1 T lime zest and add to the cookie dough 1/2 tsp English Toffee Stevia and 2 T cinnamon.

Gingersnap Cookies or Recipe for making a Gingerbread House
☆☆☆☆☆

This cookie has a lot of versatility. If made thicker, it can be used for building a gingerbread house. If made thinner and baked longer, it will be more like a gingerbread snap. If it gets soft overnight, place back in the oven the and it will firm up. Store them in the freezer and eat whenever you crave this nostalgic flavor.

Dry Ingredients
1/2 cup ground Pecans
1/2 cup Sweet Brown Rice flour
1/2 cup Sorghum flour
2 T Arrowroot flour
1 tsp Vanilla powder
2 tsp Baking powder
1 tsp Xanthan gum
1 1/2 T Cinnamon
1 T ground Ginger
1/8 tsp ground Cloves
1/2 tsp Salt

Wet Ingredients
2 1/2 T Chicory tea (1 T steeped in 1/4 cup)
5 1/2 T Aquaschata™
2 1/2 T ground Flax seeds
1/4 tsp Liquid stevia
15 drops English toffee Liquid Stevia

Frosting ideas
1 recipe Cashew Coconut Butter Cream Frosting (Page 380)
1 recipe Macadamia nut Cauliflower Risotto dessert filling (Page 381)

Suggested flavors: freeze dried fruit powders for coloring or flavoring

Cooking Instructions:
Preheat oven to 350 degrees F
1. In a food processor, pulse or process the pecans to a meal.
2. In a cup, steep for 5 - 10 minutes 1 T of Chicory crystals in 1/4 cup of boiling

water. In a small saucepan, heat up 5 1/2 T of Aquaschata™ and pour into a bowl. Add the ground flax meal making a loose flax egg. Add both regular and English Toffee Liquid Stevia to this as well.

3. In a stand mixing bowl, add the dry ingredients and mix until well combined or hand whisk before setting it up in the stand mixer. Pour in the Aquaschata™ mix and on low speed let the dry ingredients take in the wet. Turn it to medium to high speed until it becomes a dough ball. Remove and use immediately.

4. On a Silpat mat, using a rolling pin, roll out the dough to the desired thickness. For cookies, the thinner they are the more "snap" they will have. For building a gingerbread house, you can make them thicker and cut into the shapes for building the house. For cookies, use any cookie cutter size and bake in a 350 degree F oven for 20 min. They make a lot of cookies. Freezing works well. Whenever you'd like to eat them, just place them back in the oven to reheat for 5 minutes and they will crisp up again. Enjoy with or without frosting. I prefer frosting.

Pies, Meringues, Cakes, Cupcakes & Cake Pops

Deep Dish Rustic Apple Pie 326

Pecan Pie..328

Holiday Pumpkin Pie..329

Lemon Meringue Pie..331

Key Lime Pie Filling...333

Key Lime Pie Crust...334

Vegan Meringues...335

Cakes

Lemon Cake with Lemon & Raspberry Filling with
Coconut Whipping Cream..341

Orange Poppyseed Cake with Orange Hazelnut Filling &
Chocolate Whipping Cream..344

No Bake Blueberry Hazelnut Cheesecake with
Blueberry Compote...346

Hazelnut Chocolate Torte with Raspberry Coulis &
Cashew Cream..348

Basic Vanilla or Chocolate Pound Cake..................................351

Chicory Spice Cake with

Ginger Cardamom Cashew Glaze................................353

Chai Mini Cupcakes with Cashew Butter Cream Frosting...355

Cake Pops..357

Deep Dish Rustic Apple Pie *makes 1 deep dish pie*
☆ ☆ ☆ ☆ ☆

This classic Pie delivers both in flavor and crust. It's hearty and filling. Serve with Vanilla Ice cream (Page 402)) and Coconut Whipped Cream (Page 377).

Filling Ingredients
8 Honey Crisp Apples (4 cups) heaping, mounded in pie dish, depends on the size of the apples.
2 T Cinnamon
2 T Lemon juice
1/4 tsp Liquid Stevia if apples aren't sweet (optional)

Single recipe Walnut Crust - 1 deep dish **double if making a top**

Dry Ingredients
1/2 cup Roasted Walnuts
1/2 cup Sweet Brown Rice flour
1/2 cup Sorghum flour
2 1/2 T ground Flax seeds
2 T Arrowroot powder
1 tsp Vanilla powder
3/4 tsp Xanthan gum
1 tsp Salt

Wet Ingredients
8 -10 T Aquaschata™
1/4 tsp Liquid Stevia
2 tsp ground Orange Peel

Variation: *Cobbler with Oat topping and no crust*
3 cups Thick Rolled Oats
1/3 cup Teff flour
2 T Date Nectar
3/4 cups ground toasted Walnuts
1/2 cup Aquaschata™
1/2 tsp Salt
   Optional: Cinnamon to taste.

Cooking Instructions:
Preheat oven to 425 degrees F.

1. Peel and core the apples. Cut into 3/4 inch cubes or so and put in large bowl. Make sure they are consistent in size so they all cook together. Add the cinnamon, lemon juice and mix. Set aside while making the crust.
2. If you are making a top and bottom crust, **double the crust recipe.** If you are making the cobbler version, then make one bottom crust. In a mixing bowl add all the dry ingredients together. Roast walnuts at 325 degrees F for 10 minutes making sure they don't burn. In a food processor, crumb them. Don't let them turn into a paste. Mix the walnuts into the dry ingredients.
3. Combine all the wet ingredients including the 2 tsp ground orange peel. In the stand mixer on low, begin slowly pouring in the liquids. Turn the speed to medium and when a dough is formed it is done. If you doubled it, slice in half and set one inside a zip lock bag as you roll out the bottom half. Between two pieces of parchment paper, place the dough in the center and flatten into a round circle. Using a rolling pin, roll the crust to be approximately 1/4 inch thick. Flip upside down into the deep dish pie shell. Adjust the pie dough to sit nicely inside. Add the filling and heap it so it's raised with a nice giant mound of apples. Next, repeat the top half of the dough (if not making the cobbler top) and place the top half of the dough over the mound of apples. Clean up the edges by using your forefinger and thumb on one hand and your thumb on the other

hand. Make an edge forming the dough between those fingers creating a fluted edge. Poke some holes or make a design on top for venting.
4. Bake in a 425 degree F oven 10 minutes and then lower the temperature to 350 degrees F for one hour. Check halfway to see if you need to put foil over the top to prevent the crust from burning. If it's not dark enough, keep it uncovered and check again at 45 min.
5. *Cobbler Version;* Follow above directions for making and placing the bottom crust. Place all Cobbler ingredients in a bowl and mix thoroughly. Spoon onto mounded apples in the pie dish. Slightly press oat mix onto apples. Follow baking instructions.
6. When it's baked, let cool for an hour before slicing into it.

Variation: Berry and cherry pies prefer a lattice top crust.

Pecan Pie
☆☆☆☆☆
A healthy version of a decadent dessert.

Crust Ingredients
1 recipe Angel Butter, refrigerated (Page 107)

1 T Aquaschata™
1/3 tsp Liquid Stevia
1/2 cup Sweet Brown Rice flour
1/2 cup Sorghum flour
2 1/2 T ground Flax seeds
2 T Arrowroot powder
1 tsp Vanilla powder (optional)
3/4 tsp Xanthan gum
1 tsp Salt

Pie Filling Ingredients
3 cups Pecans
3 Chia eggs, triple recipe (Page 71, Number 4)

1/4 cup Date Carmel (Page 373)
1 cup Xylitol
1/2 tsp Vanilla powder
2 T Aquaschata™
3 - 7 drops English Toffee stevia
3/4 tsp salt

Cooking Instructions:
1. Preheat oven to 350 degrees F.
2. Place flours and Angel Butter in food processor and pulse to a cornmeal texture. Or in a stand mixer to the same texture. It shouldn't look moist. Pour into a 9-inch pie plate and press with fingers allowing it to come up the edge. Cook in the oven till a golden brown starts to show. Approximately 15 - 20 mins.
3. In a sauce pan, add Date caramel, xylitol, Aquaschata™ and Stevia and heat on medium. Mix the chia eggs in a bowl with the pecans and vanilla. Then, add that into the saucepan, allowing the sugars to coat everything, thoroughly.
4. Pour the pecans into the baked pie shell. Place in the refrigerator 30 minutes. It's ready to serve. Cut and serve with Vanilla Ice Cream (Page 402).

Holiday Pumpkin Pie *makes 1 pie*
☆☆☆☆☆

This traditional holiday treat will find a new meaning for healthy and delicious. This is rich without being overly sweet. Included is another different type of pie crust that continues to make for a delightful change.

Crust Ingredients
1 recipe Angel Butter Refrigerated (Page 107)
2 T Coconut Cream
1 T Aquaschata™
1/3 tsp Liquid Stevia
1/2 cup Sweet Brown Rice flour
1/2 cup Sorghum
2 1/2 T ground Flax seeds
2 T Arrowroot powder

1 tsp Vanilla powder (optional)
3/4 tsp Xanthan gum
1 tsp Salt

Pie Filling
3 1/4 cups cooked, baked or canned Pumpkin, mashed
1 cup Oat milk (or any plant-based milk)
1/4 cup Arrowroot flour
1 tsp Liquid Stevia
1 tsp Vanilla powder
1 - 2 T Pumpkin Spice (or use recipe below)
Pinch of Salt

Create your own Pumpkin Spice-Adjust to your taste buds' desire and double if necessary.
2 tsp ground Cinnamon
1 tsp ground Nutmeg
1 tsp Mace
1/4 tsp ground Allspice
Dash of ground Ginger

1 recipe Coconut Whipping Cream (Page 377)

Cooking Instructions:
1. Preheat oven to 350 degrees F.
2. Place flours and Angel Butter in food processor and pulse to a cornmeal texture. Or use a stand mixer to get the same texture. It shouldn't look moist. Pour into a 9 - inch pie plate and press with fingers for a smooth surface and allow it to come to edge of rim. Cook in the oven till a very light golden brown starts to show, do not overcook because it will need to continue cooking with the filling inside. Approximately 15 min.
3. Place pumpkin and milk in food processor. Puree, then add remaining ingredients and process to a smooth, thick cream. Pour filling into crust. Bake for 15 minutes at 425 degrees F, then reduce oven temperature to 250 degrees F and continue baking for 1 1/4 hours. Place on rack to cool and then chill before cutting. When completely chilled, pie will be firm.

Lemon Meringue Pie *1 pie*
☆☆☆☆☆

There is some versatility in this recipe. Depending on what ingredients you have on hand, you can find yourself wowing many of your friends.

Pie shell recipe. Choose one.
1 recipe pie shell - baked and cooled - two choices here

Pie shell #1
1 1/2 cup Almond flour
1/2 cup Brown Rice flour
1/3 cup Arrowroot powder
3/4 tsp Xanthan gum
5 T Aquaschata™
1/4 cup Angel Butter (Page 107)
1/2 tsp Salt

Walnut crust - Pie Shell #2
1/2 cup toasted Walnuts
1/2 cup Sweet Brown Rice flour
1/2 cup Sorghum flour
2 1/2 T ground Flax seeds
2 T Arrowroot flour
8 T Aquaschata™
1/4 tsp Stevia
1/2 tsp Salt

Lemon Curd - *makes 1 1/2 to 2 cups*
1 1/4 cup fresh Lemon Juice
1/4 cup + 3 T Oat milk
1 cup Xylitol
1/4 tsp Turmeric
1 T Agar Agar
1 1/2 tsp Tapioca Flour

1 Recipe for Meringue (Page 336)

Cooking Instructions for Lemon Curd:

1. In a saucepan heat up the Oat milk, lemon juice, xylitol and turmeric. Bring to a boil and on medium heat cook another minute.
2. In a small cup, add the tapioca flour and 2 - 3 T of cold water and mix until the flour dissolves. In another small cup have the 1 T of Agar Agar powder and add 3 T of cold water (enough to dissolve it) and set aside.
3. On medium high heat, whisk in the tapioca liquid and then add the Agar Agar liquid and continue vigorously whisking for one minute.
4. Whisk the tapioca mixture into the oat milk mixture on a medium to high heat. Continue whisking until the mixture starts to bubble. Remove from heat.
5. Once the pie shell is cooled and the lemon curd is hot, pour the curd into the shell and place it in the freezer for 45 minutes to 1 hour to set.
6. Once the pie shell is cooled and the lemon curd is hot, pour the curd into the shell and place it in the freezer for 45 minutes to 1 hour to set.
7. Make the meringue (See instructions below) or, if already made, whip it again to refresh.

- **Cooking Instructions** for Pie crust, Walnut Pastry dough (Page 362). Or use almond flour and follow similar instructions.

- **Cooking Instructions** for *Meringue (Page 335)*
  Note: If making Aquaflaxa Meringue, chill the flax water in the freezer for 30 minutes before making meringue.
  You have several options on how to apply the meringue. One way is to pipe it in medium peaks with a pastry bag. Another way is to pour it on top 2 - 3 inches and smooth it out with a spatula and then with a metal spoon touch the back side of it on top of the meringue and lift making little peaks. With a flame torch, heat the peaks with the flame and darken them. Similar to roasting a marshmallow. Serve right away.

This is not to be baked in the oven*, as it will melt the lemon curd.*

Key Lime Pie Filling *makes 1 - 10 inch spring pan, or 4 minis*
☆☆☆☆☆

This has the silkiest texture. The crust is absolutely brilliant and your guests would never know there is tofu in this. It is heavenly.

Ingredients

1 lb. Pumfu (pumpkin seed tofu) - That's 2 packages of 8 oz.
1 cup Coconut Cream (from can, refrigerated overnight - no liquid, cream/solid only)
Shy of 3/4 tsp liquid Stevia (remove 1/8 tsp from 3/4 tsp)
1/4 cup Xylitol (adjust if needed)
3/4 cups Lime Juice
3 - 4 T Lime Zest (taste and adjust)
1/4 cup Raw Cashews (soaked or ground) blended in 1/3 cup +1 T oat milk)
2 T Cold Inulin
1/2 tsp Xanthan Gum
1 tsp Citric Fiber (Natur Emul is best)
1/2 tsp Salt

Cooking Instructions:

1. In a blender or seed grinder blend cashews to liquefy. Place all remaining ingredients into food processor. Taste and adjust as needed. Does it need more lime zest? That's the big question here. More salt? It draws out the flavor. Are you using store bought lime juice vs squeezing your own. These are all important pieces that bring out the best flavor and texture in the end.

Key Lime Pie Filling is very versatile. It can also be used in Waffle Bowls, Profiteroles, Donut filling, Tortes and of course, the Key Lime Pie Crust below. Use your imagination!

Key Lime Pie Crust *1 large 10 inch or 4 minis - 4 inch*
☆☆☆☆☆

The Crust is flavored just like a graham cracker crust!

Crust Ingredients
- 1/2 cup Pecans
- 1/2 cup Sweet Brown Rice flour
- 1/2 cup Sorghum flour
- 2 1/2 T ground Flax seeds
- 2 T Arrowroot flour
- 2 1/2 T Chicory tea (1 T steeped in 1/4 cup water)
- 5 1/2 T Aquaschata™
- 1/4 tsp Liquid Stevia
- 15 drops English toffee Liquid Stevia
- 1 tsp Vanilla powder
- 1 1/2 T Cinnamon
- 1 tsp Salt

Cooking Instructions:

1. Begin by making Chicory tea. Steep it for 5 min.
2. In one bowl, mix the wet ingredients together and in a food processor, blend to mix the dry ingredients together. Add the liquid to the food processor and turn this into a wet sand texture.
3. Press into the spring pan. Bake at 350 degrees F for 15 - 20 minutes depending on your oven. You will feel it beginning to get stiff and crack. Take out and let cool.
4. If you don't have a spring pan, and have round cookie cutters, you can roll it out with a rolling pan and cut the sizes you want. You can also take foil and make your own size round and wrap it around the crust and fill. It's one way to get creative. It's less messy with a spring pan though.

And, no matter what you create with the Key Lime Filling, the best topping for this is the Cashew Cream on Page 379.

Vegan Meringues

In this section you will find 4 different recipes for making Vegan "Egg free" Meringues. Each are unique in themselves and offer a different but similar end result. They each can be whipped over and over many times and they each can have freeze dried fruit powders added to them to offer color for frosting. Two different meringues can be combined together creating another frosting like "buttercream" and can be used to frost cakes and piping flowers. However, those need to be eaten right away. The Meringue recipe for the lemon meringue pie holds up for up to two days. Although I doubt there will be any left over.

The four different recipes include one of the following. Garbanzo bean water - which is known as Aquafaba; Flax seed water - known as Aquaflaxa; Potatowhip - also known as Potato Protein; and finally, Versawhip 600K™, is a Modified Soy Protein. I will go into detail for all 4 with recipes that are successful. Again, this is another level of **Fearless in the Kitchen**. *It requires an adventurous spirit and courage to try something new. Sometimes it's just too hard to stretch outside that box. I did feel like I was a mad scientist in the kitchen working out the kinks. Meringues are known for having sugar. So, how to get around that was tricky, but I found a way. Let's get started.*

Meringues are considered delicate and difficult. In the case of Vegan Meringues, because I am using stevia, it's different. Eating air has new meaning. Dehydrating them is how you "bake them" and to me, I haven't enjoyed that because it's the "eating air" that comes through the dehydrator. Without sugar, it's just not the same thing. However, YOU CAN MAKE French Macaroons. That being said, it's worth it. It does take a lot of trial and error. I have had my fair share of "failures" in this. I have made "marshmallows" by mistakenly baking a meringue at too high a temperature. What I know is that every "failure" gives me information that is valuable ... somewhere.

IMPORTANT NOTE: When using your stand mixer bowl, there can be no trace of oil on the metal bowl whatsoever. If you've made a pastry dough with walnuts, that is considered oil. Use lemon juice to wipe it clean and then, soap and water. If you have a vanilla flavoring with sunflower oil in it, it will break the meringue. *You cannot use essential oils to flavor this. Only freeze dried powders or vanilla powder.*

◆ **Recipe for Aquafaba -** *the biggest question is "does it taste like beans?"* No, it does not. This recipe has the greatest success, but to me, isn't the healthiest. *There's a lot* *of controversy on this topic. If you are making your own garbanzo beans and saving the water, it is much safer for your gut health. However, my bigger question is, how often would you be eating a lemon meringue pie? Maybe once a year? If that's the case, then it doesn't matter. The amount ingested is so small. I have seen recipes using the liquid as an "egg wash" for pastry dough. I haven't tried that, so I don't know. I use Aquaschata™ for everything needing an egg wash.*

Ingredients
1 can of Garbanzo beans liquid - 1/2 cup liquid only
1/2 tsp liquid Stevia
1 tsp Vanilla Powder (optional)

Cooking Instructions for Aquafaba:
In a stand mixer with the whisk attachment, pour in the liquid and the stevia. Turn on low to medium speed. After it is halfway whipped, stop and add the vanilla powder and beat until you have stiff peaks. By far the quickest and easiest. However, there are people that can't or won't eat bean water.

◆ **Recipe for Flaxseed water also known as - Aquaflaxa -** *This is truly miraculous. And flax seeds are healthy. So this is my go to recipe. It works consistently ... tried and true.* ***However, you MUST put the flax water in the freezer 30 minutes before starting.***

Ingredients for making Flax water:
Makes 4 cups (enough for 4 Meringues since they can be unstable)
6 cups of water
2/3 cup Flax seed
Synthetic nut milk bag if you have one *(will make things much easier)*
or a large strainer covered with cheesecloth

Ingredients for making Meringue
1/2 cup Flax Water (Aquaflaxa)
1/8 tsp Xanthan gum
1/4 tsp Liquid Stevia
2 tsp Tapioca flour
2 tsp Cream of Tartar
1 tsp Vanilla powder
1/4 - 1/2 cup Aquafaba *(only if it doesn't come together)*

Cooking Instructions for Aquaflaxa:

1. Bring 6 cups of water to a boil.
2. Place 2/3 cup of flaxseed into a synthetic nut milk bag if you have one, it will make clean up a breeze. Take the bag with the flax seeds and place in the boiling water and cook it on medium heat (still maintaining a boil) for 30 min. You can tie the string to the handle or find a way to get it out of the way. If you don't have a bag, place seeds in the pot and boil for 30 minutes and then strain in a large strainer over a bowl. Cover the strainer with cheesecloth.
3. If using nut milk bag, simply remove and squeeze the bag with a heat protective glove. If no nut milk bag, pour the liquid on a cheesecloth over a strainer into a bowl. Bundle the cheesecloth, pull up, make a bag and squeeze out the remaining liquid. *Save the flax seeds for crackers, bread, salad dressing or even flax apple butter. Pop it in a baggy and into the freezer.*
4. The water remaining should look like egg whites. Let it cool in the fridge until you are ready to use it. Before starting your meringue, prep by placing half a cup in the freezer. If it goes too long, it will freeze, so set a timer.
5. In the mixing stand mixer, add the 1/2 cup Flax water and turn it on medium speed for 30 seconds before adding anything else. Next, turn it to high speed and let it go for another minute.
6. Next, add the 1/8 to 1/4 tsp Liquid Stevia (remember its equivalent to 1/4 cup of sugar) and mix another couple of minutes. Stop and add the tapioca flour. Scrape down sides again. You may have to scrape sides down a few times. This prevents any clumping.
7. While on high speed, sprinkle in the Xanthan gum slowly. If it's done too quickly, (like all at once), it ruins the meringue by coagulating it. It may take a couple of minutes to sprinkle it all in. The whole purpose of the Xanthan gum is for it to create the structure that holds the meringues form. So, it's really important to add it slowly. Next, add in the cream of tartar. Remember to scrape sides. You will see the soft peaks forming. At this point taste and see if it needs more stevia.
8. If you have been at this for 20 minutes and you haven't seen stiff peaks, and if you have saved some chickpea water from cooking (keep it in the freezer and thaw when you know you might need it), or open a can of beans and use the liquid. Start adding new liquid with 1 T at a time up to 4 T. It is the last resort. At this point, add the vanilla powder. It is a denser powder than some freeze dried fruits. Only add 1/2 - 1 tsp or it will collapse. If that happens, add more bean water, up to another 1/4 cup.

9. If you would like this to be a "butter cream" like frosting, for frosting a cake, add another 2/3 of a cup of Chickpea water. This will take the Aquaflaxa meringue to a whole new level of smooth and luxurious. You can add Dragon Fruit powder to make it a beautiful pink. Or a blue pea powder to make it a beautiful blue. These both are very light and will not collapse the meringue, up to a point. Meaning, you can add up to 2 tsp of powder. The 3rd will collapse it.
10. You can store this in the fridge and whip it again the next day. Whip it as many times as you need to. That is what I call "food magic."

◆ *Recipe for Potatowhip - also known as potato protein - by Sosa Products.*
"Does it taste like potatoes?" ***No, it does not!*** *Purchase at* https://supplies.gusta.ca/

This naturally occurring protein is extracted from non-genetically modified potatoes as a by-product when producing potato starch. When removing the potato starch, the remaining product contains 'potato fruit water.' This potato fruit water, as it is called in the industry, is treated with heat and acid to coagulate and separate the proteins before being dried into the powder that is potato protein.

In order to make the protein 'active' it needs to be hydrated. The hydration ratio varies depending on the intended use and so takes a little experimentation, however from what I have researched, a 6:1 water to protein, seems to be the amount for meringues.
Once combined with water, and before using, the mixture needs to be left in the fridge for 30 min. It can be used for meringues, mayonnaise, salad dressings, cakes etc. …

Since these recipes are not using sugar, and are using Stevia, instead, you can mix with freeze dried fruit powders. However, they do get heavy and can knock down the meringue. You can dehydrate or freeze them. The freezing doesn't make them completely hard, more like the texture of ice cream.

Ingredients
3/4 tsp Stevia
1 cup + 3 T water
3 to 3 1/2 tsp Potatowhip from Sosa
1/4 tsp Xanthan gum.

You need to soak the potatowhip in the water - in the fridge for 30 minutes before blending. When it is almost fully whipped, add the xanthan gum and continue whipping. You will immediately see a change in texture, the meringue will become more stable and thicker.

Ingredients for another potato whip recipe
4 3/4 fl. oz. water
4 1/2 oz. Potato protein
Large pinch of Baking soda
1/8 tsp Xanthan gum

My personal add ons:
1/4 tsp Stevia
1/4 cup Cold Inulin powder

Cooking Instructions for Potatowhip:
1. Put 4 3/4 fl. oz. of water with the potato protein   Put the bowl in the fridge for 30 minutes for the protein to rehydrate. After refrigeration, add xanthan gum into small bowl and whisk together.
2. Add this liquid to the bowl of the stand mixer fitted with the whisk attachment. Or use an electric hand mixer. Now add baking soda. Whisk the mixture for 5 min. Add the Stevia. Beat on high speed until you are able to get stiff peaks.

◆ **Recipe for faux Versawhip 600K™** - *a soy based product "Another flavorless taste"*
The term "Versawhip" usually refers to Versawhip 600K™, a proprietary, modified soy protein used to replace egg whites or gelatin in foam recipes. It's pure enzymatically treated soy protein which can be hydrated with water and whipped to make a foam. Uses less product than with egg white powder, foams are more stable, and has a better flavor release. Can be used for cold or hot foams. Advantages include consistent foam quality without risk of over-beating, greater heat and acid tolerance, and reduced microbial risk. It is claimed to be more stable and is great for baking. Versawhip 600K™ is a soy product and you use very little. I have created a recipe that gets similar results and is sugar free.

Ingredients
3/4 tsp Gellan Gum F (it will not work with other gums)
3/4 tsp Versawhip 600K™
1/8 tsp Xanthan gum
1/2 cup + 1 T water
3/4 tsp Stevia
2 tsp freeze dried Passion Fruit powder

Cooking Instructions for Versawhip 600K™

1. Add water first in the stand mixer. Sprinkle in versa whip on top of the water. Begin mixing at speed #7. At 3 min., move it to #8 for 3 more minutes until medium stiff peaks happen. At this point, add in your freeze dried fruit powder (like passion fruit) and liquid stevia. Whip until stiff peaks appear. It's a silky smooth texture.

Final Note: Alternative Meringues are a great place to get **Fearless in the Kitchen.** Try them all. Some are easier than others. Some are quite costly. Be aware of allergy restrictions. The good news is, that all of these recipes are sugar free!

On the resource page (88), I have included where you can find these Molecular Gastronomy products. They are fun and bring the chemistry and science into the kitchen. This is a great way of teaching kids how they, too, can be **Fearless in the Kitchen.**

Lemon Cake with Lemon and Raspberry Filling with Coconut Whipping Cream

☆☆☆☆☆

Lemon is one of the most versatile ingredients. It can be used in both savory and sweet recipes. This allergy friendly lemon cake is a great birthday cake for kids. This recipe makes 3 six inch cakes or 2 eight inch.

4 Egg Replacer
6 T Tapioca flour
4 tsp Baking powder
1 tsp Xanthan gum
1/2 tsp Cream of tartar
3/4 cup warm water

Dry Ingredients
1 1/2 cups Brown Rice flour
Scant 2/3 cup Arrowroot flour
1/3 cup Millet flour
1/3 cup Buckwheat flour
1/2 tsp Xanthan gum
1 tsp Vanilla powder
2 tsp Baking powder
1 cup Xylitol
1/2 tsp Liquid Stevia
3/4 tsp Salt

Wet Ingredients
1/3 cup Aquaschata™
2/3 cup + 1 T Lemon juice
1 T lemon zest (3 lemons)
3 T Oat milk
1/4 tsp Turmeric for color

Fillings and Frosting
1 Pint Fresh Raspberries
1 Recipe Lemon Pastry Cream (Page 384)
1 1/2 Recipe Coconut Whipped Cream (Page 377)

Cooking Instructions:
1. Preheat oven to 350 degrees F. Prepare 3 six inch cake pans with parchment paper or 2 eight inch cake pans or one 9 x 13 pan.
2. Zest the lemons before juicing them. Then, cut them in half and juice and strain the seeds.
3. In a bowl, add the lemon juice, Aquaschata™ and lemon zest.
4. Either using a hand mixer or using a seed grinder, place all of the egg replacer ingredients and mix until it froths. It will expand in volume. Set aside.
5. Add all the dry ingredients into a stand mixer bowl and whisk together.
6. Pour the egg replacer into the lemon Aquaschata™ liquid. Whisk until it all blends and expands twice its size. It will be quite airy and lemony yellow.
7. In the stand mixer on low, add the egg replacer and mix until it is all blended. Add the 3 T oat milk. Continue mixing on #2 setting until the batter is silky smooth. Taste the batter and adjust as needed. Does it need more lemon juice? More stevia? It should be fairly balanced at this point. If not, add what is needed.
8. Divide the batter into the cake pans and bake for 30 minutes or until they have a bounce back and clean toothpick. And are pulling away from the edges.
9. Remove from cake pans with a spatula or knife and completely cool on wire rack. Do not do anything until they are completely cooled. This may be a couple of hours.
10. In the meantime, prepare the Lemon Pastry Cream (Page 384) frosting and refrigerate. Prepare the coconut whipping cream (Page 377) and refrigerate. Other variations could be the Cashew Butter Cream frosting (Page 380) or Raspberry Coulis (Page 399).
11. Assembling, make sure the cake tops are flat. Shave off any domed part with a sharp or serrated knife. If this is a 3 layer cake, have a layer of lemon pastry cream and then add fresh raspberries on top. If you have a raspberry coulis, drizzle that on top giving the raspberries a nice glaze. If you don't have that, take some raspberry fruit jam and water down a Tablespoon or two and use that as a glaze on the berries.
12. After the layers are stacked, crumb coat the cake in the lemon pastry cream, filling in any gaps. This is a critical step in frosting cakes. It seals in moisture, and it can keep the cake fresh for days in the fridge. If you used any of the raspberry coulis in the crumb coat, the color red will bleed through the coconut whipping cream, eventually. Unless you are looking for a beautiful, pink, tie-died cake, only use the lemon pastry cream is the crumb coat.

13. Frosting with the Whipping cream is easy and fun. The coconut whipping cream should be stiff still. Make sure you have it on a 6 inch round cake board so you can transfer it later to the 8 inch cake board. A decorative plate works as well. Make sure there's plenty of frosting to pipe the border and bottom. Add some fresh raspberries on top to decorate along with some lemon zest or some tiny cut-up pieces of lemon. This will be well received!

Orange Poppyseed Cake with Orange Hazelnut Filling and Chocolate Whipping Cream
☆☆☆☆☆

Ingredients
4 Egg Replacer
6 T Tapioca flour
4 tsp Baking powder
1 tsp Xanthan gum
1/2 tsp Cream of tartar
3/4 cup warm water

Dry Ingredients
1 1/2 cups Brown Rice flour
2 T Poppy Seeds
Scant 2/3rd cup Arrowroot flour
1/3 cup Millet flour
1/3 cup Buckwheat flour
1/2 tsp Xanthan gum
1 tsp Vanilla powder
2 tsp Baking powder
1 cup Xylitol
1/2 tsp Liquid Stevia
3/4 tsp Salt

Wet Ingredients
1/3 cup Aquaschata™
2/3 cup + 1 T Orange juice
1 T Orange zest
3 T Oat milk
1/4 tsp Turmeric for color

Cooking Instructions:
1. Preheat oven to 350 degrees F. Prepare 3 six inch cake pans with parchment paper or 2 eight inch cake pans.
2. Zest the orange before juicing them. Then cut them in half and juice and strain the seeds.
3. In a bowl, add the orange juice, Aquaschata™ and orange zest.

4. Either using a hand mixer or using a seed grinder, place all of the egg replacer ingredients and mix until it froths. It will expand in volume. Set aside.
5. Add all the dry ingredients into a stand mixer bowl and whisk together.
6. Pour the egg replacer into the orange Aquaschata™ liquid. Whisk until it all blends and expands twice its size. It will be quite airy and orange.
7. In the stand mixer on low, add the egg replacer and mix until it is all blended. Add the 3 T oat milk. Continue mixing on #2 setting until the batter is silky smooth. Taste the batter and adjust as needed. Does it need more orange juice? More stevia? It should be fairly balanced at this point.
8. Divide the batter into the cake pans and bake for 30 minutes or until they have a bounce back and clean toothpick. And are pulling away from the edges.
9. Remove from cake pans with a spatula or knife and completely cool on wire rack. Do not do anything until they are completely cooled. This will be awhile.

Making the fillings:
Orange Hazelnut Filling (Page 386) Make the day before.

Chocolate Coconut Whipping Cream (Page 377)

No Bake Blueberry Hazelnut Cheesecake with Blueberry Compote
☆☆☆☆☆

5 inch diameter springform pan
This is another grain free dessert.

Ingredients
Crust:
1/2 cup Hazelnut flour
2 Medjool dates (soaked 30 minutes in 1/4 cup warm water)
1 T Hazelnut paste
9 drops Liquid Stevia

Blueberry Cheesecake:
2 cups Chestnuts - roasted, boiled, puree with 3 dates
Baby Lima bean puree - cook, blend with vanilla 1 T blueberry powder, and optional, soaked raw cashews
Add Liquid Stevia to taste

Blueberry Compote:
2 cups fresh or frozen Blueberries
1/4 cup water
1 T Arrowroot powder
9 - 15 drops Liquid Stevia

Cooking instructions:
1. *Preparing the Crust:* Add all crust ingredients in a food processor and process until mixture is combined and starts to form a ball. Transfer into a 5" spring pan and press down into a flat crust along the base. Freeze while working on the filling.
2. *Blueberry Cheesecake:* Score Chestnuts with an x using a sharp knife. Roast in oven or toaster oven at 425 degrees for 10 - 15 min. This will make peeling the chestnut easy.
3. In a medium sized pot, add the chestnuts and enough water to cover them. Boil for 45 min. until they are soft. Check water levels to prevent evaporation. When soft, place in blender and add 3 chopped dates (optional) and puree until silky smooth. Set aside.
4. Baby Lima beans can be cooked ahead of time. 1 cup in a pressure cooker on high for 30 minutes with 15 minutes release time. Or on the stove top 40 - 60

minutes simmering until tender. Place cooked beans in blender with vanilla powder, blueberry powder, soaked cashews and 1/3 water to start. Puree until smooth. Add more water if necessary.

5. Combine chestnut puree and lima bean puree and blend until creamy. Move into a bowl and add 1/4 tsp Liquid Stevia (less if using dates). Take the pan out of the freezer and add the filling into the spring form on top of the crust. Refrigerate for several hours or overnight.

6. Remove from springform pan. With a metal spatula and a cup of hot water, dip spatula into hot water and go around the sides of the cheesecake if it has any irregularities. This will smooth it out.

7. In a small saucepan, add water and blueberries. Bring to a boil and lower to medium heat until berries are cooked through. Add 1 T of arrowroot powder to 2 - 3 T of cold water in a cup and stir. Do not put arrowroot powder into hot liquid. It will clump. Add the liquid arrowroot powder into blueberry saucepan and stir for a minute or two, until thickened. Remove from heat and add Stevia to sweeten. It will sweeten more as it cools. Refrigerate. Serve 2 - 3 T of the compote on top of the cheesecake.

Notes: *Many aspects of this recipe can be prepped ahead of time. Lima Beans can be made and frozen any time you need extra. Roasting the chestnuts can be done at any time and kept in a sealed container until you are ready to boil them.*

Tapioca starch can be used in place of the arrowroot powder (my preference).

* *Kudzu root can also be used very similarly to arrowroot powder, though, it's healthier.*

Hazelnut Chocolate Torte with Raspberry Coulis and Cashew Cream
☆☆☆☆☆

This heavenly, guilt free version is without a doubt one of my favorite recipes. It has been one of my signature recipes as well. It's been reinvented to fit an oil free and sugar free diet. I describe this torte like a chocolate mousse cake. I surprise pastry chefs, amateurs, children, and most everyone with this dessert as they cannot believe there are no eggs in it. You can't go wrong with tantalizing your guests! The best part is it's so quick and easy to make in a food processor. And it can also be made completely grain free if using a nut milk.

Chocolate Hazelnut Torte:
1 lb. Soy Tofu or Pumfu (pumpkin seed tofu)
1/2 cup Cacao powder
1/2 cup Xylitol
1 tsp Liquid Stevia
2 T Chicory Crystals, steep in 1/4 cup hot water for 10 min.
1 tsp Vanilla powder
1 1/2 cups nut milk or Oat Milk
1/2 cup White bean flour (baby lima bean) (or 1/4 cup white bean flour and 1/4 cup hazelnut flour)
1 tsp Baking powder
1 tsp salt

1 pint fresh Raspberries

Chocolate Ganache:
This Ganache recipe differs from the one on page 389. All part of the big picture!
3/4 cup Cacao Paste
1 cup Oat Milk (or nut milk)
1/2 tsp Hazelnut Liquid Stevia

Cooking Instructions for the Hazelnut Flourless Chocolate Torte:
1. Preheat oven to 350 degrees F.
2. Before you begin, add 2 T Chicory Crystals to 1/4 cup boiling water and let it steep for 10 min. Strain and use the liquid.
3. Place all of the torte's ingredients into the food processor, except the melted

cacao paste and blend for 3 - 4 minutes until smooth and creamy.
4. Over a double boiler, melt the cacao paste. In another pot, bring 1 cup of plant based milk to a boil. When the cacao paste is completely melted, add in 1/2 tsp Liquid stevia and put this into the food processor with the batter and mix again until completely blended in.
5. Pour into either a 10" springform pan, 4 - 4 " springform pans, or 3 - 5" springform pans. Make sure they are non stick pans. You can add parchment paper to the bottom if you are concerned about any sticking. It's usually not an issue though.
6. Bake in the oven for 40 - 45 minutes until a toothpick comes out clean. When the cake/cakes are cooled, pour the ganache onto the top and refrigerate overnight. The next day, remove and place on the serving platter. Decorate the top as you wish. They will sink about 1/2" to an inch leaving plenty of room for the ganache.
7. Prepare the Cashew Cream and Refrigerate.
8. Prepare the Raspberry Coulis and Refrigerate.

Cooking Instructions for Chocolate Ganache:
- While it's baking in the oven, make the chocolate ganache. In a double boiler, add the cacao paste. Do not allow any water to blend with the cacao paste. Once it's completely melted add in the liquid stevia. There are many flavored ones you can use. In this case, Hazelnut Flavored. At the same time, boil the plant based milk in a pot. In a small mixing bowl, add the melted cacao paste and add the hot milk. Mix until creamy and well blended.
- There are many freeze dried powders you can use for flavor and color. There are many different coulis you can make as well. This is a very versatile and creative process. However, raspberries and cashew cream are a classic.

Cashew Cream
1 1/2 cups ground Raw Cashews *(or Macadamia or Pili Nut)*
1/2 cup water (add a little more after you have refrigerated it to thin it)
1 - 2 T Oat milk
Pinch of salt
25 drops of Liquid stevia (1/4 tsp)

Cooking Instructions for Cashew Cream:
- In blender, add cashews and water and blend to form a thick milk. Add the cooked baby lima beans until the cream thickens. Blend in vanilla and salt. Chill and serve. (Cream will thicken substantially when chilled but will not be stiff)

Raspberry Coulis
4 cups fresh or frozen Raspberries
1/2 tsp liquid Stevia
2 T Lemon Juice

Cooking Instructions for Raspberry Coulis:
- Bring raspberries to a boil with the lemon juice and stevia. Simmer for 3 or 4 minutes. Next, pour it into the blender and blend on high. Strain into a jar and refrigerate. If you need to thin it for any reason, just add a little water.

Basic Vanilla or Chocolate Pound Cake
☆☆☆☆☆

This is a good basic cake. In this unconventional style of baking, letting go of the traditional light and fluffy cake opens the door for celebrating with healthier recipes. Healthier means heavier, so quite literally, this is a "pound" cake. It is a denser cake. However, between this cake and the lemon cake recipe, these two have continuously succeeded as the most successful "birthday cake." It is the one featured on the front cover of this cookbook, Epicurean Awakening. It has a lot of versatility, which is why it is a basic cake recipe. It works great for using different ingredients to change the color, make it a chocolate cake or a berry cake. Double the recipe to make a double layer cake. Fill it with fruit and pastry cream or keep it simple and use the same frosting throughout. It is kid approved as well! And very allergy friendly.

Dry Ingredients
1 cup Baby Lima Bean flour (or Brown Rice flour)
1/2 cup Brown Rice flour *(if grain free, use Almond, Hazelnut or White bean flour)*
1/2 cup Arrowroot powder
1 cup Xylitol
1 tsp Baking soda
2 tsp Baking powder
3/4 tsp Xanthan gum
1 tsp Vanilla powder
1 tsp Salt

3 Egg Replacer
4 1/2 T Tapioca flour
3 tsp Baking powder
3/4 tsp Xanthan gum
1/2 tsp Cream of tartar
1/2 cup + 1 T warm water

Wet Ingredients
1/2 cup Aquaschata™
1/2 cup Applesauce
1 cup Mashed bananas
1/2 tsp Liquid Stevia
3/4 cup Oat Milk

Cooking Instructions:

1. In a mixing bowl, mix all of the dry ingredients. If you are making a chocolate cake, add 1/4 cup *Cacao Powder*. (Also using 4 T of *Maqui Berry Powder* here adds another variation if you wanted a dark color cake)
2. Make the Egg replacer for 3 eggs in a seed grinder or with a stand mixer.
3. Whisk the Aquaschata™ into the egg replacer and set aside.
4. Mash the bananas and mix with the applesauce, stevia and mix into the Egg Replacer bowl.
5. Using a stand or hand mixer, pour the wet ingredients into the dry mix. Adjust the batter at this point with the oat milk by slowly adding it to the desired consistency of a cake batter.
6. This cake makes three 6 inch cakes or two 8 inch cakes. You can use a 9 x 13 instead. Cut in half and make it a double layered cake. Line the cake pans with parchment paper to prevent sticking.
7. Bake in a 350 degree F oven for 40 minutes or until a toothpick comes out clean. Remove cakes and let cool completely on cooling a rack. Do not wrap these in plastic or a zip lock bag. The moisture will turn them sour.
8. There are many frosting and pastry cream recipes in this book, starting on Page 376.

Chicory Spice Cake with Ginger Cardamom Cashew Glaze
☆☆☆☆☆

This makes a delicious winter treat. The Ginger Cardamom Glaze adds to the joy of eating it. Time to enjoy one of those "puts a smile on your face" treats. It's one of my favorites.

Dry Ingredients
1/4 cup Baby Lima Bean flour
1 cup Brown Rice flour
1/2 cup Hazelnut flour
1/4 cup Sorghum flour
1/2 cup Arrowroot powder
3/4 tsp Xanthan gum
2 tsp Baking powder
1 tsp Baking soda
2 tsp Cinnamon
1/4 tsp Nutmeg (grated whole)
1/4 tsp ground Cloves
1/2 tsp Vanilla powder
1/2 tsp Salt

Wet Ingredients
1 cup Chicory Tea (1/4 cup chicory crystals steeped in 1 cup boiling water)
1 cup mashed Banana (the blacker the skin the better)
2 T Aquaschata™
1/4 - 1/2 cup Oat milk
3/4 cup Applesauce (unsweetened)
1 tsp Liquid Stevia

Ginger Cardamom Cashew Glaze
1/2 cup Raw Cashews (soaked 2 - 4 hours to soften)
1/2 cup Baby Lima Beans cooked
1 cup water
1/2 tsp Vanilla powder
9 - 12 drops Liquid Stevia
1 tsp powdered Ginger
1/4 tsp Cardamom

Cooking Instructions: Preheat oven to 350 degrees F.
1. Boil water to steep chicory crystals.
2. Mix all dry cake ingredients in a large mixing bowl.
3. In a small mixing bowl, add stevia to chicory tea. Mix bananas, applesauce, Aquaschata™ and 1/4 cup oat milk.
4. Mix wet into dry ingredients.
5. Place parchment paper on the bottom of a 9 x 13 cake pan.
6. Pour batter into 9 x 13 pan and bake in 350 degree F oven for 35 - 40 min.
7. When cooling, it appears sticky. Let sit overnight for best texture and flavor.

Note: if batter is still too sticky, add an extra 1/2 cup Brown Rice flour, 1 T at a time.

Making Ginger Cardamom Cashew Glaze

Cooking Instructions:
1. Blend all ingredients in blender – refrigerate.
2. Adjust sweetener. Thickens in fridge. Adjust consistency by adding water, 1 - 2 T.

Chai Mini Cupcakes with Cashew Butter Cream Frosting

☆☆☆☆

makes 24 minis

These Chai Mini cupcakes taste amazing. Bet you can't eat just 3 or 4 ...

Spice Mix
1/2 tsp Anise
2 tsp Cinnamon
1 tsp ground Ginger
1/4 - 1/2 tsp fresh grated Nutmeg (use whole nutmeg)
1/2 tsp Cardamom
1/4 tsp ground Cloves

Dry Ingredients
1/2 cup Millet flour
1 cup Sweet Brown Rice flour
1/4 cup White Bean flour
1/2 cup Hazelnut flour
1/2 cup Arrowroot powder
1/4 cup Sorghum flour
1/2 tsp Vanilla powder
1 tsp Xanthan gum
2 tsp Baking powder
1 tsp Baking Soda
1/2 tsp salt

Wet Ingredients
3/4 cup Applesauce
1 T Aquaschata™

1 tsp Liquid Stevia
1 cup Chicory Tea (Steep 2 T chicory crystals in 1 cup boiling water)
1/4 cup Oat milk

1 Recipe Cashew Butter Cream Frosting (Page 380)

Cooking Instructions:
1. Preheat oven to 350 degrees F.
2. Make the Chai spice mixture and store in an airtight container.
3. Make the Chicory tea and steep for a few minutes.
4. In a mixing bowl, combine all the dry ingredients. In another bowl, combine all the wet ingredients. Pour the wet into the dry.
5. Spoon the batter or pipe the batter into mini muffin tins. The Silpat mold allows these to pop out easily.
6. Bake for 20 - 25 minutes or until a toothpick comes out clean.
7. These do best without an enclosed container, so the moisture doesn't spoil them. Freezing them keeps the freshness. So, if they aren't being eaten right away, store in a container, freeze and reheat when ready to eat. If you frost them and then freeze them, allow them to naturally thaw. The toaster oven will melt the frosting.

Notes: Try other spice combinations or lemon zest or orange.

Cake Pops
☆☆☆☆☆

These were inspired from one of my sons birthday parties. He asked for donuts, and with some batter left over, I thought to put them into the truffle mold and make cake pops. The way they were decorated and displayed on the cone shaped styrofoam turned into a "Galaxy Cake" as they looked like planets were in orbit. Had the triangle styrofoam cone been wrapped in black, it would have looked like a space cake for sure. Be as creative as you'd like.

Ingredients
1 Chocolate or plain Donut Recipe (Page 293 and 291)
Long lollipop sticks*
Styrofoam Cone (or brick) to stand them in while they freeze
Toppings - Chocolate Ganache (Page 389), Raspberry Coulis (Page 399)

Cooking Instructions: Preheat oven to 350 degrees F.

1. To make cake pops, place batter in a small truffle silicon mold and smooth top to make it even. Larger one works for other creative outcomes, but for cake pops, use the smaller ones. Bake at 350 degrees F for 10 - 15 min. Once cool, trim the tops to be more even when put together. Push a stick into two half rounds, creating a ball. Do not go through the top one. Once you have made a match to all the cake tops, with a top and bottom and a stick in it, push the sticks into the styrofoam cone. Place cone in the freezer until you are ready for the next steps.
2. Once you have the toppings made, take a knife, and using the filling of choice, fill in the gaps between the two cake half rounds that are frozen together. Smooth it around. Remove any excess drip and place back on the styrofoam. Do that with the remaining pops. Put back in freezer.
3. Once the first layer is frozen, dip in a second layer. If the first layer was caramel, the second might be chocolate. Or Raspberry coulis and the next layer is chocolate. Once they are all frozen, prepare for the next step.
4. You can add a 3rd layer of decoration. There's edible gold glitter. There's white chocolate spray. If you are using crushed toasted buckwheat or toasted nuts or coconut, you will want to apply it after the second layer before freezing.
5. How to serve? It depends on what they are for. The styrofoam cone can be wrapped in gold or other colored foil. If it's at a birthday party, that's a

decorative way to display them before kids take them. They will be frozen for a little bit before they begin thawing. So, there's time, until there isn't.

Note: *If the sticks are too short, there won't be enough room to stick them in the styrofoam when you dip them and set them in the freezer. And make sure you have the room in your freezer to hold this work of art.*

Basics & Bonuses

Walnut Pastry Dough for dessert crusts or petit fours.....362

Phyllo like Pastry Dough..365

"Crunchy" Noodles……….....………………………………367

Nut Butter Filled Pretzels/Pretzel Bites…………………....368

Apple Turnover with Vanilla Ice Cream..............................370

Xylitol Simple Syrup..372

Date Caramel………………………………………………373

Bliss Balls or Energy Balls……………………………….....375

Walnut Pastry Dough for Petit Fours Cups or Dessert Crusts

☆☆☆☆☆

makes 2 dozen

This crust has so much versatility! It is used in Turtle Bars, Lemon bars, and pie dough. Change the walnuts to pecans and it's now in the Key Lime Pie or Gingerbread Cookies. It can even be made into cookies as it is an excellent support for many desserts.

Single Recipe for Pastry Cups and single pie crust.

Ingredients

1/2 cup toasted Walnuts*
1/2 cup Sweet Brown Rice flour
1/2 cup Sorghum flour
2 1/2 T ground Flax seeds
2 T Arrowroot flour
8 T Aquaschata™
1/4 tsp Liquid Stevia
1 tsp Vanilla Powder
1/2 tsp Salt

Cooking Instructions for making the dough:

1. Roast the walnuts in a 300 Degree F oven for 10 min. Once cooled, use a food processor to meal them. Do not over mix into Walnut butter.
2. In a small saucepan, heat up 8 T of Aquaschata™ and pour into a bowl. Add the ground flax meal making a loose flax egg. Add the Liquid Stevia to this as well.
3. In a stand mixing bowl, add the flour, the ground walnuts, vanilla powder and salt. Mix until well combined or hand whisk before setting it up in the stand mixer. Pour in the Aquaschata™ mix and on low speed let the dry ingredients take in the wet. Turn it to medium speed. If you are making a crust for turtle bars or a crumble crust, before this becomes a dough ball, remove and use appropriately, patting it down into the baking dish.
4. Turn on to high speed in the mixing bowl letting this become a dough ball. Remove and use immediately.

*Substitute Pecans in place of Walnuts if you are avoiding Walnuts.

Cooking Instructions for Making Pastry Petit Fours:

Preheat oven to 350 degrees F.

1. Using mini muffin pans (silicon is too soft for this), roll out about 1 inch of

dough. You will know quickly if it's too big. Find something that will act as a round wooden dowel (lemon reamer end works great), place the ball on the bottom of a nonstick mini muffin tin. Press it down with your thumb.

2. Using the end of the lemon reamer or wooden dowel with a round end, twist it back and forth pushing down to a thinner bottom. Using your thumbs, spread it evenly filling the mini muffin tin into a perfect cup. Practicing this will help make them thinner in time. Too thick, they look clunky. Too thin, they crack and break. Find the right amount of dough that will be the perfect size. It's easier to make a lot of dough balls, then work the tins for a row or two. Rather than doing one at a time. The dough won't dry out. The oils from the walnuts keep it moist. That's why this is such a perfect crust to work with.

3. Bake in a preheated oven at 350 degrees F until they are a nice golden brown. Roughly 15 - 20 minutes. Once they come out of the oven and cool down, it's easy to take a stiff spatula or a butter knife to pop them out.

Suggested uses: *Petit Fours are bite sized desserts. Fill with the Key Lime Pie or Lemon Pastry Cream topped with Coconut Whipping Cream and fresh Raspberry or Lemon or Lime Zest. Or make mini turtle bars or pecan pie filling topped with a drizzle of chocolate ganache. Make a cherry filling or a blueberry compote and top with a Cashew Cream Glaze. It really is impressive how upscale these look. Perfect for parties.*

Cooking Instructions for a Rustic Pie Dough:
Preheat oven to 425 degrees F.

1. Double the recipe for top and bottom pie dough. If using for single pie recipe like pumpkin pie, pecan pie or a lattice top berry pie, follow these instructions.

2. Form a ball of dough and place it in the center of the mat. Begin rolling out, turning the mat every now and then, keeping the dough as a circle. This is a very forgiving dough. If it tears, simply push it back into itself and roll over it again. Roll out to the size of the pie dish. Deep Dish Pie dishes require a bigger circle.

3. Next, flip the mat on top of the pie dish and peel back the mat leaving just the dough. Settle it into place. If it's a single pie, pour the filling in and finish the edges by fluting them with your right thumb and forefinger making a u shape while your left thumb pushes into that u shape making a nice clean decorated edge.

4. If you are making a double recipe, then you will be cutting the dough in half and setting one half aside and following the above instructions. After you have the filling mounded up, roll out the second dough half and again, flip it upside

down on top of the pie. Peel it back and settle the dough in place. Cut off the extra dough and set that aside for making extra pastry cups. Poke holes in the top for venting and bake at 425 degrees F for 10 minutes and then lowering to 350 degrees F for 60 minutes. Cover edges with foil after 45 minutes if it appears to be darkening.

5. When it comes out of the oven, it will sound and feel hollow and hard. As it cools, that hardness softens. Most of the pies in this book taste better the next day after completely cooling off.

Cooking Instructions for the bottom crust of Cheesecakes and Bars.
Preheat oven to 350 degrees F.

1. Follow "Making the Dough:" directions on Page 363. Before it forms into a dough ball, and is thoroughly combined and crumbly, remove from the mixer.
2. Pour into a 9 x 13 pan lined with parchment paper. Or a 10 inch springform pan or mini spring pans. Shake the pan in all directions allowing the crumble to evenly spread. Pat down with your hands until firm.
3. Bake at 350 degrees F for 15 - 20 minutes until crust is done.

Variation:
Hazelnut Crust for Bars and "Cheesecakes"
☆☆☆☆☆

Hazelnut Crust:
1 1/2 - 2 cups Hazelnut flour
4 - 6 Softened Medjool Dates chopped (or 1 cup Xylitol or 1/2 cup Date Nectar)
2 T Cacao powder
1 tsp Vanilla Powder
1 Recipe Angel Butter (1 T Aquaschata™, 2 tsp chia seeds, 1/8 tsp Turmeric and 2 T Coconut Cream)

- Use a food processor for this. Combine and pulse to a crumble. Press into pan.

PASTRY DOUGH

Phyllo-Like Pastry Dough
☆☆☆☆☆

This dough recipe makes a lot. Reduce recipe in half or freeze extra dough if you don't need as much. The versatility this pastry dough offers is as close to a phyllo dough that I've made. It doesn't tear when it gets really thin. It can be used in savory or sweet creations. It is great for my Happytizer's of Mushrooms wrapped in Phyllo. It can be used in a main entree to make a Wellington and it can even be used to make Apple Turnovers. Favorite ways to use it includes a pretzel filled bite with a nut butter or pinwheels filled with sunflower butter or hazelnut butter and "jam" bites using a Raspberry coulis to dip it in. This dough can be used for just about anything "wrapped." It will not be flaky, but it will have crunch and it will bake whatever is inside.

Dry Ingredients
1 1/4 cup Tapioca flour
1 cup + 2 T Arrowroot flour
2 1/4 cups Oat flour
1/2 cup Brown Rice flour
2 T Psyllium Husk <u>powder</u> *
2 tsp Salt

Wet Ingredients
1 3/4 cup Cashew Milk**(or any plant based milk)
1/3 cup + 2 T Aquaschata™

Cooking Instructions: Preheat oven to 400 degrees F.
1. In a small pot warm cashew milk over medium heat (just under a boil). Add Aquaschata™ once it's heated.
2. In a mixer bowl (using the dough hook) combine tapioca flour, arrowroot flour, oat flour, brown rice flour, psyllium husk powder, and salt. Mix on medium speed for 5 minutes adding in the cashew milk and Aquaschata™ liquid until it forms a nice dough ball that is sticky, but firm.
3. Remove dough onto a floured surface (I use brown rice flour). Make sure your hands are floured too. Knead for 2 more minutes, putting your body weight into it. You want the dough supple, not dry.
4. Divide into 10 - 12 using a knife or pastry cutter.

5. Depending on your use, you can freeze half the dough or set aside for what you are making.
6. Weigh all the divided pieces and make as close to 34 - 36 grams each for consistency.
7. Next, either use the pasta machine to make thin pieces or a rolling pin. This dough can be stretched to the last setting on the pasta machine and not tear. It is quite magical that way. Keeping settings to #5 or #7 seem to be sufficient with whatever was being made.
8. Once you have wrapped whatever it is you are using this for, bake in a preheated oven of 400 degrees F. Times vary based on the filling. Usually, 15 to 20 minutes is all that's needed.

Notes:
* Psyllium husk powder can be found in the bulk herbs section at natural grocery stores. This recipe only works with the powder. Not the whole fiber. I use the whole fiber for my bread recipes.

"Crunchy" Noodles
☆☆☆☆☆

These crunchy noodles taste and feel just like Chow Mein noodles. I originally learned this idea from an Australian chef. However, he made them with food grade charcoal giving them a "charcoal" look. Which is kind of funny ... as if you leave them in the oven too long, they will burn.

Ingredients
1/2 recipe Phyllo-Like Pastry Dough (Page 365)
Pasta Machine to make thin or a rolling pin to roll very thin.
Spaghetti attachment
Salt or Chili Lime powder

Cooking Instructions:
1. Divide the Phyllo-Like Pastry Dough into 5 or 6 pieces each weighing 34g - 36g (About 1 1/4 ounces).
2. Keep the unused dough in a zip lock bag as you work with each one individually.
3. Roll out a piece just enough to go through the pasta machine to thin it.
4. Bring it to #4 or #5. Then change out the attachment to the spaghetti and run it through to turn it into spaghetti shape noodles.
5. Preheat oven to 400 degrees F.
6. Line a cookie sheet with parchment paper or a Silpat mat.
7. Next, place the noodles on the cookie sheet not touching.
8. They cook quick... 5 - 7 minutes. Watch 'em!
   It's a labor of love at this point. It's worth it because you will have Some of the best crunchy noodles. I like to randomly place them crossing and making designs. Don't let them clump together. I've attempted it as a whole clump, and it doesn't work at all. You can either line them up straight in a row and the other method just explained. Season with salt, garlic salt or chili lime powder. Bake until they are golden brown. Not long at all. You will know when they are burnt. Keep your eyes on them. Remove and let cool. Place in a sealed container to keep them crunchy. If there are any left. Sprinkle them or eat as a snack. They make a very satisfying "cracker.

Nut Butter Filled Pretzels and Pretzel Bites dipped in Raspberry Coulis

☆☆☆☆☆

These bite size treats are a take on "peanut butter and jelly" and are similar to the almond butter or peanut butter filled pretzels in the store, however they are more allergy friendly. You can use sunflower butter or anything that works for your body type. The amount used can be controlled and it really is about the flavor vs the fat in this case. A little can go a long way.

Ingredients
1/2 recipe Phyllo Like Pastry Dough (Page 365)
Nut or Seed Butter of choice
Pasta Machine to make thin or a rolling pin to roll very thin.

1 recipe Raspberry Coulis or other fruit flavored "jam"

Cooking Instructions:

1. Divide the Phyllo Pastry Dough into 5 or 6 pieces, each weighing 34g - 36g. Keep the unused dough in a zip lock bag as you work with each one individually. Between two pieces of parchment paper, roll out the dough into a rectangle. As if you were making ravioli. You can either run it through the pasta machine from #1 and each time making it thinner to #2, #3, #4, and ending on #5. For what you are using this for in this recipe, this thinness works just fine.
2. Whatever nut or seed butter you are using, you will need a 1/4 tsp measurement to scoop and place on your dough in a line leaving space on each end. Make sure they are about 1 inch spaced from each other as you will be cutting in between them.
3. You are making a small, filled cracker here. It is about 1 inch by 3/4 inches once pinched closed. Keeping that in mind, fold the dough over the nut butter, wetting with water (with your finger) the area the dough you will be touching so it will stick together.
4. Once you have made enough bites, place them on a cookie sheet on parchment paper and bake at 400 degrees F for 15 minutes or until golden brown.
5. Another way to make these that is quicker, is to take your nut or seed butter and thin it down with water, if it's extra thick, as you want to make easy to spread. Not too thin. Take a round or rectangle that you have rolled

and spread the nut or seed butter and starting on one side, just like making cinnamon rolls, roll it all the way to the other side. Take a sharp knife and cut every inch and place on a cookie sheet lined with parchment paper. Bake at 400 degrees F for 15 minutes or until golden brown. Once cooled, serve with a small dipping of Raspberry Coulis.

Notes: Mix it up and have both ways of making these fun kid friendly treats.

Apple Turnover with Vanilla Ice Cream
☆☆☆☆☆

The caramelization on the apples creates a decadent dessert. A fun way to serve the vanilla ice cream it to make it in silicon truffle size molds. That way when you cut open your turnover, you can fill the inside of the hot apple dessert and with a small half truffle size of Vanilla ice cream. Having a hot and cold dessert at the same time.

Ingredients
1/2 recipe Phyllo-Like Pastry Dough (Page 365)

Filling
4 Honey Crisp Apples, chopped
1 T Cinnamon
1 T Lemon Juice
9 - 15 drops Liquid Stevia (optional) depends on how sweet the apples are.

Pasta Machine to make thin or a rolling pin to roll very thin.

Pastry Brush with Coconut milk

1 recipe Vanilla Ice cream (Page 402)

Cooking Instructions:
1. Divide the Phyllo-Like Pastry Dough into 5 or 6 pieces, each weighing 34g - 36g (1 1/4 ounces).
   Keep the unused dough in a zip lock bag as you work with each one individually. Between two pieces of parchment paper, roll out the dough into a rectangle. As if you were making ravioli. You can either run it through the pasta machine from #1 and each time making it thinner to #2, #3, #4, and ending on #5. For what you are using this for in this recipe, this Level of thinness works just fine.
2. In a large skillet, sauté the apple pieces with cinnamon and lemon juice on Medium high heat. Cook them down until they are half cooked. Somewhat Al dente, so they can continue to cook in the oven and caramelize.
3. For this recipe, you want the #6 thin layer on the pasta machine. There will be 3 layers of the same dough cut approximately 3 inches by 7 or 8 inches.

Using a pastry brush, brush each layer with coconut milk and place another layer on top, 3 layers down. Then take 1/4 to 1/2 cup of the apple filling and place at the top leaving an inch and a half from the top. Take the top and fold it over the apples and fold the sides in and roll until the seam is on the bottom. Adjust accordingly to make sure the seam is on the bottom. Place on a cookie sheet lined with parchment paper.
4. Once you have made enough turnovers, bake in a preheated oven at 400 degrees F for 15 - 20 minutes or until golden brown. The kitchen will smell like an apple pie is baking.
5. Remove from oven. When hot, cut one open and place a small round of Vanilla Ice Cream (Page 402) inside. It's absolutely delicious.

Xylitol Simple Syrup

This is an easy recipe and works wonderfully when needing a "syrupy" texture. In fact, it's perfect for replacing corn syrup. The weird cooling flavor xylitol is known for, disappears, in the same way it does when used with any citrus.

Ingredients
1.5 cups granulated Xylitol
1 cup filtered Water

Cooking Instructions:
1. In a small pot, add the water and xylitol. Be careful and avoid any splashing of the xylitol crystals hitting the sides of the pan. If they don't dissolve, they trigger the liquid xylitol to recrystallize.
2. Simmer on medium heat until all the xylitol has dissolved into a liquid state, approximately 4 - 5 minutes. Please don't stir, any contact of the sides may end up recrystallizing later.
3. Once all the xylitol is in liquid form, reduce the heat to medium low and simmer for 1 minute to reduce and thicken to a syrup. Be sure to watch the pot while making the xylitol syrup as it can overflow if you don't reduce the heat, just like a regular simple syrup.
4. Pour into a clean container that has no granulated xylitol residue in it.
5. Cover and keep in the refrigerator up to 10 days.

Date Caramel *makes 2 cups*
☆☆☆☆☆

This is oh, so good. If you can't have dates ... try Yacon syrup.

Ingredients
15 Medjool Dates
1 cup Hot water
1/3 cup + 1 T ground Raw Cashews*
3 T Oat milk
1/4 tsp Vanilla powder
3 T Coconut Cream (out of the Refrigerator solids only)
Pinch of salt
And a lot of patience

Unless you double the recipe, you need to be patient with how much back and forth may happen between seed grinder and blender. A stick blender will make this go much easier!

Cooking Instructions
1. Soak dates in a mason jar with 1 cup boiling water. Let sit for an hour or overnight. Keep the liquid! Remove the pits from the dates and place in blender.
2. In a blender, add the cashews, dates, 1/2 of the date liquid, oat milk, vanilla powder and salt and blend on high (like it's being whipped) for a minute or so. If there isn't enough liquid, you won't have any traction. This is why I suggest doubling the recipe. If you transfer it to a seed grinder, do it in batches so it has space to whip. When it's broken down and you see the date bits, add it back to the blender. If you add all the water back, it can be too runny. So. start with smaller amounts.
3. Next, add in 3 T of coconut cream. At this point in the blender, you may need to add another 2 - 3 T water to get it whipping. You want to blend it on high to get it "whipped." This is what makes the difference in both texture and looks. You will notice that all the date flecks are no longer visible. That is what you are aiming for.
4. This is the "base" caramel recipe that is used in the ice cream or the pecan bars. If it's a candy like caramel your after, then there is this option that requires cooking it on the stovetop. You can use 2 T

Arrowroot flour with 4 T water and 3/4 tsp ground Chia Seeds. Heat Caramel and add 2 T of the liquid mixture and stir. Then add 2 more T. Then stir. Finish the remaining. Stirring consistently. Pour into little candy molds or into little truffle rounds. Put in freezer. You can keep this inside the freezer and use half or whole whenever you would like a caramel chew. Let it thaw a little and it will have a chewy texture.

5. Refrigerate the basic recipe in an airtight container. It keeps for about 1 week. Place in freezer to keep longer. Freeze in 1/2 cup amounts for adding to ice cream.

Substitute with Macadamia or Pili nuts if avoiding cashews. Or make without any nut. You can also add it to the Cauliflower Ricotta recipe for Cannoli fillings, however, it will only be good for the first day. After that, the flavor of cauliflower earthiness comes through. You can freeze it to prevent that from happening. Both the cannoli or the filling.

Bliss Balls or Energy Balls
☆☆☆☆☆

These make an excellent snack for kids or take them along for a hike to boost your energy.

Ingredients
1/2 cup Amaranth cooked grain
2 T Chia Seeds
1/2 T Psyllium Husk powder
1/4 cup dried Blueberries (optional)
1 1/2 T Sunflower Seed butter (or any other nut or seed butter)
1/4 - 1/3 tsp Vanilla powder
9 - 15 drops of Liquid Stevia (any flavors)
2 - 4 T toasted Sunflower seeds (or Sesame or Pumping seeds)
1 T Hemp or Pumpkin seed protein powder (optional)
1 - 2 T Oat flour (dry toasting optional)
Another 1 T Oat flour mixed with 1 T pumpkin spice to roll in afterwards
Pinch of Cardamom seeds
pinch of salt

Cooking Instructions:
1. Cooking Amaranth is fun to watch. Fill a small pot of water and add 1/2 cup Amaranth and let boil for 15 minutes or so. It is done when it all sinks to the bottom of the pot. Strain and set aside.
2. In a mixing bowl, add the remaining ingredients.
3. Roll 1 T of dough into a ball in your hand and roll it into the spice flour mixture and place in an airtight container. Kids love them.
   Suggestions: Add cacao, or roll in coconut flakes, cinnamon, etc. Instead of dried blueberries, use freeze dried blueberries, dried cranberries or freeze dried fruit powders.

Frostings, Whipped Toppings & More

Coconut Whipping Cream...377

Basic Cashew Cream..379

Basic Cashew Butter Cream Frosting...................................380

Ginger Cardamom Cashew Cream Glaze.............................380

Macadamia Cauliflower Ricotta Cheese Dessert Filling...381

Orange Ginger Frosting...383

Lemon Pastry Cream..384

Lemon Curd...385

Orange Hazelnut Pastry Cream...386

Hazelnut Cacao Chestnut Mousse with Raspberry

Coulis and Cashew Cream...387

Chocolate Ganache..389

Delicious Turtle Bars...390

Baked Apples with Golden Raisins and RizCous/

Cauliflower Rice..392

Coconut Whipping Cream

☆☆☆☆☆

Finally, a Frosting for cakes that you can pipe and frost. It is AMAZING. This frosting is fun to work with. It can take on colors easily, and, can be used as filling for cupcakes and profiteroles. You can even pipe flowers with it! Once you try this recipe, you will have a new favorite.

Ingredients

2 cans Refrigerated Organic Unsweetened Coconut Milk (with guar gum) You will use the solids only, saving the liquid for another use.
1/2 tsp Xanthan Gum
2 T Cold Inulin
1 T Tapioca flour
1/4 tsp liquid Stevia (adjust to taste)
1 T Freeze dried Passion fruit Powder or Vanilla Powder (optional)
If you want a **Chocolate** frosting, add melted cacao paste (sweetened with stevia)
or
4 - 5 tsp Cacao Powder (add another 8 oz, milk with this option)

Cooking Instructions:

1. Refrigerate 1 or 2 cans of Coconut Milk, overnight. It will not work at room temperature. Open the can upside down to make it easy to dump the liquid into a jar and save for another use. Scoop out the Coconut Cream into a stand mixer or mixing bowl with hand mixer.
2. Add the Xanthan Gum and turn on low speed. Before adding any other ingredient, break up the density at this speed. You can use a rubber spatula to scrape the sides. Once it's not as hard as when you opened it, begin adding the Inulin and the liquid stevia. Sometimes, I'll add in the coconut liquid to get it going a little better. However, you can add any kind of milk. You only need 1 T at a time. Since the longer you let it mix, the better it creams.
3. Add the Tapioca flour and turn it on medium to high speed and let it cream for about 5 minutes. Scraping sides if you need to. At this point, you can add any food coloring, raspberry or strawberry coulis, drizzle it in for pink. Or add the freeze dried powders. You can also flavor it with liquid stevia. They have peppermint, lemon, vanilla - etc. …Vanilla powder gives a brown speckle. Liquid vanilla stevia is clear and doesn't affect the end result. You are looking

for soft peaks, not stiff. If you want more structure, the tapioca and or cacao powder will create more stiff peaks, making it easy to use with a pastry bag.
4. This keeps in the fridge for 1 week, if it lasts that long. You can fill pastries, cupcakes and frost cakes and pipe borders and flowers. Add Cacao powder to make it chocolate and stiff or melt in the cacao paste with extra stevia to give it a richness. Or drizzle the melted cacao paste on to it for a dark contrast design.

Basic Cashew Cream *makes 1 - 2 cups*
☆☆☆☆☆

This cream is rich, so only a small amount is really needed. It has no cholesterol and minimal saturated fat. This can be used over fruit, tortes, crisps and pies. It is perfect for dipping strawberries.

Ingredients
1 cup Raw Cashews (Soak for 2 - 4 hours to soften)
1 cup water
1/2 cup cooked Baby Lima Beans (add more if too thin)
15 drops Liquid Stevia (start here and add more if needed)
1/2 tsp Vanilla powder
pinch of Salt

Cooking Instructions:

- In blender, add cashews and water and blend to form a thick milk. Add the cooked baby lima beans until the cream thickens. Blend in vanilla and salt. Chill and serve. (Cream will thicken substantially when chilled but will not be stiff)

Notes: *This freezes well and can be scooped out when thawed 1/2 way. Since it will spoil 3 - 4 days in the fridge it is a good idea to freeze it if you have made more than you need.*

- *Add fresh mint, fresh strawberries or fresh mangoes to bring new flavors to light. Also adding cocoa or melted cacao paste and extra stevia work well to fill chocolate cakes. (Use less water so it is thicker).*

Basic Cashew Butter Cream Frosting
☆☆☆☆☆

Ingredients
3/4 cup Raw Cashews (soaked or ground up)
1/4 tsp Liquid Stevia
Freeze dried fruit for color (optional)
3 T Coconut Cream
1/4 cup water

- Blend in seed grinder or blender on high speed.

Ginger Cardamom Cashew Cream Glaze   *makes 1 cup*
☆☆☆☆☆
Pour this over a warm chicory spice cake and feel the indulgence.

Ingredients
1/2 cup Raw Cashews (soaked 2 - 4 hours to soften)
1/2 cup cooked Baby Lima Beans
1 cup water
1/2 tsp Vanilla powder
9 - 12 drops Liquid Stevia
1 tsp powdered Ginger
1/4 tsp Cardamom

Cooking Instructions:
- Blend all ingredients in blender. Refrigerate. Adjust sweetener. Thickens in fridge a little… adjust texture with water by adding 1 - 2 T, if necessary.

Macadamia Cauliflower Ricotta Cheese Dessert Filling

☆ ☆ ☆ ☆ ☆

Makes 2 cups

The cauliflower creams this beautifully and keeps it light and not rich. So, you can enjoy this without the heaviness or richness of dairy.

- *Basic Recipe:*
  1 1/2 Cauliflower riced (Page 106),(Cooked) = 1 head of Cauliflower*, Raw
  1 cup Macadamia nuts ground into a meal
  Salt to taste

- *Sweet Version:*
  Add fresh fruit coulis like raspberry, blueberry, chocolate, ginger, orange zest, lemon zest
  Use cacao powder to replace the nutritional yeast.
  1/2 tsp Liquid Stevia (Flavored Stevia work well here if you have a specific flavor in mind)
  1 1/2 tsp Vanilla powder

  Example of a sweet version
  Sweet Macadamia Cauliflower Ricotta Cheese recipe - makes 2 cups
  1 1/2 cup Cauliflower riced (roughly 1/2 a head)
  1/2 cup Macadamia nuts ground into a meal
  1/2 tsp Liquid Stevia (Flavored Stevia work well here if you like a specific flavor)
  1 tsp Vanilla powder
  1 1/2 cup Fresh Raspberries
  1 T Cold Inulin
  3 T Coconut Cream, cold, from refrigerator

  - Or Freeze dried Raspberry powder
  - Or Raspberry coulis

Cooking Instructions:
1. Prepare Cauliflower, depending on which version you have chosen.
2. In the food processor, add remaining ingredients. Fresh fruit, Freeze dried fruit or Coulis all work here. It tastes best the same day. After the first day the cauliflower flavor begins to show and isn't as pleasant. So, this is best to freeze and thaw to make ahead of time or to eat fresh.

**Try recipes with purple cauliflower for a stunning lavender colored filling.

Variations:
Add fresh fruit coulis like mango, blueberry or blackberry, or add 4 - 6 T of any freeze dried fruit when not in season, melted chocolate, ginger, orange zest, lemon zest ...
Use cacao powder to replace the nutritional yeast.

Orange Ginger Frosting

☆☆☆☆☆

This fragrant frosting tastes amazing with spice cake or as a filling inside a cupcake. The color is a rich amber and the flavor profile can even be added into an ice cream by steeping it in any plant based milk.

Ingredients
2 T Mulling Spice
1/2 T Chicory Crystals
1 cup boiling hot water

1/2 cup ground Raw Cashews
1 cup cooked Baby Lima Beans (or pumpkin seed tofu)
1 tsp Ginger powder
1/4 tsp Cardamom
1/2 tsp Vanilla powder
1/2 tsp ground dehydrated Orange Peels
1/4 tsp Liquid Stevia
Pinch of Salt

Cooking Instructions:

1. In a cup, steep 1 cup boiling water with the mulling spices and chicory crystals. Steep for 5 - 6 minutes. Strain and set aside the liquid. Let it cool off for 10 min.
2. In the blender, add the spiced water, and the remaining ingredients. Add more water if it needs to be thinned down.

Variations: *For an orange hazelnut frosting, substitute Hazelnut liquid stevia and omit the ginger powder. This would then pair well with the Orange Hazelnut Pastry cream. Add a little cacao to the frosting and it's now a chocolate color and ready for an upscaled cake.*

Lemon Pastry Cream
☆☆☆☆☆

Super delicious. And full of protein. No guilt, that's for sure. (For a nut free version, use the Lemon curd recipe, page 385).

Ingredients
1 1/2 cups cooked Baby Lima Beans
1/2 cup Lemon Juice
1 T ground Chia Seeds
1 - 3 T water
1/4 cup Raw Cashews
3 T Xylitol
3 - scoops of 1/32 Pure Organic Monk Fruit
1/8 tsp Turmeric, for yellow color
1 T Tapioca flour (optional if heating to get desired thickness)

Cooking Instructions:
1. Cook Lima Beans in the pressure cooker.
2. In a blender, add cooked Lima beans, lemon juice and cashews.
3. In a separate cup, add 1 - 3 T of warm water with the ground chia seeds and let that firm up a little. And then add to the blender.
4. Next, combine the xylitol and monk fruit. You need both monk fruit (there is no eurythritol in it) and xylitol to get the balanced flavor.
5. Add xylitol/monk fruit to the blender. Make it real creamy. Add more water if need be. Add a dusting of turmeric to make it yellow. It's not yellow enough without it. Refrigerate it for a couple of hours and the lemon flavor really pops.
6. Make walnut tart shells and fill with a raspberry on top. Pipe into shells and add a raspberry.

Lemon Curd *makes 1 1/2 cups to 2 cups*
☆☆☆☆☆
This delicious lemon curd has the texture of apple butter. Spread it on bread, English muffins, fill profiteroles and or make lemon bars using the Walnut pastry dough as the crust for the bars. It delivers a lot of flavor and doesn't disappoint.

Ingredients
1 1/4 cup fresh Lemon Juice
1/4 cup + 3 T Oat milk
1 cup Xylitol
1/4 tsp Turmeric
1 T Agar Agar
1 1/2 tsp Tapioca flour

Cooking Instructions:
1. In a saucepan heat up the Oat milk, lemon juice, xylitol and turmeric. Bring to a boil and on medium heat cook another minute.
2. In a small cup, add the tapioca flour and 2 - 3 T of cold water and mix until the flour dissolves. In another small cup, add the 1 T of Agar Agar powder to 3 T of cold water (enough to dissolve it) and set aside.
3. On medium high heat, whisk in the tapioca liquid and then add the Agar Agar liquid. Continue vigorously whisking for one minute.
4. Whisk this into the lemon juice saucepan on a medium to high heat until it begins to bubble.

Note: *If not using right away, pour into a canning jar, with lid, and store in refrigerator.*

Orange Hazelnut Pastry Cream *makes 1 1/2 cups to 2 cups*
☆☆☆☆☆

This pastry cream is perfect inside petit fours, Profiteroles or frost the inside layers of a cake. Combine with cacao whipped frosting and you have another creamy, delicious cake.

Ingredients
1 1/2 cup Oat milk
1 cup Orange juice
1/4 tsp Liquid Hazelnut Stevia (*or plain*)
1/2 cup Xylitol
4 T Tapioca flour
2 T Kudzu root
4 tsp Arrowroot powder
5 tsp Agar Agar

Cooking Instructions:
1. In a saucepan heat up the Oat milk, orange juice, xylitol and hazelnut stevia. Bring to a boil and on medium heat cook another minute. Taste. Is it too sweet? Not enough sweet. Adjust the flavors. Balance it out with the hazelnut stevia. You may need to add more to adjust flavors.
2. In a small cup, add the tapioca flour, kudzu root and arrowroot powder, stir and add in 1/4 to 1/3 cup of cold water and mix until all the powder dissolves. In another cup have the 5 tsp of Agar Agar powder and add 3 T of cold water (enough to dissolve it) and set aside.
3. Take the first cup of flours and add it to the liquid, mixing it with a whisk for a minute or two. It should thicken up. Take the Agar Agar and add that dissolved liquid to the mixture and mix another minute or so. Pour into a covered glass container to cool in the refrigerator for a couple of hours and let set.
4. Taste again. It gets diluted with the added ingredients. If it's too sweet, adjust with more orange juice to cut the sweet. If it's still too tart, add a drop or two of Stevia. Pour into a covered glass container or directly into a Hazelnut Crust. Place in refrigerator to cool and set.

Suggestion: *If you are using this with the Hazelnut Crust, the favor of hazelnut are already in the crust. It's optional to use it in the cream. Adding Freeze dried Passion Fruit powder to a cream topping will also cut the sweetness while adding another flavor dimension.*

Hazelnut Cacao Chestnut Mousse with Raspberry Coulis and Cashew Cream *Makes 3*

☆☆☆☆☆

This dessert delivers a wow factor. Although it is quite the unconventional method of making mousse, it shows both the resources available and the power of creativity. Plus supports you on your journey as you continue learning what it takes to be **Fearless in the Kitchen**. *There are many desserts made with tofu. Looking at lima beans that way will help bridge this for you. Try this, you will not be disappointed. Add a raspberry coulis to this and you are now in heaven.*

Ingredients
2 cups Fresh Chestnuts (jar peeled chestnuts are available)
2 cups water
2 T Raw Cashews
1 cup cooked Baby Lima beans
1/4 - 1/2 cup water
2 T Cacao powder
2 - 3 T (2/3 cup bark) melted Cacao Paste (Cacao seeds; no other ingredients)
1 tsp Vanilla powder
1/2 tsp Liquid Hazelnut Stevia
pinch of salt
thin with Oat milk once made and chilled if it's too thick.

1 recipe Raspberry Coulis (optional) (Page 399)
1 recipe Cashew Cream (Page 379) or Coconut Whipping Cream (Page 377)

Cooking Instructions:
You can prepare both the chestnuts and lima beans ahead of time to make this go quickly.

1. In a pressure cooker, cook 1 cup baby lima beans for 30 minutes (15 minutes release time). Strain and set aside. You can do this ahead of time and freeze.
2. Chestnuts can either be steamed whole or roasted. Prepare fresh chestnuts with scoring the shell with an x so it will peel apart easily when cooked. (If you don't do this step, they can explode in the kitchen going off like firecrackers!!) You can

roast at 425 degrees F for 15 minutes or until they easily come out. Or you can steam them for 30 minutes to one hour and remove shells. I find it quicker to roast and then boil them for 45 minutes in a pot of water covering them. Maybe 2 cups. Make sure you add water to the pot as it will evaporate out. The chestnut is done when it's soft inside.

3. Crumble the chestnuts to a blender or food processor, blend the chestnuts with 2 cups of water and salt. It will be completely smooth. Set aside and add 2 T cacao powder.
4. Place 1 cup of the lima beans into the blender or food processor with 2 T cashews (optional) and start with 1/4 cup water. Blend till smooth. The cashews if they aren't smooth yet will in the next step.
5. In a double boiler, heat the water until it melts the Cacao paste. Use a spoon to assist it along. There's a point where it just melts effortlessly. Add in 1/2 tsp Hazelnut Stevia. Sweeten until desired taste.
6. Add chestnut cream to the blended lima beans and add the vanilla. Blend till completely smooth. Add the melted cacao at this point and blend again.
Cacao Paste is extremely bitter. Add Stevia to sweeten to taste.
(Optional) Making Cashew Cream or Coconut Whipping Cream - Make ahead of time so it's chilled.

Serve in clear wine glasses with layers of chocolate mouse and fresh raspberries (or Raspberry Coulis), then drizzle with cashew cream on top.

Notes: *You can use the Hazelnut cacao Chestnut mousse as a filling to a cake or even frost the cake with it. It freezes well. So you can make this ahead of time.*
**Use Macadamia or Pili nuts in place of Cashew if you cannot eat cashews

Chocolate Ganache

☆☆☆☆☆

What is a ganache? Ganache is a pourable icing. The traditional recipe calls for heavy whipping cream and butter. This ganache uses more healthful ingredients but still has a rich, sweet, chocolate flavor. It is easy to make, easy to work with, versatile, and delicious. You can dip fresh fruit, such as strawberries or bananas, in it as well. It can be used to pour over cakes, pipe borders or dip cookies and donuts as a way to offer a more decadent treat. Chill it and pipe decorations on the cake or make chocolate roses.

This recipe is unconventional; however, the chemistry still works and the end result offers a decadent and delicious chocolate glaze. Due to the organic nature of the cacao paste, it is extremely bitter. It needs to be sweetened with stevia in order for it to balance out what you are making.

Ingredients for a Chocolate Ganache:
1/2 - 1 cup Oat milk
1 cup Cacao paste
1 tsp Liquid Stevia

Optional - add 1/4 tsp Hazelnut Liquid stevia, Peppermint Stevia or English Toffee Stevia

Cooking Instructions:

- With a double boiler, break up the cacao paste into pieces and melt. Once melted, turn off the heat and add the oat milk, vanilla and cacao powder. Remove from heat and then add the English Toffee Liquid Stevia. Stir in completely.

Delicious Turtle Bars *Makes 16 Bars in a 9 x 13 pan*
☆☆☆☆☆

To me, Turtle Bars represent the ultimate decadent dessert. Turtle Bars have been in my life for over 30 years and finding a way to make them sugar free, gluten free, oil free and vegan has been a continuing evolution. If you can't have dates for the caramel, to get that "caramel" flavor, the English Toffee Stevia works as a substitute. There are also two crust options to keep this fun for you. They both offer a different end result. Using the hazelnuts will invite that flavor in and using the walnuts gives it a milder flavor. Either way, they are delicious.

2 Crust options:

- Make a double recipe of the Walnut Crust pastry (Page 362)

- Or try this Hazelnut Crust:
  1 1/2 - 2 cups Hazelnut flour
  4 - 6 Softened Medjool Dates chopped (or 1 cup Xylitol or 1/2 Date Nectar)
  2 T Cacao powder
  1 tsp Vanilla powder
  1 Recipe Angel Butter (Page 107)

Chocolate Ganache: This is a specific Ganache recipe for Turtle Bars
1/2 - 1 cup Oat milk
2 cups Cacao Paste
1 tsp Liquid Stevia
Optional, add 1/4 tsp Hazelnut liquid stevia to this or
1/4 tsp English Toffee Liquid Stevia drops
1/2 - 1 cup Pecan pieces, roasting them before hand is optional

1 recipe Date Caramel (Page 373)

Cooking Instructions: Preheat oven to 350 degrees F.
1. Roast 1/2 - 1 cup pecan pieces in oven or toaster oven at 350 degrees F for 10 min. Remove and let cool.
2. **If making the Hazelnut crust, use a Food processor.** Add the crust ingredients and pulse until little pea size pieces are formed. Like

crumbs of all sizes. **If making the Walnut pastry crust**, use the stand mixer and follow those instructions and when you have the crumb like texture before the dough is formed, follow the next steps.

3. Pour Walnut dough into a 9 x 13 pan lined with parchment paper. Shake the pan in all directions allowing the crumble to evenly spread. Pat down with your hands until firm.
4. Place in the 350 degrees F oven and bake for 7 - 10 minutes, until slightly browned. Let cool completely before adding Ganache Topping.
5. With a double boiler, break up the cacao paste into pieces and melt. Once melted, turn off the heat and whisk in the oat milk, vanilla and cacao powder. Remove from heat and then add the English Toffee Liquid Stevia. Stir in completely.
6. Pour on top of the crust and swirl around to ensure all corners are covered with the melted ganache.
7. Make the Caramel recipe and drizzle that on top. Next, add the pecan pieces sprinkled on top.
8. Refrigerate several hours. Cut into 16 bars 32 bars if you want them smaller. This freezes really well.

Baked Apples with Golden Raisins and RizCous or Cauliflower Rice

☆☆☆☆☆

RizCous is exactly like couscous but made with brown rice. This is a yummy cobbler that has nutritional value and is delicious at the same time.

*To make this grain free, use Cauliflower rice and almond flour or hazelnut flour and follow the instructions (Page 106). Omit the milk and oats for cooking and use the flavoring. Add only enough plant based milk to mix it appropriately with the remaining cobbler topping.

Ingredients

1 pound Golden Delicious Apples or Honey Crisp Apples (cored and thinly sliced)
3 cups Oat Milk
1/2 tsp Liquid Stevia
1 1/2 cups RizCous (Page 69) or 3 cups Cauliflower riced (cooked to 1 1/2 Cups, Page 106)
1 tsp Vanilla powder

Topping

1/2 cups rolled Oats (or walnuts or pecans for grain free)
1/3 cups White Bean flour (for grain free) or sorghum flour
1/3 Xylitol
1 tsp ground Cinnamon
1/2 tsp ground Nutmeg
1/2 cup Angel Butter (Page 107) (Double recipe for 1/2 cup)

1/3 cup Golden Raisins (or dark), soaked
1 recipe Cashew Cream (Page 379)
English toffee Stevia (opt)

Cooking Instructions: Preheat oven to 375 degrees F.
1. Prep the Angel Butter. Combine milk and stevia in a 2 quart saucepan over high heat, stirring often. Stir in RizCous and vanilla. Cover and set aside.
2. Combine oats, flour, cinnamon, nutmeg, 1/3 Xylitol and Angel Butter in food processor.

3. In a 9 x 13 casserole dish, at least 2 1/2 inches deep. Pour the RizCous mixture into the prepared dish. Smooth and level the RizCous. Place the apples on top of the RizCous evenly and in layers. Sprinkle raisins over the apples and the RizCous.
   Cover with foil and bake at 375 degrees F for 20 minutes or until apples are tender.
4. Remove foil and sprinkle oat mixture over fruit. Bake, uncovered, 15 to 20 minutes longer, or until topping is golden brown.
5. Serve warm, with Cashew Cream flavored with pumpkin spice stevia or English Toffee stevia.

Cold Treats & Drinks
Ice Creams & Sorbets

Raspberry Sorbet..398

Raspberry Coulis..399

Marionberry and Blueberry Coulis........................400

Blueberry Compote..401

Vanilla Ice Cream..402

Blueberry Sumac Ice Cream..404

Lemongrass Lime Ice Cream...405

Cardamom Cinnamon Ginger Oat Ice Cream...............407

Drinks

Blueberry lavender Lemonade...408

Chai Tea, Caffeine Free...409

Ice Cream, Sorbets, Popsicles, Ice Cream Bars and Ice Cream Truffles

Remember when you were a kid and heard the ice cream truck and all its playful music it came with? Life can trigger us into some kind of memory when it comes to food. Especially when food is about birthdays and celebrations ... foods that were just plain fun. One of my favorite memories of my youngest son, is sitting on a log at 4 years old at camp with all his buddies eating popsicles. And the teacher would send a photo and call it the "Popsicle log." This is summer!

Living a dairy free life is much easier nowadays with all the milk alternatives, however living a sugar free life does come with some tricks and tips to still enjoy these summer festive moments. These recipes I have developed are easily loved by all ages. They deliver flavor, creaminess and amazingly, they are sugar free. Create some new memories!

In the beginning of the book, I shared all about Inulin. There are many new products on the market that have taken popsicles and ice cream bars to a whole new level. First let's begin with sugar free ice cream. I've read a lot on this topic and almost everywhere I read, it says you cannot make ice cream using only Stevia as the sweetener. Let me tell you that is simply not true. You can! And these recipes in the book prove it over and over again. It's all in the chemistry, and I have practiced and practiced and practiced perfecting this for you. As you embark upon creating this amazing "ice cream," you'll find the sugar replacer is also the fat replacer.

The next key to making a creamy delicious ice cream is the emulsifier. Fat is what makes ice cream taste so creamy. So how do you replicate that without the creamy nut milks? Without dairy? The product I have found as another key element for great non dairy ice cream is Citric Fiber (Purchase at http://supplies.gusta.ca/). Used with Xanthan gum, it gives it the structure that it requires. There are some sorbets that are so creamy already they don't need these two ingredients; Strawberries, Marionberries and Mangoes, to name a few, make for a very, very creamy sorbet. It's simple, as you will see in the recipes. So, how is it that people haven't figured this secret out yet? It's simple, we are programed to believe it's not possible. It's that simple. Changing our belief systems takes courage and faith. And with cooking, I say, **Be Fearless in the Kitchen**. When kids learn that there are delicious allergy friendly ice creams and parents learn they can be sugar free, there's a perfect solution for both the kids and adults. Just because you've never heard of Inulin doesn't mean it's something to turn your head away from. In fact, it's not only ideal, it's also a prebiotic for the digestive track. Meaning, it is a major support to our digestion! Now that's a turn of events. Eating your ice cream and healing your gut! I bet you didn't see that coming.

Before I jump in with my favorite recipes and show you the magic of creating this at home, let's look at the new and improved popsicle molds. I grew up with a paper cup and a popsicle stick. Now, they have fun shapes like rockets, animals, and even aliens! What's even more impressive are the silicon molds that are designed for both juice popsicles and ice cream bars. Then you have the small truffle silicon molds that are easy to come by at craft stores. The world of silicon molds has created an upscale delivery of these frozen treats that were once served in a paper cup.

There are small ice cream bar molds for kids' hands. There are large with round corners and square corners that have lines in them making marks for "chocolate candy bars." There are so many different types of silicon molds that you can choose from that up your style. And, with these new recipes, you are finally upgrading your boring, cardboard diet you felt imprisoned by when the doctor says you can no longer eat sugar or dairy. I'm here to bring the joy back in your summer treats.

Raspberry Sorbet (or any other berry)
☆☆☆☆☆

Notice these are the same ingredients for the Raspberry Coulis? Minus the milk part. That's a trick I'm about to share.

Ingredients
4 cups frozen or fresh of any one kind or a blend of Raspberries,
 Strawberries, Blackberries
2 T Lemon Juice
1/4 - 1/2 tsp Liquid Stevia
Oat milk, Cashew milk, Coconut milk or Macadamia nut milk (optional)

Cooking Instruction
- In a saucepan, bring to a boil the raspberries, the lemon juice and stevia. Cook on medium heat for 3 - 4 minutes. Pour into a blender and then pour into a shallow container and place it in the freezer for several hours. Once it freezes, place back into the blender with some plant based milk (oat milk is very creamy) and blend again and it should be firm but not hard. The amount of milk you add into it depends on how frozen it is. It may not need it if you caught it in time.
- Serve in a waffle bowl (Page 240) or by itself, or in a popsicle mold.

Variations: *Any berry works for this.*
Strawberry Sorbet, Marionberry Sorbet, Blackberry Sorbet, will all make an exceptionally creamy sorbet when done this way. Same amount of ingredients and same technique. It's delicious!

If you want to get fancy and roast beets and blend them together, or add special flavors like rose water, lavender, mint, using either essential oils or crushing the leaves yourself, you can add them into the blender for new and exciting flavors. Or stick with traditional flavors. Experiment!

Fruit Coulis

*What is a Coulis? Is it similar to a compote? No they are different. A **coulis** is made from cooking the fruit, blending it and then straining it. There are no seeds and it has a shiny glass - like appearance and you can taste the essence of the fruit in it's pure concentrated form. They are perfect for glazing donuts, decorating dessert plates, filling inside cakes and pastries or can be blended into ice cream, cream cheese, whipped cream and meringues. You can even make vegetable coulis like roasted red peppers, carrots and beets.*

*A **compote** is a whole fruit, not blended. Not pureed. They taste significantly different in desserts. Compotes are excellent in Crepe fillings, on yogurt, on ice cream, on pancakes and waffles and even on fresh fruit itself.*

Raspberry Coulis

☆☆☆☆☆

This is considered to be liquid gold. It's absolutely divine. If you have never made this, you are in for a treat. And being made with stevia, you are not missing out. It is delicious!

4 cups fresh or frozen Raspberries
1/2 tsp liquid Stevia
2 T Lemon Juice

Cooking Instructions:

- Bring raspberries to a boil with the lemon juice and stevia. Simmer for 3 or 4 minutes. Next, pour it into the blender and blend on high. Strain into a jar and refrigerate. If you need to thin it, just add a little water.

Marionberry Coulis

☆☆☆☆☆

4 cups Fresh or Frozen Marionberries
2 T Lemon Juice
1/2 tsp Liquid stevia

Cooking Instructions:

- Bring Marionberries to a boil with the lemon juice and stevia. Simmer for 3 or 4 minutes. Next, pour it into the blender and blend on high. Strain into a jar and refrigerate. If you need to thin it, just add a little water.

Blueberry Coulis

☆☆☆☆☆

4 cups Fresh or Frozen Blueberries
2 T Lemon Juice
1/2 tsp Liquid stevia

Cooking Instructions:

- Bring blueberries to a boil with the lemon juice and stevia. Simmer for 3 or 4 minutes. Next, pour it into the blender and blend on high. Strain into a jar and refrigerate. If you need to thin it, just add a little water.

Blueberry Compote

☆☆☆☆☆

4 cups Fresh or Frozen Blueberries
2 T Lemon Juice
1/2 tsp Liquid stevia
1 1/2 tsp Arrowroot powder
2 tsp cold water

Cooking Instructions:
1. Bring Blueberries to a boil with the lemon juice and stevia.
2. Simmer for 3 minutes or so.
3. For making compote, add the water to the arrowroot powder in a small cup and mix to make it a liquid. Then pour it into the blueberries. Mix until it's thickened. It generally takes about 10 - 20 seconds. If it's not thickening, add more arrowroot powder mixed with water. Never by itself. It will clump in the pot.
4. Pour into an airtight container and refrigerate before using.

Vanilla Ice Cream

☆☆☆☆☆

This is a basic recipe that can be used to inspire any flavors you desire. Using both freeze dried fruit powders, essential oils, such as lavender and lemongrass, or turning this into chocolate ice cream. Some recipes you will replace the vanilla powder with the other flavors.

Ingredients
1 heaping tsp Vanilla Powder
4 T Cold Inulin
1 T Citric Fiber (Natur Emul is what I use)
3/4 cup Raw Cashews (optional, and soaked)
2 cups water
1 can Organic Coconut Milk (with guar gum)
1/2 tsp Liquid Stevia
3/4 tsp Xanthan Gum
Pinch of salt

If Nut allergy, replace water and cashews with 2 cups Organic Oat Milk

Cooking Instructions:
1. Add everything into a powerful blender and blend on high for several minutes. Refrigerate for several hours if not overnight.
2. Make sure the ice cream maker is in the freezer overnight. The paddle and attachment also go in the freezer an hour or so beforehand.
3. Attach the ice cream maker to your kitchen aid if that's what you have. If you have a free standing one, make sure everything is in place before pouring in the soon to be ice cream.
4. Set on low and pour the liquid in slowly. Once it's all in, turn to the appropriate setting. Follow the directions of your ice cream maker to your desired consistency. It may finish like soft served ice cream. Once in the freezer it gets hard and you will have to take it out to thaw a little for it to get creamier. I suggest scooping it into balls with your ice cream scooper and place it on parchment paper on a cookie sheet. And they will harden and freeze. They are pre scooped for ease! They fit perfectly in the waffle bowls (Page 240) now.

Variations:

Chocolate ice cream *- 1/2 cup + 2 T cacao powder mixed with 2 T Coconut Cream, or use Chocolate Flavored Stevia, or Use 1/3 cup crushed chocolate mint leaves.*

Strawberry ice cream *- add 2 T Strawberry freeze dried powder, or Strawberry flavor stevia*

Mint chocolate chip *- add fresh ground mint leaves and cacao nibs, or Use 1/3 cup crushed chocolate mint leaves.*

Lemongrass and lime juice *- on medium low heat, infuse lemongrass into the milks for 30 minutes and let sit for 2 hours. You can add essential oil to pop the flavor even more.*

Ginger ice cream *- Add 1 heaping tsp powdered ginger, or steep several ginger tea bags in milk (boil and cool) for 2 hours, or use 6 drops ginger essential oil.*

Caramel ice cream *- add 1/2 cup of Date Caramel (Page 373) to the blended mix. Or English Toffee Liquid Stevia*

Pour into Silicon Ice Cream Bar molds
They come in many shapes and sizes. You can drizzle the different coulis on it, or dip them in all together and freeze and then add a layer of chocolate. Try drizzling raspberry coulis and chocolate together and freeze. Blueberry coulis, mango coulis, strawberry coulis, Marionberry coulis ... You can swirl it into the mold making a marbled effect. Crush nuts and sprinkle on the outside of the chocolate, or Toasted Buckwheat for added crunch.

Note* *Do not add the liquid to the ice cream maker unless its turning. Once the liquid goes in, it begins to freeze and the paddles won't be able to turn. If this happens, there's no turning back. You will have to mix it by hand.*

Blueberry Sumac Ice Cream

☆☆☆☆☆

The color and vitality of this ice cream is off the charts. The health benefits of both blueberry and sumac make this a perfect healthy treat. Blueberries are one of the lowest glycemic fruits and can usually be eaten by everyone. Nutritionally, it is full of Anthocyanins which are an antioxidant and anti-inflammatory. Sumac also has an added bonus of being very beneficial for those with type 2 diabetes. Sumac, having a slightly tangy and citric flavor, compliments the blueberry and balances out the taste.

Ingredients
2 T organic freeze dried Wild Blueberries
2 tsp Sumac powder
4 T Cold Inulin
1 T Citric Fiber (Natur Emul is what I use)
3/4 cup Raw Cashews (optional, soaked for a couple of hours)
2 cups water
1 can Organic Coconut Milk (with guar gum)
1/2 tsp Liquid Stevia
3/4 tsp Xanthan Gum
Pinch of salt

Cooking Instructions:
1. Add everything into a powerful blender and blend on high for several minutes. Refrigerate for several hours if not overnight.
2. Make sure the ice cream maker is in the freezer overnight. The paddle and attachment also go in the freezer an hour or so beforehand.
3. Attach the ice cream maker to your kitchen aid if that's what you have. If you have a free standing one, make sure everything is in place before pouring in the soon to be ice cream.
4. Set on low and pour the liquid in slowly. Once it's all in, turn to the appropriate setting. Follow the directions of your ice cream maker to your desired consistency. It may finish like soft serve ice cream. Because this gets hard in the freezer and you will have to take it out to thaw a little to get creamier.

Notes: Replace Cashews and water with 2 cups of Oat milk if any nut allergies. Do not add the liquid to the ice cream maker unless its turning. Once the liquid goes in, it begins to freeze and the paddles won't be able to turn. If this happens, there's no turning back. You will have to mix it by hand.

Lemongrass Lime Ice Cream

☆☆☆☆

Ingredients

2 cups Cashew Macadamia nut milk blend (1/4 cup Raw Cashews, 1/4 cup Macadamia nut)
2 cups Filtered water
1 can Coconut milk
6 inch Lemongrass stalk
2 T Lime Juice
1 1/2 tsp lime zest
3/4 tsp Liquid Stevia
4 T Cold Inulin
1 T Citrus Fiber (I use Natur Emul)
Pinch of Salt
6 drops of Lemongrass essential oil

Cooking Instructions:

1. In a blender, add the cashews and Macadamia nuts with water and blend on high for a couple of minutes to make the Cashew Macadamia nut milk.
2. With the back of a knife, or something heavy, pound the end of the lemon grass stalk to break up the fibers and activate the fragrance of the lemon grass. In a pot, add nut milk and Coconut milk. Bring to a boil and add lemongrass and lime juice. Let steep on low for 30 minutes and then turn off heat and let sit for 2 hours. Strain before putting everything into the blender.
3. Add everything into a powerful blender and blend on high for several minutes. Add any essential oils at this point if you would like a stronger flavor. Refrigerate for several hours if not overnight.
4. Make sure the ice cream maker is in the freezer overnight. The paddle and attachment also go in the freezer an hour or so beforehand.
5. Attach the ice cream maker to your kitchen aid if that's what you have. If you have a free standing one, make sure everything is in place before pouring in the soon to be ice cream.
6. Set on low and pour the liquid in slowly. Once it's all in, turn to the appropriate setting. Follow the directions of your ice cream maker to your desired consistency. It may finish like soft serve ice cream. Because this gets hard in the freezer and you will have to take it out to thaw a little to get creamier, I suggest scooping it with an ice cream scooper and place it on parchment paper on a

cookie sheet. They will harden and freeze. And they fit perfectly in the waffle bowls.

Note* Do not add the liquid to the ice cream maker unless it's turning. Once the liquid goes in, it begins to freeze on the side walls and the paddles won't be able to turn. If this happens, there's no turning back. You will have to mix it by hand.

Cardamom Cinnamon Ginger Oat Ice Cream
☆☆☆☆☆

This is a modified version of chai tea. Only frozen. If you would like to have a full chai flavor, use the spice recipe on page 355.

1 heaping tsp Vanilla powder
4 T Cold Inulin
1 T Citric Fiber (Natur Emul is what I use)
2 cups Oat milk
1 can Organic Coconut Milk (with guar gum)
1/2 tsp Liquid Stevia
3/4 tsp Xanthan Gum
1 - 2 Ginger tea bag, depends on how much flavor you'd like
   (or 3 inch Ginger slice)
10 - 15 crushed Green Cardamom pods
2 Cinnamon sticks, 2 - 3 inches long
Pinch of salt

Cooking Instructions:

1. In a pot, add Oat milk and Coconut milk. Bring to a boil and add 10 - 15 crushed cardamom pods, Ginger tea bag(s) and cinnamon sticks. Let steep on low for 30 minutes and then turn off heat and let sit for 2 hours. Strain. You want only the liquid.
2. Put milk liquid and remaining ingredients into a powerful blender and blend on high for several minutes. Refrigerate for several hours if not overnight.
3. Make sure the ice cream maker is in the freezer overnight. The paddle and attachment also go in the freezer an hour or so beforehand.
4. Attach the ice cream maker to your kitchen aid if that's what you have. If you have a free standing one, make sure everything is in place before pouring in the soon to be ice cream.
5. Set on low and pour the liquid in slowly. Once it's all in, turn to the appropriate setting. Follow the directions of your ice cream maker to your desired consistency. It may finish like soft serve ice cream. Because this gets hard in the freezer and you will have to take it out to thaw a little to get creamier, I suggest scooping it into balls with your ice cream scooper and place it on parchment paper in a cookie sheet. And they will harden and freeze. They are pre scooped for ease! They fit perfectly in the waffle bowls now.

Blueberry Lavender Lemonade

☆☆☆☆☆

The purple color of this refreshing drink is divine. This lavender lemonade recipe is the ultimate party drink. Great for baby showers, wedding showers, summer BBQ's and just because. Since we eat with our eyes, this drink is exciting because it's all about that!

Ingredients
6 cups filtered water
1/2 cup Xylitol
1/4 tsp Liquid Stevia (Adjust to taste)
1 - 3 T dried Lavender (personal preference)
2 cups Lemon juice
1 T Blueberry Freeze Dried powder

Cooking Instructions:

1. In a large pot, add the water and bring to a boil. Add the xylitol, lemon juice and lavender and turn off the heat. Let the lavender infuse for 30 minutes using a tea infuser.
2. Remove from heat, and cool. Add Blueberry Freeze Dried powder, stevia and refrigerate. Serve with a slice of lemon or a fresh lavender stem for decoration.
   Suggested variations: *Use other Freeze dried fruits such as Blackberry, Raspberry, Strawberry or Mango for different flavors equally delicious.*

Chai Tea *6 servings*
☆☆☆☆☆

This recipe is caffeine free. To make it with black tea or rooibos red tea, add a tea bag or loose tea to boiling water.

6 Cups Filtered Water
2 Whole Star Anise Pods
2 Cinnamon Sticks
1 T grated fresh Ginger
1/2 tsp grated Nutmeg (use whole nutmeg)
8 crushed Green Cardamom Pods
4 Whole Cloves
1 cup Plant Based Milk
1/4 tsp Liquid Stevia

Cooking Instructions:

1. In a large saucepan, bring the water to a boil over high heat. Add the anise, cinnamon, ginger, nutmeg, cardamom, and cloves. Reduce heat and simmer for 10 min.

2. Stir in the milk and add stevia. Adjust the taste if needed with adding more drops.

3. Pour the chai through a strainer or nut milk bag into a cup.

Notes

Index

A

About the Author · 19
Acknowledgments · 1
Aioli · 114
    Basil · 114
    Basil Artichoke · 115
    Cilantro Garlic · 114
    Garlic · 114
    Roasted Red Pepper and Smoked Paprika · 115
All about Crackers · 171
Alternatives A-Z · 69
    Agar agar 77
    Apple Pectin 77
    Baking Powder · 69
    Binder · 71
    Butter · 70
    Buttermilk · 70
    Caramel · 69
    Cashews · 69
    Citrus Fiber Powder 77
    Coffee · 69
    Cornstarch · 69
    Couscous · 69
    Egg Replacements · 70
    Egg Wash · 71
    Egg whites · 71
    Guar Gum 77
    Kudzu Root 76
    Leavening · 71
    Milk · 70
    Miso, Dark · 70
    Oil 83
    Potato 78
    Potato Starch 77
    Psyllium Husk/Powder 78
    Sour cream · 70
    Sweeteners 78
    Xanthan Gum 77
Apple Turnover · 370
Angel Butter 107

Aquaschata™ 35
Artichoke Spinach Jalapeño Dip · 136
Artichoke Sun-dried Tomato Basil Dip · 131

B

Baking Tips · 284
Basics & Bonuses · 360
Bliss Balls · 375
Blueberry Compote · 346, 401
Bread · 183
    Biscuits with Green Onions · 212
    Cauliflower Pizza Crust · 216
    Challah · 202
    Cinnamon Raisin Bagels · 219
    Cinnamon Raisin Bread · 187
    Corn Bread · 213
    English Muffins · 185
    Farmhouse Bread · 193
    Farmhouse Bread Version 2 · 195
    Herb Dinner Rolls · 208
    Multi Grain Sandwich Bread · 196
    Naan · 214
    Onion and Dill Dinner Roll · 210
    Onion Poppyseed Bagels · 222
    Pizza Crust · 215
    Pretzel · 227
    Pumpernickel Bagels · 225
    Pumpernickel Bread · 198
    Rosemary Breadsticks · 206
    Spiced Pumpkin Bread · 189
    Spicy Banana Bread · 191
    Sun-dried Tomato and Olive Bread · 200
Breakfast Style Entree
    Crepe · 237
    Crepes with Nectarine and Raspberry Coulis · 239
    Fluffy Pancakes · 241
    Jalapeño Sweet Potato Pancake · 244
    Mini Waffle Bowls · 240
    Potato Latkes · 243

C

Cake · 341
    Cake Pops 357
    Chai Mini Cupcakes · 355
    Chicory Spice Cake with Ginger Cardamom Cashew Glaze · 353
    Galaxy Cake · 359
    Hazelnut Chocolate Torte · 348
    Lemon Cake with Lemon and Raspberry Filling · 341
    No Bake Blueberry Hazelnut Cheesecake · 346
    Orange Poppyseed Cake with Orange Hazelnut Filling · 344
    Vanilla or Chocolate Pound Cake · 351
Cashew Butter Cream Frosting · 313, 380
Cashew Cream · 348, 379
Cashew Gravy 254
Chocolate Ganache · 389
Chocolate Whipping Cream · 344
Choosing You · 51
Coconut Whipping Cream · 341, 377
Cold Treats · 394
    Blueberry Compote · 401
    Blueberry Coulis · 400
    Blueberry Lavender Lemonade · 408
    Blueberry Sumac Ice Cream · 404
    Cardamom Cinnamon Ginger Oat Ice Cream · 407
    Chai Tea · 409
    Fruit Coulis · 399
    Ice Cream, Sorbets, Popsicles, Ice Cream Bars and Ice Cream Truffles · 396
    Lemongrass Lime Ice Cream · 405
    Marionberry Coulis · 400
    Raspberry Coulis · 399
    Raspberry Sorbet · 398
    Vanilla Ice Cream · 402
Juicing Combinations for Well Being · 98
Comfort Foods · 45
Conversion Table- Sugar to Stevia · 82

Index

Crackers · 172
    Basic Cracker · 172
    Black Lentil · 175
    Everything cracker · 174
    Multi Grain cracker · 173
    Onion cracker · 172
    Protein cracker · 173
    Rebekah's Crackers- Pizza Flavor · 178
    Rebekah's Herb Crackers · 180
    Saltine · 177

D

Dairy Alternatives · 103
    Cream Cheese · 110
    Cream Cheese with Chives · 111
    Cream Cheese with Fresh Basil leaves · 111
    Cream Cheese with Fresh Cilantro · 112
    Faux Lox Cream Cheese · 112
    Hazelnut Cream Cheese · 112
    Macadamia Cauliflower Ricotta Cheese · 109
    Pumfu · 111
    Vegan Buttermilk · 108
    Vegan Sour Cream · 108
Date Caramel · 373
Dedication · ii
Dessert Crusts · 362
Desserts · 282
    Apricot Puree and Raspberries · 289
    Basic Muffin Mix · 286
    Cacao Hazelnut Pinwheel Cookies · 314
    Chocolate Donut recipe · 293
    Chocolate Hemp Cookies · 307
    Cinnamon Holes · 295
    Cinnamon Rolls · 297
    Cookie Recipe · 309
    Cream Filled Cookies · 311
    Donut Recipe · 291
    Gingerbread House · 321
    Gingersnap Cookies · 321
    Hemp Teff Cookies · 305
    Millet and Sweet Rice Muffins · 289
    Oatmeal Walnut Currant Cookies · 303
    Profiteroles and Mini Éclairs · 300
    Raspberry Cannoli · 317
    Spiced Squash Nut Muffins · 288

Dinner Style Entrees
    Main Dish · 247
        Black Bean Yam Quesadillas 257
        Classic Vegan Burger 262
        Classic Vegan Chili 259
        Coconut Lemongrass Thai Dish 266
        Falafels 264
        Falafel Waffle Bowl 265
        Gardenesque Burger 261
        Mexican Style Millet Polenta 258
        Pecan Patties 255
        Portabella Wellington with Cashew Gravy 253
        Sunlight Burger 260

    Side Dish · 247
        Barbeque Quinoa 250
        Corn on the Cob with "Butter Sauce" 248
        Jasmine Rice with Lemongrass 251
        Millet Stuffing with Cashew Gravy 252
        Taco Salad 256
        Vegan BBQ Sauce with Jack Fruit 268

Dr. James Said, ND, DC · 8

E

Egg Replacer · 86
Energy Balls · 375
Entrees
    Breakfast Style · 236
    Main Dish · 247
Entrées · 236, 247

Equipment · 84
Extracts · 72
    Essential Oils · 72
    Freeze Dried Fruit · 72
    Fresh Herbs · 72
    Herbal Teas · 72
    Vanilla Powder and Vanilla Bean · 72

F

Fearless in the Kitchen · 63
Finally Free · 60
Flours · 73
    Almond flour 73
    Amaranth flour 74
    Arrowroot powder 74
    Sweet Brown Rice flour 74
    Brown Rice flour 74
    Buckwheat flour 74
    Cassava flour 74
    Chickpea flour 74
    Coconut flour 74
    Corn flour 76
    Cornmeal 75
    Hazelnut flour 75
    Jerusalem Artichoke flour 75
    Millet flour 75
    Oat flour 75
    Pecan flour 75
    Potato flour 75
    Purple Yam Flour 78
    Quinoa flour 75
    Sorghum flour 75
    Soy flour 76
    Brown Teff flour 76
    Golden Teff flour 76
    Tapioca flour 76
    White Bean flour 76

Food Alignment - Food Frequencies · 47
Food Coloring · 78
Food Magic · 67
Foreword · 8, 17
    Dr. James Said 8
    Kari Halligan · 17
Frostings & Whipped Toppings · 376

Index

G

Gelatin · 78
Ginger Cardamom Cashew Cream Glaze · 380
Guacamole · 141

H

Hazelnut Cacao Chestnut Mousse · 387
Health and Vitality · 42
Herbs for Bread · 119
Herbs for Savory Cooking · 119
Herbs for Soup · 119
Herbs for Sweets · 119
Hummus · 134
    Beet or Butternut Squash · 134
    Kalamata · 135
    Roasted Red Pepper · 134
    Sun-dried Tomato · 135

I

Introduction · 25
    Jessika Neuert · 25
Inulin · 79

J

Juice Machines · 93
Juicing · 91
    Symptoms of Healing · 101
Juicing Combinations for Well Being 98

L

Lemon Curd · 385
Lemon Pastry Cream · 384
Let's get Started! · 39
Let's Get Started!
    Basic Starter Kit · 40

M

Macadamia Cauliflower Ricotta Cheese Dessert Filling · 381
Macadamia Cheese Dip; Plain or Basil Collard Pesto · 140
Main Dish
    Black Bean Yam Quesadillas · 257
    Classic Vegan Chili · 259
    Coconut Lemongrass Thai · 266
    Falafel Waffle Bowl · 265
    Falafels · 264
    Gardenesque Burger · 261
    Mexican Style Millet Polenta · 258
    Pecan Patties · 255
    Portabella Wellington with Cashew Gravy · 253
    Sunlight Burger · 260
    Taco Salad · 256
    Vegan BBQ Sauce with Jack Fruit · 268
    Vegan Burger · 262
Mayonnaise · 113
Menu Planning · 44
Meringues · 72, 335
    Aquafaba · 335
    Flaxseed water · 336
    Potatowhip · 338
    Versawhip 600K · 339
Mini Pizzas on English Muffins · 130

O

Orange Ginger Frosting · 383
Orange Hazelnut Pastry Cream · 386

P

Pasta · 270
    Cannelloni with Béchamel Sauce · 275
    Herbed Brazil Nut Cream Sauce · 280
    Lasagna · 273
    Lemon Basil Pesto Ravioli · 278
    Pasta Dough · 272
    Pumpkin Ravioli · 280
    Sun-dried Tomato Basil & Mushroom Ravioli · 279
Personal Accountability · 56
Pesto Dips with Crackers · 140
Pesto Plus · 156
    Artichoke Pesto · 158
    Basil Collard Pesto · 159
    Dill Pesto · 156
    Lemon Macadamia Basil Pesto · 158
    Lemon Mint Pistachio Pesto · 157
    Macadamia Basil Pesto 275
    Sun-dried Tomato & Roasted Garlic Pesto · 157
Petit Fours Cups · 362
Phyllo Like Pastry Dough · 365
Phyllo Stuffed Mushrooms · 137
Pies · 324
    Apple Pie · 326
    Key Lime Pie · 333
    Key Lime Pie Crust · 334
    Lemon Meringue Pie · 331
    Pecan Pie · 328
    Pumpkin Pie · 329
Pizza Bites · 129
Pretzels and Pretzel Bites · 368

R

Raspberry Coulis · 350, 399
Resources · 88
Risk Taking · 63

S

Salads · 146
    Broccoli with Mint Pesto Sauce · 150
    Carrot Beet · 146
    Pistachio-Apple Macaroni · 148

Index

Rainbow Avocado Raisin · 147
Rebekah's Famous Pasta Salad · 151
Tofuna · 149

Salad Dressings · 152
Avocado Cucumber Mint 154
Caesar · 152
Creamy Cucumber- Dill · 154
Creamy Dijon · 155
Creamy Ranch · 153
Mustard Dill · 153
Sesame Cream · 156
Sesame Garlic · 155
Spicy Mango or Lime Mango Poppyseed · 153

Salsa 118
Green Salsa · 125
Mango Salsa · 124
Pico de Gallo · 124

Salt · 78
Herbamare® · 78

Sauces · 118
BBQ Sauce · 124
Dark Cherry BBQ Sauce · 125

Seasoning Blends · 120
Chai Spice Mix · 123
Everything Seasoning · 123
Garam Masala · 121
Herb Salt · 122
Italian · 122
Korma Seasonings (Curry) · 121
Pate Seasoning · 120
Taco · 121

Side Dish
Barbecue Quinoa · 250
Corn on the Cob with "Butter Sauce · 249
Jasmine Rice with Lemongrass · 251
Millet Stuffing with Cashew Gravy · 252

Smoothies · 95
Banana Maple Pecan · 96
Blueberry · 96
Flax Seed Shake · 97
Maple Pecan Banana Swirl · 96
Oat Nogg · 96

Soup's On · 160
Carrot 164
Corn Chowder · 163
Cream of Asparagus · 162
Experiment #1 · 161
Fall Harvest · 166
Kale and Sweet Potato · 167
Lentils and Quinoa · 160
Moong Dal · 169
Orange Dal · 168
Pirate Stew · 165

Spaghetti Noodles · 78
Sugar =Liquid Stevia · 88
Sun-dried Tomato, Basil and Mushroom Filling · 138
Sweeteners 79
Date nectar 79
Inulin 79
Maple syrup 79
Monk Fruit Sweetener · 80
Stevia · 82
Xylitol · 81

T

Table of Contents · 4, 5, 6, 7
Therapeutic Diets · 32
Tortilla Pinwheels with Cream Cheese Filling · 139
Tortillas · 229
Coconut Flour · 231
Grain Free · 230
Corn · 232

Turtle Bars · 390

V

Vanilla Ice Cream · 402

W

Walnut Pastry Dough · 87, 362
What is Aquaschata™? · 35

Professional Grade Recipe · 38
Aquaschata™ Recipe · 38

What is disease · 31
White Bean Dip · 132
White Sauce 276
Wraps · 229
Cauliflower · 233
Collard Green · 235

X

Xylitol Simple Syrup · 372

Y

Your Awakening Begins · 29

Notes

Epicurean Awakening™

Presents ...

Epicurean Delights

Coming Spring 2024!